# EVELYN WAUGH

*a reference guide*

*A*
*Reference*
*Guide*
*to*
*Literature*

Ronald Gottesman
*Editor*

# EVELYN WAUGH

## *a reference guide*

MARGARET MORRISS
D. J. DOOLEY

G.K. HALL & CO.

70 LINCOLN STREET, BOSTON, MASS.

**Library of Congress Cataloging in Publication Data**

Dooley, D. J. (David Joseph), 1921-
  Evelyn Waugh, a reference guide.


  Includes index.
    1.   Waugh, Evelyn, 1903-1966—Bibliography.   I.   Morriss,
Margaret.   II.   Title.
Z8953.5.D66   1984        016.823'912        83-26689
[PR6045.A97]
ISBN 0-8161-8341-4

*This publication is printed on permanent/durable acid-free paper*
MANUFACTURED IN THE UNITED STATES OF AMERICA

# Contents

# The Authors

Margaret E. Morriss is a professor of English at Ryerson Polytechnical Institute, Toronto, where she is a specialist in Canadian literature.  She was educated at St. Michael's College and the Graduate Department of English, University of Toronto.  Her doctoral dissertation, completed in 1980, examines the evolution of Evelyn Waugh's literary reputation.

D.J. Dooley received his B.A. from the University of Western Ontario, his M.A. from the University of Toronto, and his Ph.D. from the State University of Iowa.  He has taught at Creighton University, St. Francis Xavier University, and the Royal Military College, and has been a professor of English at St. Michael's College, University of Toronto, since 1960. Besides articles on fiction and satire, his publications include The Art of Sinclair Lewis (1967), Compton Mackenzie (1974), Contemporary Satire (1971), and Moral Vision in the Canadian Novel (1979).

# Preface

Besides the obvious purpose of calling the attention of students of Waugh to interesting discussions of his works, life, and personality, this reference guide is also designed to illustrate the development of his reputation and the breadth of interest in him. We have had to be very selective; even Waugh's early novels were widely reviewed, and we have had to exclude far more reviews than we included. From about 1948 on, substantial critical evaluations of him began appearing (most notably F.J. Stopp's book, 1958.A2), and the entries for a given year consequently become much more numerous than they have been. Given the amazing development of interest in Waugh in recent years, we have had to continue to be selective; it is safe to say that for 1981 alone we could have found as many items as are included in the entire bibliography. Throughout, our intention has been first, to list items of intrinsic importance; second, to indicate by a representative selection of items how widely Waugh was reviewed and discussed at a given time; third, to illustrate the growth of his reputation.

The enormous amount of interest generated by the television production of Brideshead Revisited is reflected in the entries for 1981 and 1982; Waugh devotees may well have been amused by the attention paid him by such non-academic journals as Vogue, Gourmet, and the house organ of the Exxon Corporation. But even though this flurry of interest is bound to subside, the evidence provided by new books published and new books announced suggests that Waugh's reputation is becoming more and more solidly established. The English edition of one of these books, Jeffrey Heath's The Picturesque Prison, was widely reviewed in the British Isles. Besides illustrating various critical approaches to Waugh's writing, together with the degree to which views of Waugh's life and personality still enter into judgements of his writing, the reviews demonstrate how seriously Waugh was regarded by the critics at the time of completion of this reference guide.

The first Waugh Checklist (1972.A1) formed the basis for the bibliographic search undertaken; our copy of it has been so well thumbed and amended and interleaved that it is falling apart. We are also indebted to a number of bibliographic articles, such as the one by Thomas Gribble in the Evelyn Waugh Newsletter (1972.B14) and the one by Alain Blayac in <u>The Book Collector</u> (1976.5), together with the running bibliography in the <u>Newsletter</u>.

The organization is chronological, year by year, with the entries arranged alphabetically and numbered consecutively within a year. In years during which books and theses entirely on Waugh are cited, these are put into an <u>A</u> category, and shorter writings into a <u>B</u> category. Asterisks preceding entry numbers designate items we were unable to obtain for examination; in such cases, the annotation indicates the source of our citation. The index gives entry numbers for individual items rather than page numbers. Waugh's books are listed under his name in the index; under his name also appear various subject headings related to him, such as biographical information, assessments of his career, and his political and religious views.

Margaret Morriss was very fortunate in having a librarian sister, Mrs. Joan Lusczek, to make suggestions about methods of research and ways of compiling and sorting out information. Among numerous other librarians to whom we are indebted are Mrs. Margaret McGrath, of the St. Michael's College Library; Ellen Dunlap, of the Humanities Research Center at the Austin campus of the University of Texas; Challice Reed of the B.B.C. Script Library in London; and numerous other helpful people at the Library of Congress, the British Museum, the Newspaper Library at Colindale in London, and the Catholic Central Library at Westminster in London.

From a colleague, Jeffrey Heath, we have received a great many suggestions about materials to investigate and include. We would also like to acknowledge the receipt of financial assistance from Ryerson Polytechnical Institute for clerical and photographic work. To the secretary in the English office at St. Michael's, Mrs. Audrey McDonagh, must go our very warm and special thanks for all her work on the manuscript. This preface must sound to her like the "all clear": with great good luck, she may in future be able to call not only her desk, but her filing cabinet, her own.

# Introduction

A chronological study of the evolution of Evelyn Waugh's literary
reputation reveals an interesting series of contradictory opinions regarding his literary merits, his thematic consistency, his characteristic attitudes, and his authorial point of view. Throughout his
career, a genuine understanding and appreciation of Waugh's literary
aims and method was hampered by critics who praised or condemned him
for the wrong reasons, or who focused on one aspect of his writings
to the detriment of other, equally significant elements. The common
view of Waugh's development divides his career sharply at 1945, with
the appearance of Brideshead Revisited; many readers and reviewers express preference for Waugh's early satiric comedies over the later,
more serious fiction, though some will argue that his career followed
a consistent line of development. Even though his work has now received a substantial amount of critical attention, the arguments about
early Waugh versus late Waugh still go on--as does the debate about his
stature as a novelist. It is worth noting, however, that the critical
approach to him has become much more technically sophisticated in recent years, even though many writers are still led away from the works
themselves by considerations of his abrasive, self-created "public"
personality, or of the militant conservatism of his social, political,
and religious beliefs.

Born in 1903, Evelyn Waugh was the second son of Arthur Waugh,
editor, man of letters, and managing director of Chapman and Hall, the
publishing firm. Waugh always described his childhood as extremely
happy. He attended Heath Mount School, London, and expected to go on
to the prestigious public school, Sherborne, as his father and elder
brother Alec had done before. But shortly after leaving Sherborne
under a cloud of scandal, Alec published The Loom of Youth (1917) an
eyebrow-raising exposé of public school life. Therefore Evelyn's
parents sent him to Lancing College, Sussex (founded to promulgate
High Anglican principles), having noted his predeliction for religion.
The result, Waugh later noted, was to turn him to agnosticism. While
at Lancing he developed his interest in drawing, design, and illumina-
tion. Waugh also demonstrated his taste for belles lettres in start-
ing the Dilettanti, a club devoted to conversation and debate, and his
love of anarchy in forming the Corpse Club (for the apathetic) and in

disrupting the drills of the Officers Training Corps.

Winning a scholarship to Hertford College, Waugh went up to Oxford in 1922. There he continued his work in decorative drawing, contributed short stories and reported debates to university magazines, and experimented with a broad range of activities with an increasingly heterogeneous group of friends. Perhaps Waugh's most intriguing achievement during this time was the production of a silent film, The Scarlet Woman, with Terence Greenidge, John Sutro, and Elsa Lanchester. Though never publicly shown, the film demonstrates Waugh's appreciation of the technical potential of cinematic devices.

After leaving Oxford without a degree in 1924, Waugh made various attempts to establish himself as an artist, a printer, a carpenter, a journalist, and a schoolmaster. He even considered becoming "a parson." All of these efforts proved unsuccessful. Waugh's literary efforts thus far (several youthful novels, begun and abandoned; school poems and a play; undergraduate stories) constituted merely a promising juvenilia. In 1927, his first publication ("The Balance," a short story) appeared in Georgian Short Stories, edited by Alec Waugh. But as yet Waugh had little thought of a literary career. However, while recuperating from a sprained ankle, he amused himself by researching and later writing a monograph on the Pre-Raphaelite Brotherhood. On the strength of this privately published essay, the publishing firm of Duckworth commissioned Waugh, then quite low in funds, to write a biography of Dante Gabriel Rossetti to commemorate the 1928 centenary of the artist's birth. In the same year Waugh wrote his first novel, the sparkling Decline and Fall; his literary career was brilliantly launched.

So fashionable was Decline and Fall that Winston Churchill chose it as his Christmas gift to friends. Indeed, the biography and novel were both well received, garnering popular success and critical acclaim. The anonymous reviewer in Life and Letters perceptively noted Waugh's fusion of satirical exploitation of weakness with high aesthetic standards, and declared that "his future hangs on a choice of subjects admitting of this combination" (1928.2). When Waugh published Vile Bodies in 1930, his reputation as a brilliant, fashionable novelist, satirizing the vices and follies of London society with his acute observation and barbed wit, was securely established. Moreover, he was confirmed in his role by the judgement of Arnold Bennett (1928.4, 1930.6) and Rebecca West (1930.22). The immediate success of Waugh's first two novels, however, was to prove a mixed blessing. Critics who admitted to uncertainty regarding the author's serious satiric tone and intention nonetheless applauded his comic invention and exuberant manner. For the rest of his literary career, some of his commentators, such as Malcolm Bradbury and Orville Prescott, were consistently to lament Waugh's departures from his early fictional mode of comic satire.

The failure of Waugh's first marriage (to Evelyn Gardner) in 1929 and his conversion to Roman Catholicism in 1930 were crucial events in his life. For the next decade, his travels to Europe and Africa,

South America and Mexico, led to both travel books and fiction, the one genre illuminating the meaning and purpose of the other. Labels (American title, A Bachelor Abroad, 1930), Remote People (American title, They Were Still Dancing, 1932), and Ninety-Two Days (1934) rounded out the image of Evelyn Waugh as a sophisticated, if somewhat jaded, observer of exotic scenes and situations, the traveler to distant and primitive countries which somehow counterpointed the decayed civilization of his native England. This juxtaposition of the barbaric and the civilized informed Waugh's next novel, Black Mischief (1932), which clearly articulated his criticism of social decline. But critical bewilderment regarding his satire appeared most dramatically when Earnest Oldmeadow, editor of the Tablet (a prominent English Catholic newspaper), attacked Black Mischief for its alleged immorality and blasphemy (1933.3). Although Waugh defended his literary and religious integrity, this response to his novel demonstrated the satirist's vulnerability to misinterpretation. However, the appearance of A Handful of Dust (1934), generally regarded as the masterpiece of Waugh's early work, if not of his entire career, represented a rare moment of harmony between author and audience. Critics such as Edwin Muir (1934.14), Peter Quennell (1934.18), and Gerald Gould (1932.7) perceived and approved his humanist satiric purpose and ironic literary method. All the same, some, like Michael de la Bedoyere (1934.10) and Earnest Oldmeadow (1934.16), still noted his apparent lack of humanity and of a moral center.

In the early part of his career, Waugh was often compared to Ronald Firbank, Sir Max Beerbohm, Aldous Huxley, and Graham Greene. Some commentators placed him in the tradition of Jonathan Swift, Alexander Pope, and even Jane Austen. While the precision and excellence of his prose style were generally acknowledged, critics often misread his ironic tone. In Edmund Campion (1935), Waugh in Abyssinia (1935), and Robbery under Law (American title, Mexico: An Object Lesson, 1939), the author discarded his ambiguous fictional persona and clearly articulated his Roman Catholic convictions, his right-wing political sympathies, and his distrust and fear of communism. On all three counts he aroused the antagonism of leftist intellectuals. In fact, hostility to Waugh's religious, political, and social opinions was to color his literary reputation for the rest of his professional life, obscuring judgement of his novelistic skills. Nigel Dennis (1943.2) explored this aspect of Waugh's reputation, defending his literary merit in the face of those who undervalued his work, but blaming the author for his own predicament.

Those dismayed by the attitudes expressed in Waugh's nonfiction were reassured by the publication of Scoop (1938) and Put Out More Flags (1942), novels in which he appeared to return to his earliest manner. But these books marked the start of his long period of literary transition (1939-1952), during which he displayed new interest in the conflicting demands of public and private life, undertook technical experiments with first-person narration and interior monologue, tried a stylistic softening of his precise, economical prose, and moved closer to the "real" world. Critics bewildered by his apparent changes of direction were unsympathetic to his genuine literary advances, particularly in ironic expression. The most notable sign of their puzzlement appeared in response to Work Suspended (1942). Reviewers in the Spectator (1943.4) and the Times Literary Supplement (1943.1) ignored Waugh's use of first-person narration, his abandonment of the Mayfair world, his greater subtlety in characterization and his more realistic treatment of contemporary life, and concentrated instead on the author's behavior in publishing so curious a fragment. Antagonism to Waugh's characteristic attitudes was already growing; Brideshead Revisited (1945) precipitated a critical attack on the seriousness of his religious and social beliefs and on his literary integrity. Moreover, his first explicit use of Catholic themes was greeted with dismay by both his early admirers and even some of his coreligionists, who expressed distaste for his somber presentation of their faith. Although some critics admired Waugh's development, most were outraged.

Randolph Churchill (1945.5) tried to prepare the American reading public for Brideshead by stressing its author's deliberate provocation of the left-wing intelligentsia, but nothing could protect Waugh from a barrage of contradictory responses to his explicit Catholicism, his aristocratic bias, his nostalgic, romantic tone, and his use of the sentimental Charles Ryder as the novel's narrator. The selection of Brideshead by the Book-of-the-Month Club established Waugh's popularity in America almost overnight. But critical opinion was divided among those like Sterling North (1946.14), who admired Waugh's skill as a stylist but abhorred his snobbery, inhumanity, and doctrinaire religion; those like Diana Trilling (1946.22), who condemned outright the intrusion of Waugh's opinions; and those like John K. Hutchens (1945.8) and Thomas Sugrue (1946.19), who saw Brideshead as the logical and admirable development of Waugh's literary career. Harold C. Gardiner (1946.8-9) praised the novel for its Catholic theology, a well-intentioned defense which further confused judgement of its literary merits. In England praise for Brideshead from the Spectator (1945.6), from Desmond MacCarthy in the Sunday Times (1945.9), and from Edwin Muir in the Listener (1945.11) was balanced by condemnation from Peter Quennell (1945.12), Henry Reed (1945.13), and the Manchester Guardian (1945.3). The most disappointed of Waugh's early admirers was Edmund Wilson. In 1944 he had hailed Waugh as the only first-rate comic genius since George Bernard Shaw (1944.1); when Brideshead appeared, Wilson bitterly denounced its author's loss of ironic detachment, wit, and comic exuberance (1946.24).

Generally regarded as the turning point of Waugh's literary life, Brideshead prompted critics to reassess his earlier writings in the light of his latest shift of direction in fiction. Critics of considerable stature reiterated the judgements of popular reviewers. In 1946, Rose Macaulay wrote that Waugh belonged in a circus-tent world; when he strayed from it to the real world, he succumbed to romantic nostalgia and was lost (1946.12). About the same time, D.S. Savage described Waugh's "innocence" as his failure to rise above the values of adolescent sentimentality (1947.9); and Conor Cruise O'Brien [Donat O'Donnell] attacked his "alien pieties"--his unpalatable fusion of snobbery, romanticism, and Catholicism (1946.15). Focusing on Waugh's changes of literary interest rather than on his consistent development, commentators frequently exhorted him to return to his earliest mode of comic satire. Meanwhile, Waugh continued to explore new possibilities, and to find new things to say.

In 1937, Waugh's marriage to Laura Herbert had given serenity and stability to his life, perhaps facilitating his new attention to his own literary development. Although Waugh had greeted the outbreak of World War II with enthusiasm, regarding it as the essential defense of the values of Western civilization against growing anarchy, he soon grew disillusioned. The futility of mechanized, bureaucratized warfare, his own failure to find a purposeful place in battling the modern age, and Britain's alliance with Russia all played their part in cooling his ardor. His deep pessimism, born in the confusion of the thirties and nurtured by the anomalies inherent in his war experience, reached full growth in the postwar world, where he saw barbarism triumphant in the age of the common man. Scott-King's Modern Europe (1947), The Loved One (1948), and Helena (1950) constituted Waugh's examination of the social and moral bankruptcy of Europe and America, past and present. The first was received with regrets for the decline of Waugh's satiric brilliance. George Orwell (1949.14) condemned Waugh's confused and superficial view of politics, which marred his satiric message. The second was acclaimed as the epitome of his mordant wit; the third was regarded as a loose hodge-podge of history and satire, religion and social criticism, although it was to remain Waugh's favorite novel for the rest of his life. Glancing at the future in Love Among the Ruins (1953), Waugh completed his bleak survey of the hopeless plight of genuine civilization. Reviewer response to this novella prompted Waugh to assail the critics for abdication of their proper function in an article which epitomizes the author's cool relations with many of his reviewers ("Mr. Waugh Replies," Spectator, 3 July 1953, pp. 23-24).

Sometimes described as his most unproductive period, the postwar years revealed his sharper castigation of decaying culture, balanced by his emerging concern for the predicament of the lost but questing individual. Thus his long, intermediate phase of uncertainty slowly moved into a final phase of greater confidence in his role as a writer, though he did not always feel capable of fulfilling it. Waugh's new sense of direction appeared in Men at Arms (1952), the first of a proposed trilogy dealing with the experience of one individual in World War II. Critics tended to suspend their judgement of this novel, awaiting further installments; some praised his blend of realism and satire, while others expressed confusion about his tone and purpose. When Officers and Gentlemen (1955) was published, Waugh announced that his continuation of the war saga was in doubt, and that the first two novels should be considered as a single, unified structure. The general reaction of critics and reviewers was to question this. Moreover, uncertainty over his aim prevailed; some thought he was trying to write satire, and failing to do so, while others criticized the intrusion of incongruous comic episodes into serious fiction.

During the fifties, therefore, Waugh's literary reputation was undecided. While his "public image" of conservative, Catholic country squire, at odds with all aspects of contemporary life, amused and provoked his readers, Waugh's writings were beginning to be granted serious attention by scholarly and academic critics. In 1958, Frederick J. Stopp's full length book, Evelyn Waugh: Portrait of an Artist (1958.A2), appeared; it was specifically aimed at correcting misreadings of his work. The author, however, remained unpredictable to both his champions and detractors. The confessedly autobiographical Ordeal of Gilbert Pinfold (1957) provided fuel for the fires of both camps. Hostile critics rejoiced in Waugh's self-revelations, while his admirers praised his ironic self-portrait. Ronald Knox (1958) caused controversy over Waugh's treatment of the prominent churchman, prompting accusations that the biographer had projected his own misanthropy onto his subject. A Tourist in Africa (1960), an admittedly pedestrian piece of travel literature, merely increased critical irritation at Waugh's image of himself as an aging, cantankerous observer of contemporary life.

Responses to Unconditional Surrender (American title, The End of the Battle, 1961), however, demonstrated a new appreciation of his literary talents. This final volume of the war trilogy begun nine years earlier was praised as the essential completion of the war saga, which in turn was hailed as the crowning achievement of his career. The three volumes were edited and united in Sword of Honour (1964; US, 1965), described by some as the only writing to come out of World War II which was likely to survive. During the interim, critics such as Bernard Bergonzi (1963.B4, 1964.B12) and Frank Kermode (1960.B21, 1962.B19) began to perceive that Waugh's social, religious, and political opinions, so long regarded as damaging intrusions into his fiction, in fact constituted a powerful and productive "aristocratic myth," which gave lasting significance to his writing. In discussions of Unconditional Surrender, and of the first (and only) volume of Waugh's autobiography, A Little Learning (1964), his emerging tolerance and compassion were recognized, and his ironic detachment received new acknowledgement (Bradbury [1964.B14], Burgess [1964.B16], Hart [1964.B29]).

Nevertheless, hostility to Waugh's personality and writings remained, and conflicting evaluations of his literary status marked the obituaries of his death in 1966, further complicated by observations on his private personality and behavior. Since his death, nonetheless, critical interest in his writings has gradually increased, stimulated by the fresh information and insights provided by Christopher Sykes's biography (1975), The Diaries of Evelyn Waugh (ed. Michael Davie, 1976), Evelyn Waugh: A Little Order: A Selection From His Journalism (ed. Donat Gallagher, 1977), and The Letters of Evelyn Waugh (ed. Mark Amory, 1980).

*Introduction*

To follow the course of Waugh criticism is both exhausting and fascinating. Critical misunderstanding of his attitudes and misinterpretations of his writings persisted late into his career—balanced by an ironic contrast between what he was in fact doing, and what he was perceived to be doing. A chronological study of Waugh's novels discloses this disparity between critical responses and his actual aims and achievements. Of course, this gap was widened by his militant Catholicism in a traditionally anti-Catholic society, by his often provoking private personality, and by his ambiguous literary persona. The critics, therefore, were not always to blame for their misreadings. Waugh's nonfiction, especially his journalism and book reviews, revealed his life-long convictions regarding his criteria of literary excellence and his faith in the historical synthesis of Christianity and civilization. Such a fusion, Waugh believed, fostered genuine aesthetic traditions, a diversified but integrated society, and homogeneous social and moral standards. On the other hand, audience appreciation of Waugh's outrageous comedy hindered recognition of his satiric purpose, encouraged readers to resist any changes, and delayed awareness of the sincerity of his denunciation of declining civilization.

With the benefit of hindsight, however, and the help afforded by the diaries, letters, and other material not formerly available, we can now see Waugh's sense of his own career; the points at which he decided to try new directions can be observed, along with the phases of his uncertainty and confidence.

Many critics still praise Waugh's early comedies and disparage his later, serious novels, supposedly marred by declining ironic detachment and increasingly explicit dogmatism and pessimism. Yet such a view ignores his consistent moral purpose. Even in the early novels, Waugh used satiric fantasy to expose the decay of society. The interplay of fantasy and realism animating his early fiction naturally evolved into his later vision of the interaction of human and divine purposes. His focus on anarchic society slowly changed to interest in the individual cast adrift in the modern age. His ironic detachment, often regarded as lost forever after Brideshead Revisited, developed into a more humane irony that included commitment. But the history of Waugh's literary reputation demonstrates the extent to which critics were confounded by the development of his writing. On the simplest level, dislike for the attitudes clearly expressed in his nonfiction sometimes led to hostility for his less provocative fiction. More subtly, critics often misinterpreted his use of fantasy, his satiric viewpoint, and his external techniques of narration and characterization. They misread his growing thematic concern with the conflict and congruence of public and private life, of acceptance or denial of the world of action, and of specific and universal truths.

Waugh's early success in comic satire enclosed him in a pleasant but restricted realm from which readers were reluctant to release him. So were many critics. In fact, Graham Martin wrote that Waugh was definitely a period writer: "He is essentially a pre-war novelist,

and the post war interest in him is a kind of hang-over, a nostalgic
reaction, socially, but not critically interesting" (1961.19). Any
Waugh bibliographer must heartily wish at times that it were indeed
so: it is becoming impossible to keep up with Waugh scholarship. Instead of declining after his death, his reputation continued to grow;
it is probably higher now than it ever was. The Evelyn Waugh Newsletter,
begun in 1966 by Paul Doyle, has continued to provide a focus of interest in him and a running bibliography of scholarship on him. The essential bibliographic studies of manuscripts, typescripts, and various
editions are now well advanced; the detailed examinations of characteristic themes and techniques are proceeding with all the seriousness and
meticulousness which major authors demand. In fact, twenty years after
Martin's pejorative pronouncement we find Norman Snider writing a column headed "A Nasty Man Joins the Ranks of the Exalted," in which he
laments that somehow or other Waugh seems to have become numbered among
the immortals.

Reactions to the biography and the diaries, the collected journalism and the letters, show that interest in Waugh remains substantial.
Major critics of the novel, such as Frank Kermode, David Lodge, Malcolm
Bradbury, and Bernard Bergonzi, continue to treat him with respect.
In addition, he has become the object of specialized attention. The
year 1981 brought announcements of a revised checklist of primary and
secondary material, a catalogue of the Waugh holdings at the University
of Texas, and major critical studies by Robert Murray Davis and Jeffrey
Heath. Both of these studies are the fruit of years of work, both draw
on unpublished material in the Waugh archives at Texas, and they are
convincing evidence, if such were needed, that Waugh's reputation has
not been nearly as ephemeral as Martin anticipated it would be: it is
firmly established.

# Evelyn Waugh's Major Works

1928 Rossetti: His Life and Works (biography)

1928 Decline and Fall (fiction)

1930 Vile Bodies (fiction)

1930 Labels: A Mediterranean Journal (travel); American title: Bachelor Abroad: A Mediterranean Journal

1931 Remote People (travel); American title: They Were Still Dancing

1932 Black Mischief (fiction)

1934 A Handful of Dust (fiction)

1934 Ninety-two Days (travel)

1935 Edmund Campion (biography)

1936 Mr. Loveday's Little Outing, and Other Sad Stories (short stories)

1936 Waugh in Abyssinia (travel)

1938 Scoop (fiction)

1939 Robbery under Law: The Mexican Object-Lesson (travel); American title: Mexico: An Object Lesson

1942 Put Out More Flags (fiction)

1942 Work Suspended (fiction)

1945 Brideshead Revisited (fiction)

1946 When the Going was Good (anthology of prewar travel writing)

1947 Scott-King's Modern Europe (fiction)

1948 The Loved One (fiction)

1949 Work Suspended and Other Stories Written before the Second World War (short stories)

1950 Helena (fiction)

1952 Men at Arms (fiction)

1952    The Holy Places (travel)

1953    Love Among the Ruins: A Romance of the Near Future (fiction)

1954    Tactical Exercise (short stories)

1955    Officers and Gentlemen (fiction)

1957    The Ordeal of Gilbert Pinfold (fiction)

1959    The Life of the Right Reverend Ronald Knox (biography)

1960    A Tourist in Africa (travel)

1961    Unconditional Surrender (fiction); American title: The End of the Battle

1964    A Little Learning (autobiography)

1965    Sword of Honour (fiction)

1976    The Diaries of Evelyn Waugh, ed. Michael Davie

1977    Evelyn Waugh: A Little Order, ed. Donat Gallagher (collection of journalism)

1980    The Letters of Evelyn Waugh, ed. Mark Amory

1983    Work Suspended and Other Stories (short stories); American title: Charles Ryder's Schooldays and Other Stories

# Abbreviations

AI        American Imago
ABR       American Benedictine Review
BR        Bulletin of Bibliography
CathW     Catholic World
CE        College English
ColQ      Colorado Quarterly
ConL      Contemporary Literature
CritQ     Critical Quarterly
DA        Dissertation Abstracts and Dissertation Abstracts International
DR        Dalhousie Review
DQR       Dutch Quarterly Review of Anglo-American Studies
EA        Etudes anglaises
ELH       English Literary History
ELN       English Language Notes
ES        English Studies
ESA       English Studies in Africa
ESC       English Studies in Canada
EWN       Evelyn Waugh Newsletter
GaR       Georgia Review
HudR      Hudson Review
JML       Journal of Modern Literature
KanQ      Kansas Quarterly
LCUT      Library Chronicle of the University of Texas
MFS       Modern Fiction Studies
MLJ       Modern Language Journal
MLQ       Modern Language Quarterly
MQ        Midwest Quarterly
MQR       Michigan Quarterly Review
NY        New Yorker
PBSA      Papers of the Bibliographical Society of America
PLL       Papers on Language and Literature
PQ        Philological Quarterly
PR        Partisan Review
QQ        Queen's Quarterly
RMS       Renaissance and Modern Studies
RQ        Riverside Quarterly
SAQ       South Atlantic Quarterly

| | |
|---|---|
| SatR | Saturday Review and Saturday Review of Literature |
| SHR | Southern Humanities Review |
| SNL | Satire Newsletter |
| SoR | Southern Review |
| SoRA | Southern Review (Adelaide) |
| SR | Sewanee Review |
| SSF | Studies in Short Fiction |
| SWR | Southwest Review |
| TLS | Times Literary Supplement |
| TM | Temps modernes |
| TQ | Texas Quarterly |
| TSLL | Texas Studies in Language and Literature |
| UTQ | University of Toronto Quarterly |
| YR | Yale Review |

# Writings about Evelyn Waugh, 1919-1983

1   WAUGH, ARTHUR. "To Evelyn Arthur St. John Waugh." In Tradition
    and Change. London: Chapman & Hall, pp. vii-viii.
        A moving dedication from father to son, describing Waugh's
    youth and home background, and suggesting the basis of his later
    conservatism.

1928

1   ANON. "Dominie Candide." Glasgow Herald, 1 November, p. 5.
        The audacity of Decline and Fall takes the breath away, while
    its amused commentary upon the ironies of contemporary life is both
    tonic and stimulant. It is a fantastic and brilliant caricature
    of English life.

2   ANON. Review of Decline and Fall. Life and Letters 1
    (December):724-25.
        Sees the novel as a true satire, with some intrusion of
    personal grudges. Predicts Waugh's literary success will come from
    a fusion of technical ability with exploitation of weakness, so as
    to illustrate morality.

3   ANON. Review of Rossetti: His Life and Works. Scotsman
    (Edinburgh), 5 July, p. 2.
        This is a remarkably competent study of a difficult subject;
    it would be hard to point to any estimate of Rossetti which has
    really been more successful.

4   BENNETT, ARNOLD. "Turning over the Autumn Leaves." Evening
    Standard (London), 11 October, p. 5.
        Describes Decline and Fall as a brilliantly malicious satire,
    and Waugh as a genuinely new humorist.

5   CAMPBELL, ROY. "Rossetti." Nation and Athenaeum 43 (19 May):
    212.
        Discusses the anti-Victorianism of the present generation
    and the ironic tone of modern biography. Waugh, fully aware of

Rossetti's comic aspects, does not patronize him, though he over-
estimates the value of his art.

6    CONNOLLY, CYRIL. "New Novels." New Statesman 32 (3 November):
     126.
          Refers to the fashionable, metallic humor of Decline and Fall,
     whose farcical zest arises from cynicism and "the charm of the in-
     corrigible."

7    CRAVEN, THOMAS. "The Master of the Pre-Raphaelites." New York
     Herald Tribune Books, 2 September, p. 2.
          "Unfortunately," Waugh writes, "there is singularly little
     fun to be got out of Rossetti." Perhaps this explains the cold
     squeamishness with which he recounts Rossetti's unsavory habits:
     it is not often that a biographer chooses a subject whose person-
     ality disgusts him. But the excuse for the book is Waugh's faith
     in Rossetti's art.

8    GOULD, GERALD. "New Novels." Observer (London), 23 September,
     p. 8.
          Decline and Fall is roaringly funny, but the fun goes off
     after the school part; sexual degradation and penal systems do not
     lend themselves to Mr. Waugh's light treatment and ingenuousness
     of manner.

9    GRIFFITH, HUBERT. "Books of the Week." Daily Express (London),
     8 November, p. 8.
          Decline and Fall is called an "illustrated novelette," but
     it is really a fantastic, amusing, and slightly improper nightmare.
     All of it is phantasmagoric, and three-quarters of it is funny.

10   MATTHEWS, HERBERT L. "Dante Gabriel Rossetti, Poet, Painter
     and Man." New York Times, 24 June, p. 5.
          Says it is written with a zest, cynical humor, and gift of
     characterization which make absorbing reading. A better picture
     of this turgid and perverse genius has surely never before been
     given.

11   [MOORE, T. STURGE.] "Dante Gabriel Rossetti." TLS, 10 May,
     p. 341.
          Noteworthy for getting Waugh's sex wrong; the author compares
     him to "some dainty miss of the sixties." An essay on Rossetti
     rather than a review of the book. Admires the liveliness of the
     biography but criticizes the author's "slightly astigmatic" mental
     eye, reluctant dependence on Roger Fry's aesthetic stance, and
     neglect of Rossetti's poetry. Drew an acid reply from Waugh (17
     May, p. 379). Reprinted in part: 1978.B25.

12   QUENNELL, PETER. Review of Rossetti: His Life and Works.
     New Statesman and Nation 31 (12 May):160.
          We could have spared Waugh's lengthy analysis of Rossetti's

pictures, as against a detailed and elaborate representation of the
whole pre-Raphaelite group, for a collective portrait is what is
needed.  But Waugh approaches his subject with alacrity and zeal.


## 1929

1    ANON.  "English Society Satirized."  New York Times, 7 April,
     p. 6.
          Calls Decline and Fall a satiric cross-section of English
society, which makes very amusing universal reading even if there
is not a great deal in the book that is startlingly original.

2    MATTHEWS, T.S.  "The Cocktail Hour."  New Republic 58 (17 April):
     259.
          In Decline and Fall, the author has the happy inspiration of
taking nothing seriously, and least of all himself; the result is
a book which makes more sense than most.  He makes us snicker more
often than laugh, but it is not his fault that he is an Englishman.

3    ROSS, MARY.  Review of Decline and Fall.  New York Herald Tribune
     Books, 31 March, p. 3.
          Compares Waugh with Aldous Huxley, though says that Waugh's
"juvenile gusto" is alien to Huxley's romantic bitterness.


## 1930

1    ALDINGTON, RICHARD.  "A Regionalist Novel."  Sunday Referee,
     9 February, p. 6.
          Review of Vile Bodies, describing Waugh as the "regional
novelist" of Mayfair and spokesman for the post-war generation.
Both appealing to, and satirizing, British snobbery, Waugh amuses
yet conveys a vision of impotent futility.

2    ANON.  "Current Literature:  New Novels."  New Statesman 35
     (8 February):572.
          Vile Bodies is "a revue between covers"; Waugh has a keenly
observant eye, but lacks the capacity for design.

3    ANON.  "The Looking-Glass."  Glasgow Herald, 6 February, p. 4.
          Vile Bodies is not a good novel, but it is immensely funny;
it is spoiled by at least one bad lapse from good taste, and the
caricature is sometimes overdone.  But the air of fable is well
maintained.

4    ANON.  Review of Vile Bodies.  Scotsman (Edinburgh), 13 February,
     p. 2.
          It is difficult to believe that the Bright Young People of
London are really anything like the distasteful characters in Vile
Bodies.  It seems a pity that the author, who can do better things,
wasted so much time on them.

5   ANON. "Travelling for Pleasure." Observer (London), 12
    October, p. 7.
        It would be difficult to imagine a more devastating exposure
    of modern travel than Waugh's Mediterranean journal; merely turning
    over his pages we suffer all the fatigue and disgust of being trans-
    ported from one disappointment to another.

6   BENNETT, ARNOLD. "Laughter--and a Lobster Supper." Evening
    Standard (London), 30 January, p. 9.
        Discusses humor and humorists; Waugh, chief comedian of the
    younger generation, is less successful in Vile Bodies than in
    Decline and Fall.

7   COXE, HOWARD. "Tidings from London." New Republic 62 (7 May):
    333.
        Vile Bodies shows English society in a state of disintegra-
    tion, using fantastic comedy as a satiric method. Waugh laments
    the passing of the old London of virtue and stability.

8   ERVINE, St. JOHN. "Books of the Week." Daily Express (London),
    30 January, p. 6.
        Vile Bodies is a hateful book about hateful people of whom
    the best that can be said is that they are too fantastically hor-
    rible to be real.

9   FAUSSET, HUGH l'A. "Novels of the Week." Yorkshire Post,
    22 January, p. 8.
        Vile Bodies is riotously funny, but in it Waugh runs with
    the hare instead of hunting with the hounds:  he does not really
    suggest a judgment upon the worthless characters he depicts.

10  FITTS, DUDLEY. "O Bright Young People!" Nation 130 (21 May):
    602.
        Though modeled on the early Huxley, Vile Bodies lacks Huxley's
    wit and substance. Distorting farce into tragicomedy, Waugh fails
    as a satirist because of personal intrusion.

11  GOULD, GERALD. "Post War and Pre-Waugh." Observer (London),
    2 February, p. 8.
        Vile Bodies presents a strange, youthful world, whose vul-
    garity Waugh chronicles with disgust.

12  GREENE, GRAHAM. "Plenty of Good Novels." Everyman, 30 October,
    pp. 419-20.
        Defends the value of contemporary novels, mentioning Vile
    Bodies as promising still better fiction from Waugh.

13  GREENIDGE, TERENCE. Degenerate Oxford?  A Critical Study of
    Modern University Life. London:  Chapman & Hall, pp. 71-117,
    143-49.
        While not discussing Waugh or his works, this study gives

a fascinating picture of Waugh's Oxford, particularly in dealing
with the "aesthetes" and the status of religious belief.

14   HARTLEY, L.P. "The Literary Lounger." Sketch, 29 January, p.
       214.
          Calls Vile Bodies a very entertaining book in which Waugh
presents life with the blood coursing through its veins: his humor,
irresponsible and irreverent, responds eagerly to life at every
turn. Finds him more refreshing, therefore, than Ronald Firbank
or Aldous Huxley, even though he is their inferior as an artist.

15   HORGAN, PAUL. "Mr. Waugh." New York Herald Tribune Books,
       23 November, p. 18.
          Describes the author as the center of attraction in Labels
(A Bachelor Abroad). Like Beerbohm, Waugh bases his fantasies on
the complex realities which attract him, such as the flamboyant
architecture of Gaudi.

16   JAMES, STANLEY B. "Evelyn Waugh's Apologia." Missionary 44
       (December):415-17.
          Sees Waugh's conversion to Catholicism as proof that youth
is not universally pagan. Deservedly termed the spokesman of the
postwar generation, Waugh comes from a literary family and shows
promise of a fine career. Refers to Waugh's Daily Express article
("Converted to Rome: Why it Happened to Me," 20 October, p. 10),
which equates Christianity with civilization.

17   NICOLSON, HAROLD. "Books This Week." Daily Express (London),
       3 October, p. 8.
          Review of Labels, describing Waugh's mind as acquisitive and
inquisitive. His blend of humor and scepticism, intelligence and
flippancy, makes him the best example of the postwar spirit.

18   PRITCHETT, V.S. "Warnings." Spectator 144 (18 January):99.
          Calls Vile Bodies a piece of savage satire; says he laughed
at it until he was driven out of the room. Unfortunately Waugh
feels obliged to moralize occasionally. Also, unsure about the
final world catastrophe which is Waugh's judgment upon his revels.

19   WAUGH, ARTHUR. One Hundred Years of Publishing. London:
       Chapman & Hall, pp. 305-6.
          A history of Chapman and Hall by Waugh's father, who tells
the story of the acceptance of his son's first novel in his absence,
and expresses his satisfaction in having Evelyn published by the
firm.

20   WENT, STANLEY. "The Younger Generation." SatR 6 (5 April):
       891-92.
          Sees Vile Bodies as a true "saturikon," mocking the younger
generation. The epigraphs from Alice in Wonderland and the setting
of the novel in the future are the clues to its meaning.

21   WEST, REBECCA. "A Letter from Abroad." Bookman (New York) 70
     (January):551-52.
        Discusses "the dandyism of the arts" by which young writers
     like Waugh and Robert Byron pursue high Victoriana. Predicts con-
     spicuous but idiosyncratic achievement for both.

22   _____. "A Letter from Abroad." Bookman (New York) 71 (March):
     81-86.
        Speculates that Waugh will be the Max Beerbohm of his genera-
     tion. He is a satirist because he is a disappointed romanticist;
     Vile Bodies shows the amazing intricacy of his design in rendering
     social incoherence.

23   _____. "A Study in Disillusionment." Fortnightly Review, n.s.
     127 (February):273-74.
        Describes Waugh's intricate technique in Vile Bodies in terms
     of a card game. Though authentically comic, the novel is one more
     contribution to the contemporary literature of disillusionment that
     began with Eliot's Waste Land. But Waugh's exuberance suggests
     there is an end in sight. Reprinted: 1931.7.


                              1931

1    ANON. "Remote People." TLS, 5 November, p. 864.
        Waugh's manner in Remote People is unsuited to his matter;
     his view of Africa is superficial, and his technical skill fails
     to interest by itself.

2    KUNITZ, STANLEY J. [Dilly Tante]. Living Authors. New York:
     H.W. Wilson, pp. 426-27.
        A brief biographical and critical account, in which it is
     noted that Waugh has a remarkable reputation for one so young, and
     that he plans to write a life of Swift and visit the United States.

3    PRYCE-JONES, ALAN. "Remote People." Weekend Review, 28
     November, p. 696.
        Praises Waugh's keen observation and vivid characterization,
     but criticizes his discontent.

4    R[OBERTS], R. E[LLIS]. "A Comedy of Masks." New Statesman and
     Nation 2 (17 October):478.
        Review of dramatized version of Vile Bodies, commenting on
     the Lord Chamberlain's ban and the change to a happy ending.

5    SALTMARSHE, CHRISTOPHER. "Some Latter-Day 'Decadents.'"
     Bookman (London) 80 (July):196-97.
        Sees postwar decadence as imitative and trivial, with border-
     line decadents like Waugh, Noel Coward and Beverly Nichols becoming
     so through their success. Having profoundly influenced their gen-
     eration through satires against their own circles, they are now
     turning towards sincerity and becoming duller.

6   WAUGH, ARTHUR. One Man's Road. London: Chapman & Hall, 390 pp.
       This biographical account by Waugh's father includes reminis-
    cences of Waugh's boyhood and youth, including the reasons why he
    could not go to Sherborne and the choice of Lancing for him "be-
    cause he had always shown a deeply religious temperament."

7   WEST, REBECCA. "Evelyn Waugh." In Ending in Earnest:  A
    Literary Log. Garden City, N.Y.: Doubleday, Doran, pp. 217-26.
       Reprint of 1930.23.

8   _____. "Picture of Travel Through Many Varied Lands, Pageant
    of the Near and Middle East." Daily Telegraph (London), 4
    December, p. 18.
       Remote People shows Waugh's inadequate concept of the travel
    book; he regards events personally rather than as parts of a total
    structure.


                              1932


1   ANON. "Hilarity in Africa." New York Times Book Review,
    2 October, pp. 12-13.
       Compares Black Mischief favorably with treatment of the same
    material in Waugh's travel books, declaring that fiction gives
    greater scope to his talent for creating astonishing absurdities.

2   ANON. "New Books and Reprints." TLS, 13 October, p. 736.
       Black Mischief confirms Waugh as the laureate of the Bright
    Young People.

3   ANON. Review of Black Mischief. Scotsman (Edinburgh), 13
    October, p. 2.
       Black Mischief is a pungent satire on the idea that the best
    thing to do with the coloured man is westernize him as quickly as
    possible.  The story would be a wild and hilarious farce were it
    not for its underlying irony.

4   BALFOUR, PATRICK (LORD KINROSS). Society Racket, A Critical
    Survey of Modern Social Life. London:  John Long, 288 pp.
       A valuable account of Waugh's youthful milieu, emphasizing
    his "romanticism," "snobbery," and "Edwardian nostalgia."  Cites
    the remark in Black Mischief that Basil Seal will turn serious as
    the epitome of the spirit of the thirties (p. 67).  Describes
    Waugh as a true satirist whose work will likely survive (pp. 160-
    61).

5   CANTWELL, ROBERT. "Mr. Waugh's Humor." Nation 135 (12 October):
    335.
       Black Mischief, a trivial satire on the more droll results
    of European imperialism, indicates Waugh's respect for factual
    reality and his grim sense of humor.

6    COWLEY, MALCOLM. "Decline and Fall." New Republic 73 (16
     November):22-23.
         In fiction, Waugh deals wittily with the Bright Young People;
     in travel books he changes from a cosmopolitan to a modern Colonel
     Blimp. Black Mischief, a fictional rendering of the travel experi-
     ences recorded in They Were Still Dancing, is a transitional work
     showing a change from comic exuberance to serious traditional loyal-
     ties.

7    GOULD, GERALD. "White Mischief and Black." Observer (London),
     9 October, p. 6.
         In Black Mischief, Waugh has done a wholly admirable thing
     in seeking to extend his domain; the new and more serious method
     is perhaps not entirely successful here, but the novel shows a
     range of capacity greater than that of Waugh's earlier works.

8    HARTLEY, L.P. "The Literary Lounger." Sketch, 19 October, pp.
     134-35.
         Black Mischief has its faults, but it is brilliant and enter-
     taining and gives food for thought. Waugh's is a curious talent;
     he only gets a kick when the simmering futility around him touches
     boiling point and scalds someone.

9    HERBERT, ALICE. "Evelyn Waugh and Pearl Buck." Yorkshire Post,
     5 October, p. 6.
         For farce of the more intelligent kind, kept up without a
     single drag to the end, Black Mischief is the best thing the re-
     viewer has read for years. It could, and covertly does, point a
     moral or two.

10   LEWIS, WYNDHAM. The Doom of Youth. New York: McBride, p. 108.
         Refers to two articles Waugh had written in the Evening
     Standard on the attitude of mind of the younger generation, and
     concludes that the only reality recognized here is a chronological
     reality; time is Waugh's god.

11   MARSHALL, HOWARD. "Evelyn Waugh Writes in a New Vein." Daily
     Telegraph (London), 4 October, p. 16.
         In Black Mischief, Waugh becomes a more serious satirist;
     this transitional novel shows his uncertainty in moving away from
     the jester's role.

12   MAXWELL, WILLIAM. Review of Black Mischief. New York Herald
     Tribune Books, 9 October, p. 7.
         Discusses Waugh's double-edged irony in fusing imaginative
     narrative with the factual detail of the travel books. The gro-
     tesque humor of the conclusion recalls Jacobean drama.

13   PARKES, HENRY BAMFORD. "Travel Disappointments." Nation 134
     (24 February):232.
         Review of They Were Still Dancing (Remote People), noting

the evolution of Colonel Blimp to the present. Waugh began with a
sophisticated humor which turned savage; this light book, however,
is perfect of its kind. The review is an early deprecation of
Waugh as "Catholic and cynic."

14   PRIESTLEY, J.B. "The Odd Little World of Mr. Evelyn Waugh."
     Evening Standard (London), 6 October, p. 11.
          Review of Black Mischief, discussing Waugh's influence on his
     younger contemporaries. He creates an idiosyncratic fictional world
     of comic but nightmarish inconsequentiality, through odd but sharp-
     ly observed detail, particularly in dialogue.

15   PROTHERO, J.K. "The Drama." G.K.'s Weekly, 14 May, p. 156.
          In spite of the sentimental "happy ending" it has been given,
     the dramatic version of Vile Bodies is more amusing than the novel.


                              1933


1    D'ARCY, Rev. MARTIN, S.J., et al. "Letter to Editor:  Mr.
     Evelyn Waugh." Tablet 161 (21 January):85.
          Father D'Arcy and eleven other prominent Catholics protested
     against an attack on Black Mischief by Earnest Oldmeadow, editor
     of the Tablet (1933.3). They said that it was going too far to
     call the book blasphemous and immoral, and also pointed out that
     the author could not defend himself because he was out of the
     country.

2    HANDFORD, BASIL W.J. Lancing:  A History of Ss. Mary and
     Nicholas College, Lancing, 1848-1930. Oxford:  Basil Blackwell,
     pp. 275, 278, 279.
          Discusses Waugh in relation to the Dilettanti and the Corpse
     Club, and the iconoclastic postwar attitude to the Officers'
     Training Corps.

3    OLDMEADOW, EARNEST. "New Books and Music--to Buy or Borrow or
     Leave Alone." Tablet 161 (7 January):10.
          Describes Black Mischief as "a disgrace to anyone professing
     the Catholic name." (See 1933.1 for a reply.) Oldmeadow responded
     with further condemnation of the book for its immodesty and irrever-
     ence. The controversy continued, with arguments on both sides
     (28 January, p. 116; 4 February, p. 149; 18 February, p. 212).

4    _____. "A Recent Novel." Tablet 161 (18 February):213-15.
          Oldmeadow defends his condemnation of Black Mischief against
     Waugh's supporters. As a Catholic writer, Waugh has a special re-
     sponsibility; he has written a scandalous and outrageous novel.
     The controversy stimulated Waugh to a rare defense of his moral
     and literary integrity, and a skillful demolition of Oldmeadow's
     criticisms. (An Open Letter to His Eminence the Cardinal Arch-
     Bishop of Westminster. London and Tonbridge:  Whitefriars Press.)

5   \_\_\_\_. "A Recent Novel." Tablet 161 (18 March):348.
   More in sorrow than in anger, Oldmeadow prints an excerpt
from Blackfriars criticizing the Black Mischief controversy.

6   STOPES, MARIE C. Letter to the editor on "A Recent Novel."
   Tablet 161 (4 February):149.
   The prominent birth-control advocate congratulates the editor
for attacking a novel in which her name has been used gratuitously.


1934

1   ANON. "Books: Fiction." Truth, 12 September, p. 406.
   A Handful of Dust is clever but insubstantial, ingeniously
witty but fantastical.

2   ANON. "A Handful of Dust." TLS, 6 September, p. 602.
   Discusses Waugh's consistency of attitude and purpose in
this study of futility.

3   ANON. "Gathering Wisdom." New Statesman and Nation 7 (17
   March):420.
   Ninety-Two Days shows Waugh's maturity, and his liking for
borderline countries where cultures are in conflict. Comments on
his religious preference and his mastery of deflation and irony.

4   ANON. "Hard Luck Story." SatR 11 (29 September):142.
   Waugh's purpose in A Handful of Dust is hard to determine;
his blend of the hilarious with the horrible results in a sense
of disgust.

5   ANON. "New Novels: A Cosmopolitan Collection." Glasgow
   Herald, 13 September, p. 4.
   At first one feels like acclaiming this as the author's
masterpiece, but second thoughts reveal a strange incongruity between character and incident. Brenda's and Tony's actions are out
of keeping with their characters; these may be Mr. Waugh's creatures, but he cannot create real people and then expect to do what
he likes with them.

6   ANON. "Ninety-Two Days." TLS, 15 March, p. 178.
   Praises Waugh's writing skill and consistency of mind in
Ninety-Two Days. His attitude to travel is the epitome of "dis-
gusto," and his eye turns inward rather than to the external scene.

7   ANON. Review of A Handful of Dust. Scotsman (Edinburgh),
   6 September, p. 13.
   The question of how Waugh was going to develop is most satis-
factorily answered by A Handful of Dust--perhaps a bitter book, but
the work of a man who has an original mind and has acquired a technique of unusual efficiency. Few authors writing in English today

can so successfully combine tragedy and comedy, the real and the fantastic.

8   ARMITAGE, GILBERT. "Youth, Youth!" Bookman (London) 86 (May): 120.
      Review of Ninety-Two Days, comparing Waugh to Jane Austen in wellbred observation of the author's own milieu.

9   BROWNE, WYNYARD. Review of A Handful of Dust. Bookman (London) 87 (October):44.
      Waugh's irony raises his humor to satire, but the novel is painful, and serious comedy is not Waugh's métier.

10  de la BEDOYERE, M. "Waugh-Mongering." Catholic Herald, 22 September, p. 11.
      Review of A Handful of Dust, noting the moral haze which has obscured evaluation of Waugh's work. Here the moral is labored and the tone too serious for Waugh's style.

11  DRIBERG, TOM [William Hickey]. "These Names Make News." Daily Express (London), 3 September, p. 6.
      Cites a letter from Waugh responding to Oldmeadow's Tablet attacks on Black Mischief. Waugh accepts literary criticism but rejects a presumptuous moral lecture.

12  HOLLIDAY, TERENCE. Review of A Handful of Dust. New York Herald Tribune Books, 23 September, p. 10.
      The British upper classes are no longer material for romantic melodrama, but instead for satiric extravaganza. Behind Waugh's extraordinary comic talent lies a serious moral intent.

13  ILES, FRANCIS. "Distinction in Three Novels." Daily Telegraph (London), 7 September, p. 7.
      Waugh is both inventor and prime exponent of a new literary method. In A Handful of Dust, humanity softens his satiric savagery; his laconic understatement blends the solemn and the outrageous.

14  MUIR, EDWIN. "New Novels." Listener 12 (19 September):507.
      A Handful of Dust demonstrates Waugh's technical skill in creating serious moral statements implicitly.

15  NILES, BLAIR. "Evelyn Waugh's Travels." New York Times Book Review, 27 May, p. 12.
      Sees Waugh as returning in Ninety-Two Days to the grand tradition of travel literature, admires his approach to literary raw materials, and notes the connection between his nonfiction and his fiction.

16  OLDMEADOW, EARNEST. "The Pity of It." Tablet 164 (8 September): 300.
      Continuing his attack on Waugh, he maintains that A Handful

<u>of Dust</u> fails as satire because it wavers between tragicomedy and
farce, the conclusion is "diabolically cruel," and snobbery mars
the whole. Waugh misuses his indubitable talent.

17    PRITCHETT, V.S.  "'Sweetly Toned.'"  <u>Christian Science Monitor</u>,
      25 April, p. 10.
         Review of <u>Ninety-Two Days</u>, remarking on Waugh's sophistica-
tion as a veneer. His true personality and talents emerge as he
matures.

18    QUENNELL, PETER.  "New Novels."  <u>New Statesman and Nation</u> 8
      (15 September):329.
         <u>A Handful of Dust</u> reveals the pensive melancholy under Waugh's
delicate comic equilibrium. Satirist and Catholic moralist fuse to
create a tragicomedy of blended pain and hilarity. Finding
Oldmeadow's criticisms (1934.16) surprising, Quennell admires
Waugh's economy, stern implied morality, and method of almost complete heartlessness.

19    SHERMAN, BEATRICE.  Review of <u>A Handful of Dust</u>. <u>New York
      Times</u>, 30 September, p. 7.
         The novel shifts abruptly from bright sophistication to a
dull travel account; Waugh's urge to tragedy is ill-considered.


                              <u>1935</u>

1     ALEXANDER, CALVERT.  <u>The Catholic Literary Revival</u>. Milwaukee:
      Bruce, pp. 290-93.
         Makes Waugh a pivotal figure in a chapter on satire, dividing
authors into "pre-Waugh" and "post-Waugh." In <u>Black Mischief</u>, Waugh
is too intent on making his readers hate modern life; it is not a
successful Catholic satire. Calls <u>A Handful of Dust</u> the most powerful satire since <u>Brave New World</u>.

2     ANON.  "The Life and Death of <u>Edmund Campion</u>." <u>Sunday Times</u>
      (London), 13 October, p. 8.
         Assuming an intelligent reader, Waugh uses rapid scene
shifts and swift-paced narrative in his novels. In this biography,
he employs technical precision and clarity to write naturally of
one who achieved heroic sanctity.

3     ANON.  Review of <u>Edmund Campion</u>. <u>Listener</u> 14 (13 November):887.
         Praises Campion's character and Waugh's craftsmanship, but
criticizes his scholarship and sense of the historical background.
He reiterates the "Catholic account" of the effects of the
Reformation on English society.

4     BURNHAM, PHILIP.  "Books:  About a Saint." <u>Commonweal</u> 23
      (27 December):247-48.
         A rare recognition of the consistency among Waugh's novels,

biographies, and travel books--in style, formal elegance, and
point of view. His mastery of experience is shown in his blend of
realism and fantasy; his moral stance is implied but unmistakable.

5    GLEN, ALEXANDER R. Young Men in the Arctic: The Oxford
     University Arctic Expedition. London: Faber & Faber, pp.
     227-60.
        An account of an expedition to Spitsbergen, on which Glen
was accompanied by Hugh Lygon and Waugh. Describes Waugh's distaste for skis and pemmican, his pessimistic philosophy, and his
gift for conversational fantasy.

6    OLDMEADOW, EARNEST. "News and Notes." Tablet 166 (12 October):
     451.
        Refers to Waugh's notoriety as a novelist, with further crit-
icism of Black Mischief. Notes Waugh's unsuitability as a war correspondent for the Daily Mail in the Abyssinian War, since Waugh is
"churlish" in his anti-Abyssinian stance. A further jibe at Waugh's
reporting appears 19 October, p. 490.

7    WOOLLCOTT, ALEXANDER. The Woollcott Reader. New York: Viking,
     pp. 1009-10.
        Introducing A Handful of Dust, says room was made for it in
this collection in the belief that a distinguished minority of
American readers would find it profoundly moving; it had dropped
into the bookshops of the United States unnoticed. It is a heart-
sick book whose gaiety has the desperate jauntiness of an orchestra
fiddling on a sinking ship.


                                1936

1    ANON. "In Abyssinia." Scotsman (Edinburgh), 16 November, p.
     17.
        In Waugh in Abyssinia, the author puts the case for Italian
intervention effectively.

2    ANON. "Italy in Abyssinia." Tablet 167 (13 June):750-51.
        A report of Waugh's address to the Newman Society of Oxford,
presenting his views on the Abyssinian War. A valuable gloss on
Waugh in Abyssinia, since it explains the reasons for Waugh's un-
popular support of Italy.

3    ANON. "Light on a Dark Place." Tablet 168 (14 November):672.
        Waugh in Abyssinia indicates the volatile and unreliable
qualities of the press; its author demonstrates his knowledge of
Abyssinia and shows how the "gulf between words and realities"
colors public information regarding the country.

4    ANON. Review of Waugh in Abyssinia. G.K.'s Weekly, 5 November,
     pp. 172-73.

Waugh's knowledge rests on experience. Sardonically noting the practices of the press and the moral indignations of the public over Abyssinia, the reviewer praises Waugh's dispassionate account.

5    ANON. "Sad Stories." TLS, 4 July, pp. 561-62.
     Describes Waugh's narrative detachment, his skill in creating tales from ephemeral nothings, and his expressed consciousness of futility in Mr. Loveday's Little Outing.

6    BOWRA, C.M. "Mr. Waugh's Short Stories." Spectator 157 (10 July):70.
     Praises Waugh's varied talents in Mr. Loveday's Little Outing, stating his unique "painful" comedy arises out of the ironic development of situations and exploitation of failure.

7    CONNOLLY, CYRIL. "Three Shelves." New Statesman and Nation 11 (4 January):25-26.
     With Powell, Hemingway, and Fitzgerald, Waugh ranks among the "Firbank derivatives." He is a naturally gifted novelist and satirist, but his development toward the Right dooms his anarchic charm to ultimate peevishness.

8    de la BEDOYERE, M. "Abyssinian War in Perspective: The Nature of Italian Occupation: Evelyn Waugh's Account." Catholic Herald, 31 October, p. 3.
     A sympathetic review of Waugh in Abyssinia, arguing that Waugh's attitudes are based on his concrete experience and noting that there are historical grounds for his view of Italian superiority.

9    GARNETT, DAVID. "Current Literature: Books in General." New Statesman and Nation 12 (7 November):735.
     Hostile review of Waugh in Abyssinia, accusing Waugh of racism, a superficial admiration for Italian civilization, ignorance of the League of Nations Covenant, and falsification of the facts of the campaign.

10    HORNE, ROGER. "Facts, Mr. Waugh!" Cherwell, 13 June, p. 164.
     Report of Waugh's address on Abyssinia to the Newman Society at Oxford, questioning the validity of his attitude to Italian aggression and observing that his Catholicism and his humor color his presentation.

11    KENSIT, J.A. "Points from Letters: Edmund Campion." Listener 15 (30 January):221.
     A letter written on behalf of the United Protestant Council to protest Desmond MacCarthy's B.B.C. review of Edmund Campion, which treated the Jesuit as an innocent man wrongly executed. Kensit offers evidence of Campion's avowed treason. MacCarthy defends himself in the same issue (pp. 221-22), but Kensit's response (12 February, p. 319) launched a controversy lasting several months

(4 March, pp. 457-58; 18 March, pp. 552-53; 1 April, p. 642). On
26 February, pp. 410-11, Waugh wrote to defend his scholarship and
to attack Kensit for ignorance and anti-Catholicism.

12   QUENNELL, PETER.  "New Novels."  New Statesman and Nation 11
     (11 January):54.
          Waugh is the only young novelist to use satirical romance;
     his conversion suggests the moral malaise which, combined with
     awareness of the absurd, produces his remarkable satire.

13   WALTON, EDA LOU.  "Mr. Waugh's Stories."  New York Times Book
     Review, 1 November, pp. 21, 23.
          Discusses Waugh's sardonic, antisentimental humor in Mr.
     Loveday's Little Outing.  He is detached, economical, and manipula-
     tive in technique.


                              1937


1    ANON.  "Waugh in Africa."  New York Times Book Review, 13 June,
     p. 11.
          Waugh in Abyssinia is a lucid and interesting narrative of
     personal experience, and useful as a minority defense of Italian
     occupation and attack on British policy, although Waugh's enthusi-
     asm may be both extravagant and premature.

*2   METZGER, JOSEPH.  Das katholische Schrifttum in heutigen England.
     Munich: Kosel & Putstet, pp. 343-44.
          Source:  Checklist, no. 1112; 1972.A1.

3    STONE, GEOFFREY.  "War in Abyssinia."  American Review 9
     (April):114-20.
          Review of Waugh in Abyssinia, noting the disunity of the Left,
     which still dominates the press and scorns the "blindness" of the
     Right.  Waugh avoids the larger moral questions by limiting him-
     self to his personal experiences, and these give validity to his
     opinions.  Italian behavior has conformed to European practice in
     Africa, and the excitement in Addis Ababa has produced more rumors
     than truth.


                              1938


1    ANON.  "Sensation-Hunting Burlesqued."  Scotsman (Edinburgh),
     5 May, p. 15.
          Scoop will probably move readers to tears--not of sorrow but
     of mirth.  No book that one can remember has presented such an
     amusing burlesque of the methods of the sensation-loving press of
     London.

2    BULLETT, GERALD.  "Society--and Three Young Men."  Yorkshire

Post, 11 May, p. 6.
Scoop is the least idiosyncratic of Waugh's books; it is excellent entertainment but it has not the unexpectedness of his
earlier novels.

3    FERGUSON, OTIS. "Action Stuff." New Republic 95 (27 July):
      340-41.
      Waugh's corrosive ridicule shows no compassion, conviction,
or admiration of worthwhile values; yet his fertile imagination
and impeccable style are delightful and salutary.

4    HARTLEY, L.P. "The Literary Lounger." Sketch, 18 May, pp.
      364, xvi.
      Like most of Waugh's novels, Scoop is compounded of fantasy,
satire and realism; but pure farce counteracts the pessimism usually found in him, so that we are left exhilarated, not depressed.
The fabulous quality, the command of the region between exaggera-
tion and fantasy, is something Waugh's imitators cannot acquire.

5    HOLLIDAY, TERENCE. "Buggy Ride for the War Correspondents."
      SatR 18 (16 July):7.
      Waugh's loathing of sensational journalism in Scoop gains
validity from the experiences recorded in Waugh in Abyssinia.

6    LAZARE, CHRISTOPHER. "Inverted Fable." Nation 147 (3 September):
      pp. 229-30.
      Waugh's comedy of bad manners, based on the revolt of his
characters against rigid social patterns, puts him in the Congreve
tradition. Scoop shows his transition from behaviorist to moralist;
this inverted fable reveals him as a "fantast with a defeated purpose."

7    McINNIS, R.J. "Clever Satirization of Present-Day Shams."
      America 59 (27 August):501
      Scoop is a satirical extravaganza attacking current shams
of journalism, British foreign policy, and war correspondents.
Though Alexander Woollcott hails Waugh as England's postwar literary genius, the author of Edmund Campion here wastes his time with
trivialities.

8    SWINNERTON, FRANK. "New Novels." Observer (London), 8 May,
      p. 7.
      Waugh's talent for stating the preposterous in simple, fas-
tidious terms, his creation of sanity by translating the real into
the idiotic, are clearly revealed in the modern Wonderland of Scoop.

9    VAN GELDEN, ROBERT. Review of Scoop. New York Times Book
      Review, 24 July, p. 6.
      England's wittiest novelist sets a new standard for comic
extravaganza in Scoop's fusion of slapstick with pointed satire.
But he wastes his masterful prose on a trivial farce.

10    VERSCHOYLE, DEREK.  "Introducing the Boots."  Spectator 160
      (13 May):886.
          Waugh's satire on Fleet Street creates a Wonderland where
      the idiotic becomes the inevitable.  Scoop reveals Waugh's inven-
      tive intelligence, his flexible prose, and his supreme detachment,
      unsurprised and unsentimental.

                               1939

1    ANON.  "Corruption and Oppression."  Tablet 174 (1 July):15-16.
          Shrewd and entertaining, Robbery under Law still seriously
     examines the threat political mismanagement poses to precariously
     achieved civilization.  The review includes Waugh's profession of
     political faith.

2    CALDER-MARSHALL, ARTHUR.  "An Englishman Abroad."  Life and
     Letters Today 22 (September):468-74.
          Hostile review of Robbery under Law, exposing in detail
     Waugh's misjudgement of Mexico regarding labor unions and religious
     persecution.  Concludes with sarcasm against the Catholicism of
     Waugh and Graham Greene.

3    ELLIS, G.U.  Twilight on Parnassus.  London:  Michael Joseph,
     passim, esp. pp. 370-84.
          Compares Waugh to William Gerhardi, Anthony Powell, and other
     post-war writers, and also describes the influence of Ronald Firbank
     on him.  Sees him moving from the satirical absurdity of Vile Bodies
     to the fastidious despair of A Handful of Dust; what once seemed
     social satire survives in a wit that time has not blunted and in
     an underlying pessimism.

4    JAMES, EARLE K.  "Trouble below the Rio Grande."  Living Age
     357 (October):197-98.
          Review of Robbery under Law, noting Waugh's fear of the ef-
     fect of chaos on spiritual values.  Blatantly biased, Waugh occu-
     pies an inappropriate reactionary position.

5    MARETT, R.H.K.  Sunday Times (London), 9 July, p. 10.
          Robbery under Law defines Waugh's political position as a
     Roman Catholic Conservative, and is a useful balance to the flood
     of Mexican books written from a Liberal viewpoint.  Robbery of the
     Church, land and industry leaves Mexico's future hopeless, in
     Waugh's pessimistic argument.

6    MASON, H. St. LEGER.  "Robbery under Law."  Tablet 174 (15
     July):86.
          A letter to the editor, including Philip Page's review of
     this travel book (1939.7) in which Waugh is charged with revealing
     iniquities in the Mexican Church.  Waugh replied (19 August, p.
     250) with a copy of the retraction published in the Daily Mail

(11 August), in which his defense of the Mexican Church is clari-
fied.

7   PAGE, PHILIP.  "Philip Page Reviews New Books."  Daily Mail
    (London), 30 June, p. 4.
        Calls Waugh's Robbery under Law a masterpiece of observation,
and goes on to discuss reasons for the muddle in Mexico.  Waugh
took exception to one sentence:  "There is much information about
the fantastic riches of the Church, and also some repulsive stories
of the immorality of monks and nuns and of tortures inflicted which
rival those of the Spanish Inquisition."  Page printed a retraction
in his column "New Books" (11 August, p. 14), saying he had no intention of implying that Waugh believed these calumnies.

8   PARKES, H.B.  "Who Told Him All That?"  New York Herald Tribune
    Books, 24 September, p. 9.
        Waugh's high reputation as a novelist and a stylist is de-
served; but in Robbery Under Law his Catholic and conservative
prejudices falsify his observations.  Ignorance, defense of the
Church, and fear of Communism lead to Waugh's fantastic misstate-
ments.


## 1940

1   WORCESTER, DAVID.  The Art of Satire.  Cambridge, Mass.:
    Harvard University Press, pp. 106-8.
        The simple souls of Huxley and Waugh, subdued observers in
a world of startling events and people, are descendants of Voltaire's
Candide and Johnson's Rasselas.  Modern ingénu satire is a confes-
sion of the soul's bankruptcy.


## 1942

1   ABRAHAMS, WILLIAM.  "Brilliant Style, Sharp Wit in 'Put Out
    More Flags.'"  Boston Daily Globe, 20 May, p. 15.
        Cites the dedicatory letter to Randolph Churchill as the key
to the novel, which fuses irony with social interpretation.  But
Waugh's irony is too polite:  he still believes in the relevance
of the English upper classes.

2   ALLINGHAM, MARGERY.  "New Novels."  Time and Tide 23 (28 March):
    276.
        Praising Put Out More Flags highly, sees in it the distilled
essence of the 1920s, and magnificent variations on the great joke
of the period, "the absurdity of the Ultimately Awful."

3   ANON.  "De Mortuis Nil Nisi Bonum."  Lancing College Magazine
    (Christmas Term):126-27.
        Notes the twenty-first anniversary of the Corpse Club at

Lancing, formed to discourage enthusiasm. Their rituals are described, and the subsequent careers of their founders, including
Waugh.

4    ANON. "The Great Bore War." Time 39 (25 May):90.
     Put Out More Flags is a funny, cruelly searching image of
contemporary England by one of the most deadly serious moralists
of the time.

5    BOWER, ANTHONY. "Waugh and Peace." Nation 154 (6 June):658-59.
     Waugh is unique as a satirist of the English aristocracy in
the twenties; Put Out More Flags is a familiar satire, with under-
tones of regeneration and a hint that Waugh has outgrown his characters.

6    CERF, BENNETT A. "Evelyn Waugh's Satiric Epitaph on a Footless
     Generation of British Café Society." New York Herald Tribune
     Books, 24 May, p. 5.
     Put Out More Flags is the epitaph for the postwar generation;
Waugh, their self-appointed historian, is the finest contemporary
satirical writer, though his work is too British and sophisticated
for American bestseller lists.

7    DANGERFIELD, GEORGE. "Waugh. . . ." SatR 25 (30 May):7.
     Compares Waugh to Saki. The latter never grew up, but Waugh's
apparent cruelty and irresponsibility cover a serious purpose--an
attack on the society which made Basil Seal possible.

8    HAYNES, E.S.P. "Put Out More Flags." Truth, 3 April, p. 270.
     His intelligence and precision establish Waugh as a throw-
back to the eighteenth century. Living in an age of chaos, he has
turned life into a harlequinade, but war has made it stranger and
more ridiculous than fiction.

9    MAGUIRE, C.J. "Catholic Letters Waste a Weapon." America 68
     (10 October):17-18.
     Asks why Catholic literature neglects its satirists, and
answers it is because they disturb complacency. Depicting the in-
anity of a life style, Waugh reduces it to anguished futility;
though his work seems scandalous, it constitutes true tragedy.

10   MARLOWE, JACK. "A Reader's Notebook--II." Penguin New Writing
     14 (July-September):133-40.
     Put Out More Flags makes cutting fun of the war. But Waugh
is an angry moralist and prophet, as well as a superb comedian;
there is a dark thread running through the novel.

11   PRYCE-JONES, ALAN. "For Adults Only." New Statesman and Nation
     23 (11 April):245-46.
     Waugh's popularity rests on his adult sophistication; Put Out
More Flags excels in destructive satiric attack. Waugh's point of

view has gradually emerged--Catholic, solitary, romantic, unrelent-
ing, snobbish.

12   QUENNELL, PETER. "Selected Notices." Horizon 5 (May):348-49.
        Put Out More Flags is a middling Waugh satire, showing his
gifts of comic improvisation, exuberance, and surprise, as well as
his occasional flaw of romantic partiality.  His viewpoint is
Catholic, romantic, conservative; as always, the satirist's reme-
dies seem strangely futile compared to hsi brilliant recriminations.

13   WRIGHT, CUTHBERT. Review of Put Out More Flags. Commonweal 36
        (12 June):185.
        The last of the great literary dandies, Waugh possesses taste,
irony, snobbery, and an aptitude for shocking the bourgeoisie.  He
has always been Catholic-minded in his revolt against the English
social environment.


                            1943

1   ANON. "War Intervenes." TLS, 23 January, p. 41.
        A fragment published in a limited edition, Work Suspended is
more important to the author than to the public.  Waugh is amusing,
acute, sometimes decorative and sometimes too shrill.

2   DENNIS, NIGEL. "Evelyn Waugh:  The Pillar of Anchorage House."
        PR 10 (July-August):350-61.
        Unjustly neglected because his dexterity is judged frivolous,
Waugh is England's foremost contemporary comic novelist.  His snobbery, comic cruelty, and technique of deflation also mislead the
public; he consistently uses the great house to symbolize the passing of the landed gentry.  When he turns from satire to tragedy as
in A Handful of Dust, he is too shallow to succeed; the fragment
Work Suspended is really his best work.  In Put Out More Flags,
the playboys are reborn as knight commandos, while the younger
English intellectuals fall into permanent ghosthood.  The conflict
between the aesthete Ambrose Silk and Basil Seal, the man of action,
really represents Waugh's own inner tension.

3   HALE, LESLIE. "New Novels." Sunday Times (London), 10 June,
        p. 3.
        In the fragment Work Suspended, Waugh moderates his more ex-
travagant fancy and blends feeling with his satire.

4   HAMPSON, J. Review of Work Suspended. Spectator 170 (15
        January):60, 62.
        States that Waugh devotees are saddened by the loss of his
"world" in Work Suspended, but also curious about the purpose of
this fragment.

<u>1944</u>

1    WILSON, EDMUND.  "'Never Apologize, Never Explain':  The Art of
     Evelyn Waugh."  <u>NY</u> 20 (4 March):75-76.
         Sees Waugh as "the only first-rate comic genius" since Shaw;
     his art combines the audacious and outrageous with the plausible.
     Surveying his career, Wilson shows Waugh's progress towards con-
     ventional fiction; because of its sustained impression of terror,
     <u>A Handful of Dust</u> is his masterpiece.  Because he approaches the
     aristocracy from the outside, his snobbery works; his political,
     religious, and moral opinions do not mar his fiction.
         Reprinted:  1950.27.


<u>1945</u>

1    ANON.  "Books of the Week:  A Great Catholic Novel."  <u>Tablet</u>
     185 (9 June):273-74.
         Calls <u>Brideshead Revisited</u> a major achievement in British
     fiction; its intricate design describes the struggle of the world
     and the flesh with God's grace.  Asserting the significance of the
     invisible order, the novel is a great apologetic work.

2    ANON.  "Pagan World."  <u>TLS</u>, 2 June, p. 257.
         In <u>Brideshead Revisited</u>, the prejudices of a Catholic apolo-
     gist and romantically conservative preacher engulf the comedy.
     Though sometimes brilliant, the style is flawed by a preconceived
     idea.

3    BERESFORD, J.D.  Review of <u>Brideshead Revisited</u>.  <u>Manchester
     Guardian</u>, 1 June, p. 3.
         Admires Waugh's gifts, but disparages the material he uses
     in <u>Brideshead</u>.

4    BRADY, CHARLES A.  "Contemporary Catholic Authors:  Evelyn
     Waugh:  Shrove Tuesday Motley and Lenten Sackcloth."  <u>Catholic
     Library World</u> 16 (March):163-77, 189.
         Relates Waugh's biographies and travel books to his fiction
     in order to show his evolution from comic  to religious writer and
     novelist of love.  His intellectual detachment is often mistaken
     for amorality, his conservatism for fascism.  He combines the
     outrageous with the comic, but he is always serious about the hu-
     man verities--as in the companion novels <u>A Handful of Dust</u> and
     <u>Brideshead</u>.

5    CHURCHILL, RANDOLPH.  "Captain Evelyn Waugh."  <u>Book-of-the-Month
     Club News</u>, December, pp. 4-5.
         Discusses Waugh's pleasure in provoking controversy among
     Bloomsbury intellectuals, who suffer from "proletarian snobbism."
     Describes Waugh as Catholic, Tory, reactionary, and idiosyncratic.

6    CLINTON-BADDELEY, V.C.   Review of Brideshead Revisited.
     Spectator 174 (8 June):532.
          Stresses the importance of the frame story in Brideshead, as
     well as the brilliant narrative method and characterization.   The
     novel is both witty and deeply serious.

7    CONNOLLY, CYRIL.   "The Novel-Addict's Cupboard" and "Where
     Engels Fears to Tread."   The Condemned Playground. Essays:
     1927-1944.   London: Routledge, pp. 116, 136-53.
          Describes Waugh as a novelist in a predicament:  he is the
     most naturally gifted novelist of his generation, but his develop-
     ment has taken him into right-wing satire, which is always peevish.
     In "Where Engels Fears to Tread," novels dealing with the Bright
     Young People (here "The Bald Young People") are parodied, with
     special attention to Waugh's method of characterization by snippets
     of allusive dialogue.

8    HUTCHENS, JOHN K.   "Evelyn Waugh's Finest Novel."   New York
     Times Book Review, 30 December, pp. 1, 16.
          Brideshead marks a transition from farce to realism, though
     Waugh retains his stylistic precision and moralistic stance.   Hav-
     ing reached perfection as a satirist, he naturally moves to more
     spacious spheres.   His religious and political opinions do not mar
     his artistry.

9    MacCARTHY, DESMOND.   "A Fine Novel."   Sunday Times (London),
     3 June, p. 3.
          Describes Brideshead Revisited as Waugh's finest achievement,
     objectively exploring the relation of Catholics to the modern world.

10   MORLEY, CHRISTOPHER.   "The January Selection."   Book-of-the-
     Month Club News, December, pp. 1-4.
          Discusses Brideshead Revisited as a "seductive sardonic
     novel" about an aristocratic Catholic family lapsed from grace.
     Testifies to Waugh's accuracy as a social historian.

11   MUIR, EDWIN.   "New Novels."   Listener 33 (28 June):772.
          Brideshead Revisited makes explicit Waugh's consistent liter-
     ary seriousness and humanity.   Waugh describes the characters' so-
     cial setting effectively, and his "objective complexity" produces
     surprising effects of wit, but the religious pattern loses credi-
     bility as it becomes clearer.

12   QUENNELL, PETER.   "Waugh and Peace."   Daily Mail (London),
     2 June, p. 2.
          Brideshead demonstrates both Waugh's brilliance and his
     faults; a romantic Tory with increasingly aggressive prejudices,
     he is sometimes guilty of overwriting, he hates and fears the
     modern world, and he flees reason for dogma.

13   REED, HENRY.   "New Novels."   New Statesman and Nation 29

(23 June):408-9.
     Waugh's literary seriousness becomes explicit in Brideshead,
a deeply moving novel flawed by vulgar snobbery.  Its theme is
God's watchfulness over both Christian and pagan sinners; but, un-
like Mauriac, Waugh lacks human sympathy.

14   SPECTORSKY, A.C.  "Waning of a British Catholic Family."
     Chicago Sun Book Week, 30 December, p. 1.
          Reviews Brideshead as a seriously flawed novel.  The roman-
ticism of Oxford and the extravagance of Brideshead indicate Waugh's
protest against the passing of the aristocracy, but his brilliance
does not hide his snobbery, anti-Americanism, and presentation of
Catholicism in its least engaging aspects.


                              1946


1    ANON.  "Scribe of the Dark Age."  Time 47 (8 April):26-27.
          Describes Waugh as a devout Catholic, snob, and aesthete--
all part of his revulsion from modernity.  Refers in detail to
Waugh's open letter to his readers ("Fan-Fare," Life, 8 April,
pp. 53, 54, 56, 58, 60).

2    ANON.  "'To Crie Alarme.'"  Time 48 (1 July):102, 104.
          Review of Edmund Campion (2d ed.), noting Waugh's identifi-
cation of supernatural grace with a certain kind of gaiety.  Suggests Waugh may sense a similarity between his mission as a comic
writer and Campion's as a priest, to point out the vice and ignorance which corrupt the times.

3    CHILTON, ELEANOR CARROLL.  "The Struggle to be 'Good.'"  SatR
     29 (5 January):6.
          Describes Brideshead as a romantically charming presentation
of a self-contained fictional world full of the stuff of life.
But the narrative viewpoint, the framework, and the strangely puri-
tanical Catholicism are barriers to the appreciation of the novel.

4    DENECKE, CHARLES S.J.  "Book of the Month Club . . . January
     Selection."  Best Sellers 5 (1 February):197-98.
          Though structurally weak, Brideshead has an appealing charm
and superior craftsmanship.  But the two halves do not cohere, and
the denouement is both too abrupt and unclear to the non-Catholic
reader.

5    FREMANTLE, ANNE.  "'Who Is Wise? . . .'"  Commonweal 43
     (4 January):311-13.
          A splendid novel, Brideshead is an abrupt change for Waugh,
particularly in characterization.  He has acquired the compassion
needed by a major novelist, but his tale is too grim for greatness.

6    GANNETT, LEWIS.  "Books and Things."  New York Herald Tribune,

2 January, p. 17.
    Brideshead is brilliant but fundamentally "decadent." A
nostalgic lament for adolescence, a recognition of worldly vanity,
a reassertion of traditional faith and values--it still adds up to
nothing. Without mellowness, the novel's brilliance fades under
analysis.

7   _____. "Follow-up on Waugh." America 74 (16 February):536.
    Continues argument of 12 January, referring to Waugh's note
in the English edition of Brideshead about his "attempt to trace
the workings of the Divine purpose in a pagan world."

8   GARDINER, HAROLD C. "'Nigh Draws the Chase.'" America 74
    (12 January):44.
    Brideshead is a profoundly Catholic work, partially flawed
by some dissonance of style and theme. Satire impinges gently on
the central theme of the Prodigal Son; Waugh shows memory replaced
by reality, and the patient watchfulness of God.

9   _____. "Waugh's Awry Critics." America 74 (12 January):409-10.
    Discusses the recent popularity of Catholic fiction and the
different criteria used by Catholic and non-Catholic critics in
evaluating it. Finds that the critics have missed the Hound of
Heaven theme in Brideshead Revisited, and confused surface with
substance. Provoked a response from J.M. Patterson (2 February,
p. 503), arguing for aesthetic evaluations of fiction rather than
theological.

10  GARRISON, W.E. "A Twitch on the Thread." Christian Century
    63 (24 April):527-28.
    Discusses the mixed response to Brideshead and Waugh's ex-
plicit statement of his intentions in Life (8 April). Waugh
preaches that the secular life leads to futility and that Christianity offers the only escape, but when he identifies Christianity
with Catholicism he narrows the effectiveness of his novel.

11  HEILMAN, ROBERT B. "Sue Bridehead Revisited." Accent 7
    (1946-47):123-26.
    Noting the similarities between Brideshead and Hardy's Jude
the Obscure, especially in the heroine's act of renunciation, finds
that Julia Flyte fails as a character because her inner conflict
is unrealized, and maintains that religious conviction dims the
novelist's sympathetic imagination.

12  MACAULAY, ROSE. "Evelyn Waugh." Horizon 14 (December):360-76.
    Surveying Waugh's whole career, praises his ability to create
his own universe of lunatic logic and anarchic fantasy; he is a
dextrous circus master, ironic, detached, and amoral. When he
abandons his circus tent, he becomes flamboyant and sentimental;
the style of Brideshead is "liquefied" by romance, snobbery, and
Catholicism. He must give up such adolescent self-indulgence and

regain his unique comic spirit and ironic tolerance.  Reprinted:
1948.18.

13  MAYBERRY, GEORGE.  "Isherwood and Waugh to Date."  New Republic
    114 (21 January):96-97.
        Rejoices that dogma has not harmed the talents of either
author and, although Catholicism and Churchillian Toryism intrude
into Brideshead, and technical flaws mar it, it still demonstrates
Waugh's enormous talent.

14  NORTH, STERLING.  "Waugh Jerks School Tie of Feudal Aristocracy
    In First Work Since War."  Washington Post, 6 January, p. 135.
        Despite Waugh's reactionary politics, snobbery, racial and
religious prejudice, and lack of compassion, Brideshead is a truly
great novel.

15  O'BRIEN, CONOR CRUISE [Donat O'Donnell].  "The Pieties of Evelyn
    Waugh."  Bell 13 (December):38-49.
        Argues that "alien pieties"--romanticism, adolescent nostal-
gia, veneration for the upper classes--mingle with Waugh's Catholicism to make it a highly eccentric system of belief.  Tolerant of
great sins by the aristocracy, Waugh condemns minor faults in the
lower orders.  Reprinted: 1947.7.  Revised: 1952.24.
        T.J. Bannington wrote a detailed defense of Waugh (February
1947, pp. 58-63); to this O'Brien responded with a reiteration of
his argument (March 1947, pp. 57-62).  Waugh himself wrote to as-
sert the good faith of his conversion to Catholicism, and to admit
his preference for the European upper classes, a preference which
influenced neither his conversion nor his writing (July 1947, p.
77).  Reprinted: 1947.7; 1951.13.  Revised: 1952.29.

16  RAGO, HENRY.  "A Study in Movement."  Commonweal 44 (30 August):
    480-82.
        In Edmund Campion, Waugh's gifts as a writer of dramatic nar-
rative, employing "a visual pattern of opposing actions," are used
to create a cinematic effect.  Taste and intelligence make him a
consummate minor artist.

17  REED, HENRY.  The Novel Since 1939.  London: Longmans, Greene,
    pp. 34-36.
        Despite its impressive design, Brideshead Revisited lacks
religious feeling; its most notable flaw is the strange tasteless-
ness of its snobbery.  Waugh is indifferent to art, and his reactionary point of view declines into irritated pettiness.

18  SOBY, JAMES THRALL.  "Writer vs. Artist."  SatR 29 (17 August):
    24-26.
        In Brideshead, Charles Ryder maligns modern art:  Waugh's
aesthetic opinions firmly define him as a reactionary.

19  SUGRUE, THOMAS.  "Evelyn Waugh, Satirist, Has Come of Age:  He

Now Sees His Generation in Serious, Mature Perspective." New York Herald Tribune Weekly Book Review, 6 January, pp. 1-2.

In Brideshead, Waugh uses familiar material--the postwar generation that saw its social edifices crumble before more utilitarian modern structures--but now describes it objectively in retrospect.

20    SULLIVAN, RICHARD. "Elizabethan Jesuit." New York Times Book Review, 7 July, p. 6.

Relates Edmund Campion to Waugh's evolving literary preoccupations. Calls attention to the vitality of Campion's personality and Waugh's insight and impeccable selection of material. Sees the biography as illustrating the universal drama of religious and political conflict, the clash of private conscience with loyalty to the state.

21    TEMPLE, PHILIP. "Some Sidelights on Evelyn Waugh." America 75 (27 April):75-76.

Contains biographical information about Waugh, discusses his literary reputation, describes his controversy with Oldmeadow over Black Mischief, and quotes extensively from his apologia for his conversion (Daily Express, 20 October 1930, p. 10).

22    TRILLING, DIANA. "The Piety of Evelyn Waugh." Nation 162 (5 January):19-20.

Brideshead is structurally and thematically incoherent. Catholics in the novel are either wicked or silly; Lady Marchmain's piety is condemned by its effects. Waugh equates Catholicism with the salvation of the English aristocracy, ignoring political and economic causes for its decline. Reprinted: 1978.B37.

23    WILSON, EDMUND. "Lesser Books by Brilliant Writers." NY 22 (13 July):73-74.

While Edmund Campion presents an impressive personality, Waugh's sense of history is trivial and over-simplified: he views the Reformation as the source of all that is despicable in the modern world. Reprinted: 1950.27.

24    ____. "Splendors and Miseries of Evelyn Waugh." NY 21 (5 January):64-67.

Scathing review of Brideshead by a former Waugh enthusiast. Breaking from the comic vein into seriousness, Waugh begins well but soon lapses into banal romantic fantasy. Snobbery is Waugh's true religion; though his novel is a Catholic tract, it lacks genuine religious experience. Waugh's comic anarchy has been disciplined and destroyed by faith. Reprinted: 1950.27.


## 1947

1    ANON. "Classical Side." TLS, 20 December, p. 657.

<u>Scott-King's Modern Europe</u> reveals Waugh's strengths and weaknesses. His emphasis on the interference of politics and materialism in individual lives detracts from his more universal theme of the triumph of barbarism in the modern world.

2   BEARY, THOMAS JOHN. "Religion and the Modern Novel." <u>CathW</u>
    166 (December):203-11.
        Discusses religion as a theme in fiction, with emphasis on the problems of the religious novelist; discusses Greene, Huxley, and Harry Sylvester, as well as Waugh. In <u>Brideshead</u>, Waugh admirably dramatizes the revitalizing power of the Catholic Church and warns against confusing the Church with its imperfect members.

3   BETJEMAN, JOHN. "The Angry Novelist." <u>Strand</u> 112 (March):42,
    44.
        The introduction to "Tactical Exercise," published in the same issue. Commends Waugh's impeccable prose style, story-telling talents, and serious purpose in comedy. The Catholic Church provided him with a needed logical framework, and his conversion has colored his work. Yet he is scholarly and methodical, impartial and unsentimental in his writing. The Osbert Lancaster caricature of Waugh appears on p. 43.

4   _____. "Evelyn Waugh." In <u>Living Writers</u>. Edited by Gilbert
    Phelps. Being Critical Studies Broadcast in the B.B.C. Third
    Programme. London: Sylvan Press, pp. 137-50.
        Includes biographical details and a comparison to Firbank. Calls Waugh the one English novelist of Betjeman's own generation certain to be remembered. Emphasizes his mental and spiritual growth; he is a whole person, with a complete philosophy of life. <u>Brideshead</u>, for example, is often called his greatest failure, but it is his greatest achievement, because of its serious theme.

5   CONNOLLY, FRANCIS X. "Books of the Week." <u>Commonweal</u> 45
    (24 January):376.
        <u>When the Going was Good</u> reveals Waugh's genuine satiric vein. His manners and style are consciously deliberate, creating a self-caricature which the public accepts as real. Refers to the critical debate over <u>Brideshead</u>.

6   HUGHES, RILEY. Review of <u>When the Going was Good</u>. <u>Columbia</u> 26
    (February):13.
        This book demonstrates Waugh's ironic, critical detachment, illustrates the connection between his satire and his Catholicism, and reveals the extent to which personal expression gets into his novels. He is the ironic observer of a Post-Reformation mechanistic world dominated by a siege mentality.

7   O'BRIEN, CONOR CRUISE [Donat O'Donnell]. "The Pieties of Evelyn
    Waugh." <u>Kenyon Review</u> 9 (Summer):400-11.

Reprint of 1946.15; the ensuing correspondence is not included. Reprinted: 1951.13. Revised: 1952.29.

8    PRESCOTT, ORVILLE. "Books of the Times." New York Times, 6 January, p. 21.
      When the Going Was Good is only interesting as apprentice work; Waugh is far more effective when he uses his travel experiences in fiction. As a traveler, he was a typical twenties sophisticate. Brideshead won him international fame, but his snobbish and witty comic satires appealed only to a small circle of enthusiasts.

9    SAVAGE, D.S. "The Innocence of Evelyn Waugh." In Focus Four: The Novelist as Thinker. Edited by B. Rajan. London: Dobson, pp. 34-46.
      As he moves closer to serious writing, Waugh reveals his sentimental nostalgia, adolescent prankishness, and romantic idealism --all qualities of immaturity. Deliberately detached from human experience, he is fundamentally puerile; his mind is inadequate to the demands of tragedy. Reprinted: 1950.20.

10    SUGRUE, THOMAS. Review of When the Going was Good. New York Herald Tribune Weekly Book Review, 5 January, p. 4.
      While the travel books provided the raw material of Waugh's fiction, their intrinsic interest lies in the nostalgia they reveal, and in Waugh's unconscious portrait of himself as a certain type of English gentleman--the type he satirizes in his novels.

11    TINDALL, WILLIAM YORK. Forces in Modern British Literature, 1885-1946. New York: Knopf, pp. 127-28. Reprint. 1949.
      Waugh is funnier and more savage than Aldous Huxley. Like Huxley, he found in religion a refuge from the world, but unlike Huxley he remained an artist, leaving sermons to the clergy. Revised: 1956.14.

12    WALL, BARBARA. "London Letter." America 77 (28 June):354.
      Replies to criticisms of Waugh's snobbery by Rose Macaulay in Horizon (1946.12) and Donat O'Donnell in Bell (1946.15).

## 1948

1    ACTON, HAROLD. Memoirs of an Aesthete. London: Methuen, esp. pp. 201-5.
      "An almost inseparable boon companion at Oxford was a little faun called Evelyn Waugh." The book contains accounts of Waugh's first marriage and the publication of Decline and Fall; it also makes the point that not all of the writing of the twenties was persiflage, for books like Waugh's Rossetti contain stronger meat than many expect.

2    ALLEN, W. GORE.  "The Shires, the Suburbs, and the Latin
     Quarter."  Irish Monthly 76 (June):260-64.
         Discusses the modern fictional approach to Catholicism and
conversion, contrasting Brideshead with a novel by Ethel Mannin.
Waugh excels in subtlety and social realism, but errs in associat-
ing the Catholic life with the aristocracy.

3    ANON.  "A Knife in the Jocular Vein."  Time 52 (12 July):86-89.
         Reviews Waugh's literary career and describes his self-
contained fictional world that is reigned over by lunacy and tragicomedy.  Brideshead lacked his outrageous ironic humor; it is found
again in The Loved One, which ridicules America's attempts to pret-
tify death and vulgarize love.  Concludes that Waugh's Catholicism
and lack of compassion limit his literary abilities.

4    ANON.  "The Waiting Ones at Bay."  TLS, 20 November, p. 652.
         Waugh is often regarded as a melancholy clown, though he
posesses all the satiric talents and excels as a flayer of society.
His religious rage is more effective than his romantic nostalgia.
The Loved One is an awe-inspiring satire on materialism and its
effects on the human spirit in love and death.

5    BARRY, IRIS.  "In a Paradise of Morticians."  New York Herald
     Tribune Weekly Book Review, 27 June, p. 4.
         Discusses the satirical, sepulchral, humorous gusto of The
Loved One, a "traveller's tale" about Hollywood burial customs and
the general oddity of America.

6    BRODIE, [C.].  "First Impressions of Literary People:  Evelyn
     Waugh:  The Writer Who is Both Very Young and Very Old."  Books
     of Today (May):6-7.
         "Elderly" in appearance, Waugh possesses a youthful outrageous
wit.  He enjoys reading his own books, and believes writing "should
be like clockmaking."  He contends that American readers of
Brideshead understood not a word of it.  Contains anecdotal background material and a useful summary of Waugh's travels.

7    CONNOLLY, CYRIL.  "Introduction."  Horizon 17 (February):76-77.
         A preface to The Loved One, published in this issue.  Fore-
casts accusations of morbidity and anti-Americanism, but calls attention to Waugh's own letter explaining his main ideas in writing
the book.  A Swiftian satire on materialism, the novel integrates
rage and nostalgia into a balanced tale of love and death.

8    CONWAY, PIERRE.  "'Almost.'"  Commonweal 48 (6 August):402-4.
         Discusses the theology of Waugh's review of Graham Greene's
The Heart of the Matter (Tablet 191 [5 June]:352-54; Commonweal 48
[16 July]:322-26).  Points out that the characters in Waugh's comic
novels do not evolve, especially in the realm of religion, and thus
falsify human experience.  Brideshead therefore represents a new
achievement.

9    GARDINER, HAROLD C. "Books: Sarcophagal Satire." America 79
     (10 July):332.
     The Loved One counteracts Waugh's denial of his satiric pur-
pose and his stated intention to write of man in relation to God.
(Life, 8 April 1946). Witty as this attack on American culture
is, it is a step backward from Brideshead in artistry and subject
matter.

10   GIBBS, WOOLCOTT. "Love in Necropolis." NY 24 (23 June):70-74.
     A logical development from Waugh's earliest work, The Loved
One exhibits Waugh's comic invention, precision of style, and misanthropy. It is a rich and subtle nightmare, but not the "Swiftian
satire" praised by Cyril Connolly (1948.7).

11   GRAHAM, W.S. "England's Old Young Men." New Republic 118
     (26 April):28-29.
     Discusses the shortcomings of recent British writing, main-
taining that few writers have developed beyond their early reputa-
tions. Waugh has never developed humanity; because compassion is
missing from The Loved One, it represents a contraction of his
powers. In fact its lack-lustre caricatures and failure of insight
bring out his literary weaknesses.

12   HANSEN-LÖVE, FRIEDRICH. "Quomodo sedet sola civitas." Wort
     und Wahrheit 3:716-20.
     Quomodo sedet sola civitas could do as a motto for all Waugh's
fiction: how lost, how abandoned by God, is modern society. The
theme is especially well developed in Brideshead, which puts Waugh
in the great tragic-comic tradition of English novelists from
Fielding to Thackeray and beyond. The Loved One, showing the
American dance of death, is one of the sharpest satires since
Swift's Modest Proposal. But Waugh must not succumb to bitterness;
he would do well to heed Kierkegaard's aphorism: "In youth Swift
built a madhouse, in old age he entered it."

13   HOEHN, MATTHEW, ed. Catholic Authors: Contemporary Biographical
     Sketches, 1930-1947. Newark: St. Mary's Abbey, pp. 778-80.
     This biographical and critical article, by the editor and an
unidentified collaborator ("D.M."), places considerable emphasis
on Edmund Campion and Brideshead as revelations of Waugh's religious beliefs. It calls Waugh one of the cleverest contemporary
writers, with a fine sense of style, but lacking the saeva indignation of the great satirists.

14   JONES, ERNEST. "Very Late Waugh." Nation 167 (31 July):132-33.
     Bright but mildly boring, The Loved One fails compared to
Waugh's earliest satires. It is as monstrous as its subject; consistently venomous, Waugh confuses nightmare and tragedy and buries
morality in the macabre.

15   KING, ROBIN. "Fiction." Spectator 180 (9 January):52-53.

The satirist's mask conceals his sentimentality; without the mask he is defenseless. After the sentimentality of Brideshead, Waugh puts the mask on again in Scott-King's Modern Europe, but despite his expertise the book is dull.

16  LEE, ROBERT. "Fiction." Spectator 180 (5 March):296.
The Loved One marks Waugh's return to satire from the romanticism of Brideshead. This macabre farce is a moral tale concerning the bankruptcy of civilization.

17  LINKLATER, ERIC. "Evelyn Waugh." In The Art of Adventure. London: Macmillan, pp. 44-58.
Describes Waugh's career and personality, stressing his presentation of himself as "an old-fashioned Oxford aesthete," his wartime adventures in contrast to this, and his preference for the upper classes. Sees in Decline and Fall his emphasis on the irrational, arbitrary, and unjust, as against Hemingway's cause-and-effect toughness. Describes his conversion as a positive assertion which found literary expression in Brideshead, a brilliant comedy filled with extraordinary sadness; his dogmatic conviction of the importance of holiness forms his novels. Discusses the links between Waugh's travel experiences and his novels, his "merciless comedy," his use of the country house as an aesthetic symbol, and the development of his style from crisp economy to a rich eighteenth-century flavor.

18  MACAULAY, ROSE. "Evelyn Waugh." In Writers of Today. Edited by Denys Val Baker. Vol. 2. London: Sidgwick & Jackson, pp. 135-52.
Reprint of 1946.12.

19  MacCARTHY, DESMOND. "The Satire of Mr. Evelyn Waugh." Sunday Times (London), 21 November, p. 3.
Sees The Loved One as a satiric exposure of the modern trend which sentimentalizes religion and denies the tragedy of man's predicament in death. With masterly precision, Waugh blends fantasy and realism to create his spiritual nightmare.

20  MORRIS, ALICE S. "Death on the American Plan." New York Times Book Review, 27 June, pp. 1, 22.
Sees Waugh's literary merits as limited by his inhumanity. But his unemotional intelligence creates great satire on the American ethos in The Loved One. Death rituals are a touchstone for the country's mass mind, which treats both love and death inhumanly.

21  POWERS, J.F. "Waugh Out West." Commonweal 48 (16 July):326-27.
In The Loved One, a certain injustice and improbability are necessary to Waugh's satiric purpose, as in his earliest fiction. He uses life and death in a specific locale, Southern California, to criticize American values.

22    PRESCOTT, ORVILLE.  "Books of the Times."  New York Times,
      23 June, p. 25.
         The Loved One combines vulgarity and cruel wit in a violent
      response to the horrors of Southern California.  Waugh's target is
      not worth the intensity of his attack, nor is his locale representa-
      tive of the nation.

23    REDMAN, BEN RAY.  "Angeleno Cult for the Dear Departed."  SatR
      31 (26 June):9-10.
         Waugh's gruesome frolic, The Loved One, deals with a pure
      product of Angeleno culture, the mortuary trade.  Mixing satire,
      farce, fantasy and grim realism, it is a clever trifle.

24    ROLO, CHARLES J.  "Reader's Choice."  Atlantic 182 (July):104.
         When he abandoned ironic detachment, Waugh lost the bril-
      liance of his early comic fantasies.  In The Loved One acrimony
      blurs his vision, producing mere caricature and cliché.

*25   SCHMID, PETER.  "Evelyn Waugh, Beter und Spötter."  Weltwoch
      (Zurich) 16 (5 March):5.
         Source:  Checklist, no. 1193; 1972.A1.

26    SMITH, R.D.  "Unique and Decadent."  New Statesman and Nation
      36 (11 December):528-29.
         The Loved One shows Waugh's comic genius in macabre, fascinat-
      ing horror; yet the novel is uneven, derivative, and inferior to
      his best.  He reveals values at variance with those he intends the
      reader to grasp.

27    WECTER, DIXON.  "On Dying in Southern California."  Pacific
      Spectator 2 (Autumn):375-87.
         Discusses the recent fad of overseas satirists examining
      Californian burial customs.  Waugh nowhere reaches the level of
      Aldous Huxley; his impressions of America rest on a few stereo-
      types.

28    WOODBURN, JOHN.  "Handful of Dust."  New Republic 119 (26 July):
      24.
         Those shocked by Waugh's preoccupation with morbid material-
      ism miss the point of The Loved One, a superb satire on a decayed
      civilization.


                                    1949

1     ALLEN, W. GORE.  "Evelyn Waugh and Graham Greene."  Irish
      Monthly 77 (January):16-22.
         Compares Waugh with Greene as a critic of contemporary life,
      noting that he punishes what he loves.  Refers to Waugh's review
      of The Heart of the Matter, where he believes Waugh misses the point
      (Tablet 191 [5 June 1948]:352-54; Commonweal 48 [16 July 1948]:
      322-26).  For both writers, faith is the ultimate reality.

2   ANON. "Waugh Lecture:  Noted British Wit Discusses Three Fellow
      Convert Writers, Chesterton, Knox and Greene." Books on Trial
      7 (April):277, 301.
         An account of Waugh's American lecture tour in 1949.  Calling
Chesterton undeservedly neglected, he said that his simplicity con-·
trasts with Ronald Knox's assumption of a common culture, which
renders him unintelligible to the average modern reader.  Graham
Greene he saw as thoroughly modern, reflecting post-World War I
horror in a Christian context.

3   ANON. "Waugh on U.S. Catholicism." America 81 (1 October):681.
         Partly congratulates and partly censures Waugh for the views
in his article on U.S. Catholicism in Life (19 September).

4   BAYLEY, JOHN. "Two Catholic Novelists." National and English
      Review 132 (February):232-35.
         Greene and Waugh use Catholicism "as a weapon and a probe,"
exploring wit and anarchy from a firm viewpoint.  Both believe in
something better than the contemporary life they portray, but their
didacticism fails when it becomes manipulation.
         D.G. Neill and F.C. Johnston responded to Bayley (p. 345),
challenging his assumption of the authors' explicit Catholicism,
didactic purpose, and partisan viewpoint.

5   BREIT, HARVEY. "An Interview with Evelyn Waugh." New York
      Times Book Review, 13 March, p. 23.
         Discusses Waugh's apparent duality of innocence and cynicism;
his detached self-criticism; his opinions of contemporary writers;
his description of his own literary method; and his plans for a war
novel.  Revised:  1957.10.

6   CAREW, DUDLEY. The House is Gone, A Personal Retrospect.
      London:  Robert Hale, pp. 80-105, 199.
         Discusses public school life at Lancing from 1917 to 1922,
when Carew and Waugh were there.  Waugh's critical detachment and
austere literary taste influenced Carew; he had a natural bent for
satire, cynicism, and debunking, all with an impassive exterior.
Describes the effect of masters like J.F. Roxburgh, the formation
of the Dilettanti Society and the Corpse Club, and Waugh's warfare
with authority.

7   COUSINS, NORMAN. "Old Order vs. the New." SatR 32 (26 February):
      12.
         Wavering among satire, allegory, farce and fable, Scott-King's
Modern Europe fails by any definition to dramatize the clash of the
old order with the new barbarism.

8   GRACE, WILLIAM J. "Evelyn Waugh as a Social Critic." Renascence
      1 (Spring):28-40.
         "The object of this essay is to consider Evelyn Waugh as a
critic of contemporary relativist society, as a satirist of a world

confused and considerably disintegrated, as an artist interested
in the presentation of Catholic values." Source:  Grace.

9   GREENE, GRAHAM. "The Redemption of Mr. Joyboy." Month, n.s.
    1 (January):55-57.
       Waugh's early novels described the absurd, pathetic antics
    of his characters. In The Loved One, the observer is no longer
    innocent; by entering the moral sphere, Waugh matures. He genuine-
    ly hates what man has become, especially in view of his Redemption
    by Christ.

10  GRIFFITHS, JOAN. "Waugh's Problem Comedies." Accent 9
    (Spring):165-70.
       The shock of the incongruous is the essence of Waugh's comedy.
    Both Brideshead and The Loved One take transfigured death as their
    theme; but Dennis Barlow's obsession with death surpasses the taste-
    less. Since Scoop Waugh has lost human sympathy; The Loved One is
    his renunciation of humanity. For all his technical skill and comic
    impact, he lacks the moral core essential to the satirist.

11  MARSH, D'ARCY. "When Evelyn Waugh Thrusts, World Cries
    'Touché.'" Saturday Night, 12 April, pp. 16-17.
       Discusses Waugh's developing reputation, defending him against
    accusations of rudeness, condescension, and pitilessness by compari-
    sons with Swift and Johnson. As a "Mediterranean man," he lacks
    sympathy with North Americans; in The Loved One, he satirizes the
    materialism of America associated with its denial of the reality
    of death. He has moved from comic farce to serious fiction.

12  MARSHALL, BRUCE. "The Responsibilities of the Catholic
    Novelist." Commonweal 50 (27 May):169-71.
       Discusses Catholic fiction, contending that Waugh and Greene
    "have got the meaning of the world right." Eschewing didacticism,
    the Catholic novelist should leave his moral in the background,
    respect reality, and practice craftsmanship.

13  NIMIER, ROGER. "Journées de lecture." La table ronde 16
    (April):664-68.
       In a light-hearted discussion focusing on Waugh's unheroic
    heroes, he complains about the injustice which ranks Shaw among
    the great English writers while neglecting Waugh.

14  ORWELL, GEORGE. "New Novels from Two British Writers:  Mr.
    Waugh Pays a Visit to Perilous Neutralia." New York Times Book
    Review, 20 February, pp. 1, 25.
       Scott-King's Modern Europe completes The Loved One as Waugh's
    attack on modern civilization, whose lunatic self-destruction pre-
    vents understanding. But Waugh's narrow political vision, treat-
    ing Left and Right as indistinguishable, diminishes the effective-
    ness of the novel.

15    PRESCOTT, ORVILLE. "Books of the Times." New York Times,
      15 February, p. 21.
          Scott-King's Modern Europe is part of Waugh's sweeping con-
      demnation of the modern world. Not a pure political satire, it
      comically contemplates the victories of barbarism; yet it reflects
      the seriousness of Waugh's faith and his conservative politics.

16    PRITCHETT, V.S. "Books in General." New Statesman and Nation
      37 (7 May):473-74.
          Waugh is "the cleverest English novelist alive." Like
      Maugham, he is assuming a professional personality, slightly marred
      by snobbery and modishness. Looking at the modern world like an
      outraged schoolboy, he is fascinated by cultures in conflict and
      ideas detached from their traditions. His comic genius is romantic;
      snobbery, religion and nostalgia can destroy it, as in Brideshead.
      In Work Suspended (1949 edition), he exploits limitations and
      atrocities with remarkable comic vitality.

17    RYAN, HAROLD F. "A Vista of Diminished Truth." America 82
      (12 November):157-58.
          The Loved One is a serious satire on love and death, misunder-
      stood in a disintegrating society lacking common moral values.
      Superficially a macabre frolic, it is actually based on a sound
      apprehension of human nature and values.

18    SHEERIN, J.B. "Waugh Appraises American Catholics." CathW 170
      (November):81-85.
          Discusses in detail Waugh's article in Life ("The American
      Epoch in the Catholic Church," 19 September); his observation is
      sometimes weak but his conclusions are correct.

19    SUTCLIFFE, DENHAM. "When Irony is Not Enough." Christian
      Science Monitor, 24 February, p. 11.
          Waugh's characteristic technique in attacking modernity is
      the ironic reversal of accepted values; his demonic laughter has
      a moral intention. But Scott-King's Modern Europe is blunt, con-
      trived and dull.

20    VOORHEES, RICHARD J. "Evelyn Waugh Revisited." SAQ 48 (April):
      270-80.
          Comments on the consistent seriousness beneath the comic mask
      Waugh uses in his early novels. Defending country-house society,
      even its eccentricities, he attacks those who try to destroy it.
      He damns folly with implied morality: lack of religious faith is
      destroying civilization. His delight in Basil Seal indicates his
      cruelty; yet only Basil among Waugh's fictional characters fully
      perceives the menace of modernity as Waugh sees it.

21    WOODBURN, JOHN. "The Knife Slips." New Republic 120 (21 March):
      23-24.
          Waugh's conservative, Catholic views provide a clear vision

of the modern world, but Scott-King's Modern Europe disappoints. The hero, fascinated and appalled by his milieu, endures endless frustrations. But the profoundly serious theme is spoiled by Waugh's haphazard treatment.

22 WOODCOCK, GEORGE. "Evelyn Waugh: The Man and his Work." World Review, n.s. 1 (March):51-56.
    Surveys Waugh's evolution as a satirist, stressing his blend of cynicism about the present with sentimental nostalgia for the past. His travel books, which reveal his desire to escape the hated modern world, show that his fiction is essentially autobiographical. His lack of compassion reveals a genuine imaginative failure.


<u>1950</u>

1 ANON. "Early Christians." Newsweek 36 (15 October):98-99.
    Calls Helena Waugh's best book since Brideshead, but says that the unreality of the addled age it depicts is perhaps the defect of the novel.

2 ANON. "The Empress Helena." TLS, 13 October, p. 641.
    Helena, recalling the Roman stories of Rudyard Kipling and Robert Graves, fails by trying to do too much in a brief span.

3 ANON. "People." Time 56 (30 October):29.
    Notes Waugh's support of Hemingway's Across the River and into the Trees in the face of critical hostility. William Faulkner wrote (13 November, p. 4) to support Waugh's view.

4 BOYLE, ALEXANDER. "Contemporary Novelists--IV. Evelyn Waugh." Irish Monthly 78 (February):75-81.
    Discusses Waugh's opinions, as deduced from his fiction. Though his urbane wit unveils the knaves who prey among the fools in the leisured classes, he antagonizes the Left. He sees those not utterly self-absorbed as having a chance of salvation; his implicit Catholic views became explicit in Brideshead, which therefore provoked critical hostility. Despite its success, its method is foreign to his satirical genius.

5 C[UNEO], P.K. "Helena." Books on Trial 9 (October-November): 123, 130.
    Helena is a compact, skilfully written novel, counterpointing the fourth century with the twentieth; Helena herself is vividly characterized to carry Waugh's theme. Includes biographical note.

6 DEVER, JOE. "Echoes of Two Waughs." Commonweal 53 (October): 68-70.
    Relates anecdotes of Waugh's American visit. Helena blends the comic Waugh with the devout Waugh; the earlier parts are more convincing than the later.

7   GARDINER, HAROLD C.  "Saint Among Sophisticates."  America 84
    (11 November):110.
       Describes Helena as a streamlined, impressionistic historical
    novel with a sense of contemporaneity, but not exactly Waugh's
    metier.

8   GAUL, CECILIA C.  "A Hypothetical Helen."  Christian Century
    67 (1 November):1297.
       Both entertaining and edifying, Helena displays Waugh's tech-
    nical and narrative craftsmanship, but also his lack of historical
    veracity and his prejudices as a Catholic Englishman.  He is a
    clever and sincere propagandist.

9   HOPKINS, GERARD.  "Fiction."  Time and Tide 31 (14 October):1025.
       Discusses Waugh's blend in Helena of ancient tale and modern
    dress, with high praise for the characterization of Helena herself.

10  HUTCHENS, JOHN K.  "Books and Things."  New York Herald Tribune,
    21 October, p. 12.
       Praises Helena for its subtle wit, eloquence and elegant
    style.  The personality of Helena is delightfully rendered; Waugh
    uses anachronism deftly; his legend passes from comedy through
    satire to seriousness.

11  HUTTON, EDWARD.  "Catholic English Literature, 1850-1950."  In
    The English Catholics, 1850-1950.  Edited by George Andrew Beck.
    London:  Burns Oates, pp. 546-66.
       The return of Catholicism as an intellectual force has begun
    to make itself felt in the novel.  Greene and Waugh do not need to
    sugar their stories with romance, as Belloc and Chesterton did, but
    can present Catholicism as it really is.

12  MARSHALL, BRUCE.  "Graham Greene and Evelyn Waugh:  Grimness
    and Gaiety and Grace in Our Times."  Commonweal 51 (3 March):
    551-53.
       Greene and Waugh share literary ability, Christian faith,
    and a clear vision of modern society; Greene chronicles graceless
    grimness, Waugh graceless gaiety.  But Waugh is much colder than
    Greene.

13  MARSHALL, DAVID, and DEMETRIUS MANOUSOS.  "Evelyn Waugh Comments
    on 'Helena.'"  Anno Domini 1950 1 (Fall):5-9.
       Waugh tells of his satisfaction with Helena, its symbolism,
    its cryptic meanings and jokes.  A European novel, it will not be
    understood in America, where reviewers have already shown their
    blindness to it.  He also comments on the creation of "good" and
    "bad" characters and on the novelist's sense of wonder.

14  MORTIMER, RAYMOND.  "A Cryptic Saint."  Sunday Times (London),
    15 October, p. 3.
       Discusses the historical background of Helena, deducing the

author's defense of Christianity as historically true. Waugh's
method is calculated to shock; commenting on the present by means
of the past, his satire is obtrusive but relatively good-humoured.

15   PRESCOTT, ORVILLE. "Books of the Times." New York Times,
     17 October, p. 29.
         Helena is a slight, well-written legend, filled with surface
impressions and episodic vignettes. It lacks Waugh's satiric
thrusts; also, though filled with religious feeling, it omits treatment of Helena's conversion and any analysis of Constantine's corruption through power.

16   RAYMOND, JOHN. "New Novels." New Statesman and Nation 40
     (21 October):374.
         A "romantic" satirist, Waugh sees the Catholic Church as a
bulwark defending civilization. Helena is disappointing, flavoured
by Waugh's adolescent nostalgia and preference for the aristocracy.

17   REED, HENRY. "New Novels." Listener 44 (9 November):515.
         The saddest literary phenomenon of recent years is the in-
sistence that Waugh be taken seriously. Helena suggests an anti-
quated radio script by a sub-scholar.

18   ROLO, CHARLES J. "An Old Legend Newly Told." Atlantic 186
     (November):98-99.
         Helena is evidence of Waugh's surprising versatility. He is
much better at audacious harlequinade, however, than at fictionalized history.

19   ROVERE, R.H. "Books:  The Trouble and the Cross." NY 26
     (21 October):116-17.
         Uniting hagiography and homiletics, Helena is amusing, but
it is a polemic against democracy and liberalism. Snobbery and
faith overpower the sense of evil in the novel.

20   SAVAGE, D.S. "The Innocence of Evelyn Waugh." Western Review
     14 (Spring):197-206.
         Reprint of 1947.9.

21   SELDIN, MARIAN. Review of Helena. Renascence 3 (Autumn):97-99.
         Links Waugh's satire on the modern age in Helena to his early
novels. His talent and material are better than his novel, which
fails in characterization and, surprisingly, in style.

22   SMITH, BRADFORD. "The Daughter of Old King Cole." SatR 33
     (21 October):17.
         Helena is charming, provided one does not believe in the
heroine's sainthood, for Waugh's urbane wit, affecting disbelief
in the value of human effort, cannot deal with full characterization and dramatic intensity.

23    SPOERRI, ERIKA.  "Der Tod in Hollywood."  Universitas 5 (Heft
      12):529-31.
          In The Loved One, Waugh depicts a world of appearances, a
world of wishful thinking.  Nowhere does he himself intrude; yet
he implies by contrast the existence of his own world, that of
Catholicism.

24    SYKES, CHRISTOPHER.  "A Legend of St. Helena."  Tablet 196
      (21 October):351-52.
          Helena excels in character creation and evocation of place,
but Waugh's stylistic economy damages the time sequence.

25    TOYNBEE, PHILIP.  "Young Miss Cole."  Observer (London), 5
      October, p. 7.
          Despite Waugh's reputation for wit, Helena is flagrantly dull,
inelegant in both its seriousness and frivolity, and unconvincing.
Waugh is immovably on the side of the aristocratic angels.

26    von PUTTKAMER, ANNEMARIE.  "Evelyn Waugh."  Frankfurter Hefte
      5 (Heft 8):869-72.
          A survey of Waugh's career, with stress on the mastery of
comic and satiric techniques which the early novels show, and on
the theme of godlessness in The Loved One.  As Edmund Campion and
Brideshead show, it would be wrong to label him a satirist; here
he deals with the workings of Providence in a heathen world.  It
is to be hoped that hostile criticism of Brideshead has not driven
him back to satire, since, if there is plenty of scope for the
latter in the modern world, there is also scope and need for major
novels bringing a message of hope.

27    WILSON, EDMUND.  Classics and Commercials.  New York:  Farrar,
      Straus & Co., pp. 140-46, 298-305.
          Reprint of 1944.1; 1946.23, 24.  In addition, he comments
adversely on The Loved One.


                                1951


1     ALLEN, W. GORE.  "Evelyn Waugh's Helena."  Irish Monthly 79
      (February):96-97.
          Waugh's literary disadvantages are inseparable from his be-
liefs, which have brought him two distinct audiences, social and
religious.  By attempting to reconcile them in Helena, he suffers,
as with Brideshead, the disapproval of those hostile to his faith
or to his conservatism.

2     ANON.  "Portrait Gallery:  Evelyn Waugh."  Observer (London),
      7 January, p. 5.
          Stresses Waugh's apparent hatred for the contemporary world,
especially for democracy.  As a satirist, he is socially and re-
ligiously a traditionalist.

3    CRONIN, ANTHONY.  "A Tribute to Evelyn Waugh."  Envoy (Dublin)
     (5 July):30-36.
          A survey of Waugh's career, praising his originality, reada-
     bility, and creation of a unique comic universe.  The early comic
     satires present genuine horror, a pattern of betrayal and inverted
     values, all with comic detachment.  But Brideshead is based on sen-
     timental nostalgia; he is losing his detachment.  Subsequently he
     has returned to comedy, but his future development is unpredictable.

4    GERVAIS, LIAM.  "More Laughter in Books."  Duckett's Register 6
     (December):167-68.
          Discusses humour in contemporary Catholic writing, describing
     Waugh as a social satirist with a superb style and sense of form.

*5   HRASTNIK, H.  "Porträt Evelyn Waughs."  Die Presse (Vienna),
     27 January, p. 6.
          Source:  Checklist, no. 1052; 1972.A1.

6    HUGHES, RILEY.  "New Novels."  CathW 172 (January):312.
          Helena combines satire and hagiography in a brilliant, frag-
     mentary essay on the position of the Church in the world of Power
     without Grace.

7    IGOE, W.J.  "Mr. Waugh's Helena."  Duckett's Register 6
     (February):20-21.
          In Helena, Waugh uses a Christian perspective on the corrup-
     tion of civilization to create a fully integrated, masterly novel.

8    _____.  "Young Man in the Waste Land."  Duckett's Register 6
     (June):81-82.
          Reviews the Penguin publication of ten works by Waugh.  His
     fiction falls naturally into pre- and post-World War II phases.
     The early novels deal with upper-class response to an amoral world,
     though A Handful of Dust reveals Waugh's moral stance.  The Loved
     One is a brilliant postwar parable.  Waugh's work is unified by
     the sense of the tragic.

9    JOOST, NICHOLAS.  "Waugh's Helena, Chapter VI."  Explicator 9
     (April):item 43.
          Analyzes Waugh's remarks, through the character of Lactantius,
     on the Christian writer's function to preserve the truth.  Helena
     is a quiet polemic, refuting Gibbon's mockery of Christianity.

10   MENEN, AUBREY.  "The Baroque and Mr. Waugh."  Month 191 (April):
     226-37.
          Argues that, despite the critical disagreement over Helena,
     it is a fine contemporary novel.  Its "fault" is in fact an extra-
     ordinary technical feat.  Like Baroque art, which must be looked
     at in parts and unified by an intellectual effort on the specta-
     tor's part, the "several-centered style" of Waugh demands the in-
     tegrative activity of the reader.

*11   NETTESHEIM, JOSEFINE.  "Gnade und Freiheit:  Ist Evelyn Waughs
       Weg zur Kirche eine Sensation?"  Die Friedensstadt (Paderborn)
       14:47-50.
          Source:  Checklist, no. 1130; 1972.A1.

12   NEWBY, P.H.  The Novel, 1945-1950.  London:  Longmans, Greene,
       pp. 27-28.
          Calls Scott King's Modern Europe and The Loved One more
       limited in scope than Huxley's Ape and Essence and Orwell's 1984,
       but more successful.  Scott-King is a witty expression of Waugh's
       distaste for the confused politics of our time, The Loved One a
       brilliant piece of writing on one aspect of life in Southern
       California.  Waugh has never done anything more brilliant than this
       little book; it is a more profound comment on twentieth-century hu-
       man beings than the casual reader may suspect.

13   O'BRIEN, CONOR CRUISE [Donat O'Donnell].  "The Pieties of Evelyn
       Waugh."  In The Kenyon Critics.  Edited by John Crowe Ransom.
       Cleveland:  World Publishing Co., pp. 88-98.
          Reprint of 1946.15; 1947.7.  Revised:  1952.29.

14   OPPEL, HORST.  "Englishche Erzählkunst.  III.  Zwischen Chaos
       und Erlösung."  Die Lebenden Fremdsprachen 3 (Heft 4):100-112.
          In a broad survey of trends in English literature, describes
       Aldous Huxley's movement from cynicism to a doctrine of non-
       attachment, and Somerset Maugham's coming upon metaphysics (from
       realism and empiricism) almost unawares.  Turning to writers with
       a positive religious belief, links Waugh and Graham Greene to Georges
       Bernanos and François Mauriac.  Classifies Waugh's early work, espe-
       cially Vile Bodies, as literature of negation:  a whole generation
       seems to be saying, "We're not living in the Victorian Age."  But
       the effect is pathos:  man simply appears and disappears.  Describes
       the step forward taken with Brideshead:  Waugh leaves us with the
       feeling that expiation and redemption wait for every man, even in
       his worst straits.

15   SCOTT-JAMES, R.A.  Fifty Years of English Literature, 1900-50.
       London:  Longmans, p. 166.
          Says that we are conscious of a critical understanding behind
       Waugh's depiction of froth and foolishness in his early novels; too
       much was lost when he became more serious in manner.  But so clever
       and versatile a writer may well prove capable of producing other
       books deserving attention.

16   SMITH, STEVIE.  "On Satire."  Penguin's Progress 14:14-17.
          Defines Waugh as a "pure" satirist, employing wit, intelli-
       gence, control and consistency as weapons in his observations on
       society.

17   SYKES, CHRISTOPHER.  "The Pocket Waugh."  Tablet 198 (7 July):
       9-10.

Reviews the Penguin publication of ten works by Waugh. Surveys Waugh's literary development from frivolous to serious, and
comments on his unpopularity with the intellectual Left, especially
because of Brideshead--which, though suffering from sentimentalism
and Catholic exclusiveness, succeeds grandly.

18    WOODRUFF, DOUGLAS. "The Works of Evelyn Waugh." Penguin's
      Progress 13:12-15.
         Survey's Waugh's literary career, finding morality as well
as entertainment in the early novels, and describing Brideshead
as his most considerable achievement. His humor is rooted in a
serious belief in man as a moral being.


## 1952

1    ANON. "The Impact of War." TLS, 12 September, p. 593.
        Men at Arms dramatizes the impact of war on a romantic middle-
aged civilian. Comedy and Catholicism combine well, but the protagonist's malaise is poorly explained.

2    ANON. "Mr. Evelyn Waugh's New Novel." Times Weekly Review
      (London), 18 September, p. 12.
        Like all Waugh comedies, Men at Arms has a serious core:
the impact of war on a fastidious, rather romantic civilian in
early middle age.

3    ANON. Notice of Men at Arms. Duckett's Register 7 (July):83.
        Discusses Waugh's war experience and his literary reputation.
Sees his tragic sense as more characteristic than his comic farce.
His postwar fiction constitutes a series of sermons from the view-
point of history and Eternity.

4    ANON. "War Revisited." Time 60 (27 October):74-75.
        As Ritchie-Hook and Apthorpe show, Waugh exemplifies the
satirist's conflict between ferocity and sentiment. Waugh cherishes
the romantic, patriotic, traditional virtues; in Men at Arms, the
regiment becomes in fact a symbol of Guy's church.

5    BEEGER, SUSANNE. "Die englische Gesellschaft zwischen den
      Kriegen." Die Neueren Sprachen, n.s. 1 (Heft 3):244-57.
        Basically retells the story of Brideshead, with emphasis on
the fact that the seeker after truth can move beyond cynicism to
affirmation.

6    BEER, OTTO F. "Englische Gegenwartsliteratur: Evelyn Waugh."
      Universitas 7:31-34.
        A survey of Waugh's novels, with special attention to their
satiric and theological implications. Waugh first became known
in Germany as a brilliant, cynical satirist akin to Huxley. With
hindsight, we can recognize that A Handful of Dust was a precursor

of <u>Brideshead Revisited</u>. He surveys his world dispassionately, but the question remains open whether or not he is on the way to becoming the great satirist of these chaotic times.

7   BRAYBROOKE, NEVILLE. "Evelyn Waugh and Blimp." <u>Blackfriars</u> 33 (December):508-12.
Discusses Waugh's concern for a world without the Incarnation. <u>Men at Arms</u> contains familiar Waugh themes and attitudes: humor; satiric barbs; the disillusioned, bewildered protagonist; religious faith; and glorious comic creations.

8   _____. "Evelyn Waugh:  An Interim Study." <u>Books on Trial</u> 10 (April):270-71, 299.
Reprint of 1952.9.

9   _____. "Evelyn Waugh:  An Interim Study." <u>Fortnightly Review</u>, n.s. 171 (March):197-202.
Though his satiric treatment has become ever keener, Waugh's consistent theme has been the radical instability in our whole world order.  Discussing his travel books and biographies, and the flaws of <u>Brideshead</u>, concludes that <u>The Loved One</u> is proof of his unimpaired powers, but that <u>Helena</u> is a step back.  Reprinted:  1952.8.

10  CALDER-MARSHALL, ARTHUR. "New Novels." <u>Listener</u> 48 (18 September):477.
Reserves judgment on <u>Men at Arms</u>; what appear as blemishes at the start of a proposed trilogy may be perfected later.  Considers Apthorpe a brilliant creation, and identifies Waugh with his protagonist, Guy Crouchback.

11  CONNOLLY, CYRIL. "Mr. Hemingway's Golden Tale." <u>Sunday Times</u> (London), 7 September, p. 5.
Compares Waugh with Hemingway in terms of isolation, energy, and creation of dialogue.  Both good-tempered and religious, <u>Men at Arms</u> is a chronicle, perfect of its kind, though dull when Waugh's "impetuous glancing ferocity" is restrained.

12  CONNOLLY, FRANCIS X. "Elegy and Restoration." <u>America</u> 88 (1 November):132-33.
<u>Men at Arms</u> is a lament for the decline of Catholic, aristocratic and classical England.  Optimism about the triumph of ideals lightens the despondency, though Crouchback's symbolic function will be rejected by many readers.

13  FITZGERALD, DESMOND. "Mr. Waugh Puts Out More Flags." <u>Tablet</u> 200 (13 September):211.
In <u>Men at Arms</u> the protagonist's self-conscious Catholicism detracts from the main theme, and his character is strangely ineffectual.

14  FRANK, JOSEPH. "For King and Country." <u>New Republic</u> 127

(10 November):19-20.

Men at Arms reveals the sad situation of a satirist who has abandoned ironic detachment. A discreet orgy of adolescent sentiment is not Waugh's métier.

15    GRAY, JAMES. "Battlefields Revisited." SatR 35 (25 October): 22.

In Men at Arms, Waugh employs extraordinary verbal facility to present the soldier's "ordeal by boredom." His cool detachment chronicles a range of experience from heroic foolhardiness to solemn eccentricity.

16    GUTTERIDGE, BERNARD. "Wine with Mr. Waugh." New Statesman and Nation 44 (30 August):233.

Reminisces about Waugh's wine-drinking during the war.

17    HILTON, JAMES. Review of Men at Arms. New York Herald Tribune Book Review, 19 October, p. 1.

Men at Arms chronicles one man's very English, slightly eccentric war, from initial romantic commitment to disillusionment. The alternation of the protagonist's pride in and disgust with his regiment leads to a tragicomic result: in war the god of irony rules. Waugh has swung spiritually to the Right.

18    HOHOFF, CURT. "Satire als Zeugnis." Wort und Wahrheit 7:39-44.

Discusses the main strains in Waugh's writing, especially the satiric and the religious, and their coming together in his masterpiece, Brideshead. Shows that satire can be a testimonial to belief--as in Waugh's use of the life of St. Helena to criticize his own age, or in the depiction of a world without grace in A Handful of Dust. Compares his approach to his material with that of G.K. Chesterton and Graham Greene, and also discusses the influence of Aldous Huxley.

19    HOPKINS, GERARD. "The Soldier's Devotion." Time and Tide 33 (13 September):1044.

Men at Arms is Waugh's most mature work; it combines shrewd observation, high polish, and profound comedy with the theme of the destruction of disciplined loyalty in an age of cynical anarchy.

20    HUGHES, RILEY. "Books: Men at Arms." CathW 176 (December): 232.

Recalls Waugh's treatment of war in earlier fiction. Men at Arms combines comic technique and rich manner to produce a new blend of Catholicism and criticism in Waugh's work.

21    HUGHES, SERGE. "A Mellower Waugh." Commonweal 57 (24 October): 78-79.

Men at Arms offers neither corrosive sarcasm nor tormented soul-searching, and so may disappoint Waugh enthusiasts. But Waugh has transmuted his sarcasm into a unique ironic commitment, while retaining all his older literary virtues.

22   IGOE, W.J.  "Considering Crouchback."  Duckett's Register 7
     (November):137-38.
          Comments on Waugh's nostalgia as a virtue; his few true her-
     oes are men at odds with the modern world.  Men at Arms shows his
     talent for telescoping time and projecting his ironic vision through
     his protagonist's kindly, disillusioned eyes.

23   JOOST, NICHOLAS.  "First Part of Trilogy by Evelyn Waugh."
     Books on Trial 11 (November):54.
          Men at Arms is a new departure for Waugh; it is a serious
     long-term project whose aims are yet to be realized.  He is attempt-
     ing to write definitively about World War II and to show the revi-
     talization of his protagonist.

24   KNOX, R.A.  "The Reader Suspended."  Month 194 (October):236-38.
          Compares Waugh to Homer in his ability to make war fascinat-
     ing.  Men at Arms transfigures boredom with realism, a quality de-
     veloped by Waugh halfway through Brideshead.  Guy Crouchback, iso-
     lated by his religion and traditional culture, is integrated into
     the army.

25   LEAN, TANGYE.  "Waugh and Hemingway."  Spectator 189 (12
     September):342.
          Men at Arms presents a boyhood dream in which the demands
     of gallantry can be satisfied only by a succession of "heroic"
     figures.  Satire punctuates the idealism.

26   MORRIS, ALICE.  "The Refuge of War."  New York Times Book Review,
     19 October, pp. 5, 38.
          War as a corrective for moral stagnation is a recurring idea
     in Waugh's fiction, entering the foreground in Men at Arms.  Waugh's
     rich satiric vein accommodates itself to a serious personal drama
     about the man of sensibility adrift in the modern world.

27   MORTON, FREDERICK.  "Evelyn Waugh's Unhappy Warrior."  Reporter
     7 (25 November):39-40.
          In his early novels, Waugh's virtuosity with the ludicrous
     exploits eccentricity and satirizes middle-class values.  Men at
     Arms proceeds by paradox, outrage, and understatement.  Guy
     Crouchback, grown indifferent to evil, is both victimized and com-
     promised by his environment; Waugh's loss of narrative detachment
     infiltrates the comedy with gravity.

28   MUIR, EDWIN.  "Two Novelists."  Observer (London), 7 September,
     p. 7.
          By striving after something more significant than before,
     both Waugh and Hemingway let imperfection slip into their novels.
     Waugh's faults arise from his aspirations towards greater serious-
     ness.

29   O'BRIEN, CONOR CRUISE [Donat O'Donnell].  "The Pieties of

Evelyn Waugh."  In <u>Maria Cross:   Imaginative Patterns in a Group
of Modern Catholic Writers</u>.  New York:  Oxford University Press,
pp. 119-34.  Reprint.  London:  Burns & Oates, 1963, pp. 109-23.
    In addition to the revisions of previous articles, examines
<u>Scott-King's Modern Europe</u> and <u>The Loved One</u> as studies of the vic-
tories of barbarism over civilization in the post-World War II
world.  Sees Waugh's artistic power as resting in his "indomitably
childish imagination," a quality utterly lacking in the shapeless
and sentimental <u>Helena</u>.  Revision of 1946.15; 1947.1; 1951.13.

30   PICKREL, PAUL.  Review of <u>Men at Arms</u>.  <u>YR</u> 42 (December):xii,
     xiv.
     <u>Men at Arms</u> is a surprising Waugh novel; the hero is both
bored and boring, disproportionate attention is accorded the character of Apthorpe, and the army seems like a boarding school.

31   PRESCOTT, ORVILLE.  "Books of the Times."  <u>New York Times</u>,
     14 October, p. 29.
     Discusses the evolution of Waugh's reputation.  <u>Men at Arms</u>
is emotionally tepid, static, and lacking in comic zest.  A traditional idealist, Guy Crouchback seeks personal fulfilment in the
army.

32   _____.  "Satirists:  Waugh, Marquand."  In <u>In My Opinion</u>.
     Indianapolis:  Bobbs Merrill, pp. 165-79.
     Waugh and Marquand rank high as satirists in contemporary
fiction.  Waugh's early satires, which both attract and repel, ex-
hibit both his technical skill and his rigid opinions.  His caustic
malice can be venomous, spiteful, and snobbish.  Later books reveal
his inflexible aristocratic, conservative, and Catholic attitudes,
and his refusal to compromise with the modern world.

33   RAYMOND, JOHN.  "New Novels."  <u>New Statesman and Nation</u> 44
     (20 September):326-27.
     <u>Men at Arms</u> is consistently funny, but has all Waugh's irri-
tating mannerisms:  adolescent nostalgia, prep-school humor, per-
vasive Catholicism.  With only traces of the old savagery, Waugh
is mainly good-tempered and thus not at his best.  Compares Waugh
to Kipling.

34   SCHWARTZ, DELMORE.  Review of <u>Men at Arms</u>.  <u>PR</u> 19 (November/
     December):703-4.
     In <u>Men at Arms</u>, Waugh's subject matter has crippled his
viewpoint and his sensibility.  The daring gaiety is gone; narrow
Catholicism rules.

35   SHEPPARD, R.C.  "Letters from England."  <u>Books on Trial</u> 11
     (November):73.
     The hero's Catholicism is an interpolation of the main theme
of <u>Men at Arms</u>.  Waugh adds a new gentleness to his extravagance,
humor and unique brutality.

1953

A. BOOKS

1    McCAY, ROBERT DALE. "Idea and Pattern in the Novels of Evelyn
     Waugh." Ph.D. dissertation, State University of Iowa.
          Defines Waugh's attitudes to philosophical and practical
     problems, and examines the techniques by which he conveys these
     attitudes. Pays particular attention to character types, such as
     the innocent and the rogue, and to plots, which do not change char-
     acters but give opportunities for satire of various aspects of
     life. See DA 13:1197.

B. SHORTER WRITINGS

1    ANON. "Jerusalem the Golden." TLS, 23 January, p. 52.
          Describes the main chapter, "The Defence of the Holy Places,"
     as an able piece of Catholic journalism. Waugh has many wise and
     sad comments on the present state of the Holy Places. His history
     is oversimplified and he has some annoying stylistic tricks, but
     he does give a vivid impression of the Holy City.

2    ANON. "An Unexpected Journey." TLS, 5 June, p. 361.
          Marvels at the variety of Waugh's accomplishments, and calls
     attention to the skill he displays in his "brief excursion into
     the terrestial world to come," Love Among the Ruins.

3    BEATTIE, A.M. "Evelyn Waugh." Canadian Forum 33 (1953-54):
     226-27, 229.
          Waugh's earliest novels create new patterns for hackneyed
     genres. His narrative virtues are speed, surprise, resourceful-
     ness, and the contrivance of outrageously amusing situations. But
     he is cruel, and he hates and despises his characters--and the
     world itself. Catholicism destroyed Brideshead; his religious
     stance provides an inadequate satiric focus. In his new trilogy,
     however, he may be changing direction.

4    BLACK, STEPHEN, interviewer. "Personal Call No. 14: Evelyn
     Waugh." London: B.B.C. Radio, 29 September. Unpublished.
          Describes Waugh's Gloucestershire home. Waugh discusses his
     family background, childhood, education, and early ambitions in
     painting and carpentry. Uninterested in self-expression, he writes
     of a decadent world. He describes his rational conversion to
     Catholicism; his attitude to his family; his admiration for crafts-
     manship of any kind; his response to modern art and architecture;
     his reaction to his own literary success; his travels in Abyssinia;
     and his war experiences.

5    BLACK, STEPHEN, JACK DAVIES, and CHARLES WILMOT, interviewers.

"Frankly Sepaking--Evelyn Waugh." London: B.B.C. Radio, 16
November. Unpublished.
    Waugh discusses his childhood, his ambitions as a "man of
action," his careers in school and the army, and his writing methods. His aim is "to make a pleasant object," as "any work of art
is something exterior to oneself." He blames Gertrude Stein and
her circle for the nullity of contemporary art. Asked about the
faults of the human race, he admits to being irritated by "bad
manners, disagreeable appearance, stupidity, egoism." He supports
capital punishment, and calls the modern welfare state a fraud and
a failure.

6    BOYLE, RAYMOND. "Evelyn Waugh: Master of Satire." Grail 35
    (November):28-32.
    Comments on the publication of Love Among the Ruins in
Commonweal; Waugh's blend of religious faith and social perception
satirizes materialistic social reformers. Gives biographical information and a review of Waugh's literary career.

7    BROOKE, JOCELYN. "Waugh-Weariness." Time and Tide 34 (30 June):
    725-26.
    Waugh's recent tendency to exchange satire for romantic nos-
talgia makes Brideshead, Helena, and Men at Arms disappointing.
His last good novel was Put Out More Flags. He seems weary; his
public wants a really annihilating satire in the old manner.

8    CONNOLLY, CYRIL. "A Sidekick: Mr. Waugh's Little Outing."
    Sunday Times (London), 31 May, p. 5.
    Love Among the Ruins, like Brave New World and 1984, shows
old-fashioned lovers in conflict with the progressive state. But
Waugh's novelette, though filled with neat paradox and brilliant
timing, is pure slapstick.

9    FRASER, G.S. The Modern Writer and his World. London: Derek
    Verschoyle, pp. 109-13, 331.
    Divides the main English novelists of the 1930s into four
categories, taking Waugh and Anthony Powell as examples of the
fourth--writers of social farce or comedy, not stressing political
or social disorder but upper-class frivolity. Says the underlying
mood is wistfully or cynically conservative. Analyzes Waugh's flat,
noncommittal manner, calls his way of turning our obsessions into
farce effective, but complains about his lack of charity and unre-
sponsiveness to those outside his own class. Revised: 1964.B24.

10    GARDINER, HAROLD C. Norms for the Novel. New York: America
    Press, pp. 11, 44-45, 109, 135-36, 147, 157.
    Looking at novels from a theological perspective, uses
Waugh's phrase "man in his relation to God" as a touchstone for
Catholic writers. Says that mordant satires like The Loved One
are really saying, "The truth is not here, it is elsewhere; let
this picture send you elsewhere to seek it."

11    GORDON, CAROLINE.  "Some Readings and Misreadings."  <u>Sewanee</u>
      <u>Review</u> 61 (July):384-407.
          Discussing modern Christian fiction, argues that the writer's
      imagination operates more easily in the pattern of Christian sym-
      bolism, especially of sacrifice, than in the pattern of contempo-
      rary thought.  Waugh is noteworthy for his religious bent and real-
      ism, but he is an incomplete novelist; his greatest achievement is
      <u>Brideshead</u>.

12    HOLLIS, CHRISTOPHER.  "Mr. Waugh Looks Ahead."  <u>Tablet</u> 201
      (27 June):563.
          Reviewing <u>Love Among the Ruins</u>, observes that, unlike nine-
      teenth-century projections of the future, twentieth-century ones
      show it as inhuman and dreary.  Waugh shows a society in transi-
      tion, gradually losing its faith and traditions.

13    KENNY, HERBERT A.  "Evelyn Waugh and the Novel."  <u>Magnificat</u> 92
      (May):278-80.
          A survey of Waugh's fiction, culminating in <u>Men at Arms</u>,
      shows that he uses Catholicism deliberately in it.

14    LEAN, TANGYE.  "Fiction."  <u>Spectator</u> 190 (29 May):712.
          <u>Love Among the Ruins</u> is a concentrated satiric tale, a side-
      line to Waugh's increasingly serious major work.  Lacking hope,
      sympathy, and laughter, Waugh looks ferociously at the future,
      and concludes with resigned despair.

15    MOSLEY, NICHOLAS.  "A New Puritanism."  <u>European</u> 3 (May):28-40.
          A reply to 1953.16.  Argues that Catholicism is not "a cur-
      rent philosophy," and that the Catholic novelist is not a propa-
      gandist.  A.J. Neame reveals his own romantic snobbery; Waugh
      satirizes the aristocracy, but is never irreverent to his religion.

16    NEAME, A.J.  "Black and Blue:  A Study in the Catholic Novel."
      <u>European</u> 3 (April):26-36.
          Discusses Graham Greene and Evelyn Waugh as post-Mauriac
      Catholic writers.  Greene specializes in squalor and moral theology,
      Waugh in the eccentricities of the old Catholic aristocracy, as in
      <u>Brideshead</u> and <u>Men at Arms</u>.  At times Waugh exasperates with his
      blend of snobbery and religion.  See reply, 1953.15.

17    NOTT, KATHLEEN.  <u>The Emperor's Clothes</u>.  London:  Heinemann,
      pp. 310-11.
          Says when Waugh writes as a Catholic, as in <u>Brideshead</u> and
      <u>Helena</u>, he also writes about Catholic theory; it seems easier for
      Catholic writers born Catholic, like Mauriac, to stick to psycho-
      logical truth than for converts.  Waugh's satiric novels are suc-
      cessful because they are written outside the scope of Catholic
      dogmatism.

18    O'FAOLAIN, SEAN.  "On Being an Irish Writer."  <u>Spectator</u> 191

(3 July):25-26.

Commenting on Cyril Connolly's observation on the necessity for the satirist to "eat his own shadow" (digest his own emotions completely), observes that Waugh is one of the great comic writers of English literature because in his best work he has concealed his own bitterness.

19    PAKENHAM, FRANK. Born to Believe. London:  Jonathan Cape, pp. 115-16, 122-23, 134-35.

Chapter 14, "The Household of the Faith," describes the influence of Waugh on the author's conversion to Catholicism and that of his wife Elizabeth.  The following chapter describes divergent views on social questions, the author trying to make the world a better place, and Waugh (in his own words) "trying to spread alarm and despondency."

20    SPENDER, STEPHEN.  "The World of Evelyn Waugh."  In The Creative Element:  A Study of Vision, Despair, and Orthodoxy among Some Modern Writers.  London:  Hamish Hamilton, pp. 159-74.

Surveys Waugh's career as a serious comedian.  His early novels all deal with a world of innocent sophistication poised between a dream of the past and the nightmare of the present.  His Catholicism forces him to reject the modern world and retreat into the past, and his own spiritual quest, a valid subject for a novel, is not projected into any of his characters.  Brideshead Revisited marks a revolution in theme and technique for him; but the novel is ruined by his loss of comic detachment and the character of Charles Ryder.

21    SPIEL, HILDE.  "Enfant terrible der Katholizismus."  In Der Park und die Wildnis.  Munich:  C.H. Beck'sche Verlagsbuchhandlung, pp. 81-87.

Asks, Where is the satirist of our times? and answers that it is now difficult to write satire.  By an extended analysis of Helena, concludes that Waugh has given up passionate hatred for the writing of missionary tracts, and can no longer be ranked among the satirists.  Nor is he a prophet.  He is only a brilliant example of the hubris of our age.

22    STOPP, FREDERICK J.  "Grace in Reins:  Reflections on Mr. Waugh's 'Brideshead' and 'Helena.'"  Month 196 (August):69-84.

As a comparison of Helena and Brideshead reveals, the presumed duality of the "serious" and "frivolous" Waugh represents a real congruity between the natural and supernatural levels of perception.

23    TODD, OLIVIER.  "Evelyn Waugh ou le faux ennemi."  TM 8:1406-23.

In a rambling essay, discusses many aspects of Waugh's work —his escape into the past from a world of displaced persons, his presentation of little lessons in filigree instead of preaching morality, his great crusade to re-Christianize Great Britain and

the United States. Maintains that he is a true satirist only in
The Loved One; he is usually full of affection for what he censures.

24   TRACY, HONOR. "New Novels." New Statesman and Nation 45
     (13 June):109.
          As he turns to literature, Waugh uses his wit sparingly. But
     Love Among the Ruins crackles drily in defence of authority, tradi-
     tion and privilege, though Waugh's snobbery dulls his irony.

25   W[OODRUFF], D[OUGLAS]. "The Faithless Generation." Tablet 201
     (February):110-11.
          Notes in The Holy Places Waugh's gift for concision and his
     feeling for shades of expression. He describes his youthful de-
     sire to write of England's connection with the Holy Land, now em-
     bittered by British foreign policy. Comments as well on Helena
     and on Waugh's ideas about the Holy Sepulchre.


                              1954


A.  BOOKS

1    HOLLIS, CHRISTOPHER. Evelyn Waugh. Writers and Their Work,
     no. 46. London: Longmans, Green, 40 pp.
          Surveys Waugh's work with the special intention of clearing
     up misunderstandings about individual novels and the process of his
     development, especially his growing emphasis on religion. Considers
     Edmund Campion the turning point in his career, since it taught him
     not so much the truth of Catholicism as the sundering nature of its
     claims. Revised: 1958.A1; 1966.A2; 1971.A3.

*2   SKERLE, LISELOTTE. "Das Wesen der Satire Evelyn Waughs."
     Ph.D. dissertation, University of Graz.
          Source: Checklist, no. 839; 1972.A1.


B.  SHORTER WRITINGS

1    BARR, DONALD. Review of Tactical Exercise. New York Times
     Book Review, 19 October, pp. 6, 36.
          Review of Tactical Exercise, surveying Waugh's literary repu-
     tation and his various reputations as satirist, snob, and sentimen-
     tal bigot. Work Suspended marks the transition from "early" to
     "late" Waugh, though his diversity is unified by his abiding bar-
     barousness, charity and snobbery--in fact separate aspects of a
     single quality.

2    BLUMENBERG, HANS. "Eschatologische Ironie. Uber die romane
     Evelyn Waughs." Hochland 46 (Heft 3):241-51.
          Beginning with A Handful of Dust, refers to the grim irony

of Waugh's ending, which would be blank cynicism if it were not for a glimpse of the truth. Says eschatological irony can be found as early as Vile Bodies, which leads up to a war. Sees Brideshead as an ironic conversion novel, and The Loved One as a novel in which beasts and men are paired, to point up one of the fundamental errors of modern man. Sees Helena as an illustration of British scepticism and empiricism: with beautiful simplicity, Helena puts aside speculation about the Absolute and the Unattainable, and goes straight to the fact of the Cross.

3   [BRIEN, ALAN]. "Profile: Evelyn Waugh Among the Ruins." Truth, 8 October, pp. 1242-43.
     Compares Waugh to Alexander Pope in wit, religious, social aspiration, and bogus social status. Waugh's life reveals the dullness of his origins, his literary lionization, and his self-aggrandizement; his snobbery is "hysterical." Waugh replied to this attack merely by contradicting the statement that his home was open to the paying public.

*4   CARSTENSEN, BRODER. "Evelyn Waugh und Ernest Hemingway." Archiv für das Studium der neuren Sprachen und Literaturen 190: 193-203.
     Source: Checklist, no. 905; 1972.A1.

5   CHASTAING, MAXIME. "Les romans humoristiques d'Evelyn Waugh." Esprit 22 (August-September):247-66.
     This "little lexicon" for the lover of novels discusses Waugh's fiction under eighteen different headings, ranging from style and form to themes like death and hell. Pays special attention to his detachment and impersonality, and to his comic and satiric techniques. Translated into German: 1955.B11.

6   COSMAN, MAX. Review of Love Among the Ruins. Arizona Quarterly 10 (Summer):169-74.
     Waugh's consistent quarrel with the present arises from his neofeudalist attitude to politics, religion and social stratification, an outlook increasingly evident in his writing. Love Among the Ruins shows him at his most cantankerous; his revulsion overpowers his judgment.

7   COXE, LOUIS O. "A Protracted Sneer." New Republic 131 (8 November):20-21.
     Tactical Exercise will do little for Waugh's reputation. Generally satirical, the collected stories reveal Waugh's lack of love and moral focus, despite his wit and style. Passed over by the modern age, he takes refuge in Catholicism, snobbery, and the past.

*8   DeVITIS, A.A. "The Religious Themes in the Novels of Rex Warner, Evelyn Waugh, and Graham Greene." Ph.D. dissertation, University of Wisconsin, 267 pp.
     Source: Checklist, no. 833; 1972.A1.

9   FIELDING, DAPHNE. <u>Mercury Presides</u>. London:  Eyre &
    Spottiswoode, pp. 105, 202, 214.
        Memoirs of the former Marchioness of Bath, mentioning Waugh's
    Oxford years, his service with No. 8 Commando, and a proposal (de-
    clined) that Waugh write the history of Longleat House.

10  MIKES, GEORGE. <u>Eight Humorists</u>. London:  Allan Wingate, pp.
    131-46.
        Notes there has been no break in Waugh's career, only a
    straight and logical, but not entirely happy, development.  The
    satirist in him is in conflict with the missionary; he is a power-
    ful satirist, but only a mediocre missionary.  Analyzes <u>The Loved
    One</u> and <u>Brideshead</u> in some detail.

11  PICK, JOHN.  "Waugh Revisited." <u>Renascence</u> 7 (Autumn):39-40.
        <u>Love Among the Ruins</u> is a frightening and funny fantasy, a
    logical projection of contemporary trends into the future.  The
    Greco-Roman line drawings enhance Waugh's theme that civilization
    without Christianity is always a contradiction.

12  ROLO, CHARLES J.  "Evelyn Waugh:  The Best and the Worst."
    <u>Atlantic</u> 194 (October):80, 82, 84, 86.
        A comprehensive appraisal of Waugh's achievement, praising
    his creation of a unique comic universe, the product of an audacious
    and macabre imagination.  He consistently rejects modernity for tra-
    ditional social and religious hierarchies; his loss of ironic de-
    tachment, however, reveals his nostalgia for medievalism, snobbery,
    and lack of compassion. <u>Brideshead Revisited</u> marks the turning
    point in his career.  Revised:  1958.B10-11.

*13 STOPP, FREDERICK J.  "Das Groteske als Form der Wirklichkeitsdar-
    stellung bei Greene und Waugh." <u>Jahres- und Tagunsbericht der
    Görres-Gesellschaft 1953</u>. Cologne:  Buchemin Komm, pp. 14-26.
        Source: <u>Checklist</u>, no. 1240; 1972.A1.

14  _____ .  "Der katholische Roman im heutigen England:  Graham
    Greene und Evelyn Waugh." <u>Stimmen der Zeit</u> 153 (March):428-43.
        Discusses the problems faced by the Catholic writer in bring-
    ing a Christian emphasis into a realistic novel.  Describes the
    pattern of movement from order to disorder and back to order in
    early novels, and the change that takes place about the time of
    World War II; Waugh comes closer to Graham Greene in the introduc-
    tion of a transcendental dimension, as in <u>Helena</u>, his most techni-
    cally accomplished work.

15  _____ .  "The Circle and the Tangent:  An Interpretation of Mr.
    Waugh's <u>Men at Arms</u>." <u>Month</u> 198 (July) : 18-34.
        When the romantic crusader Guy Crouchback prepares to meet
    the Modern Age, he must undergo a process of acclimatization.  In
    <u>Men at Arms</u>, Apthorpe personifies Guy's longing for comradeship,
    and Brigadier Ritchie-Hook his adventurous romanticism.  These

two figures struggle for his loyalty, the one as his double and
the other as his military ideal.  Apthorpe's death is essential
to liberate Guy from his internal conflicts.


## 1955


A.  BOOKS

*1    DAUCH, ALFRED.  "Das Menschenbild in den Werken Evelyn Waughs."
      Ph.D. dissertation, University of Cologne.
      Source: Checklist, no. 832; 1972.A1.


B.  SHORTER WRITINGS

1     AMIS, KINGSLEY.  "There's Something about a Soldier."  Spectator
      195 (8 July):56-59.
          Officers and Gentlemen shows that Waugh's literary decline
      has been reversed.  Discursive, episodic, only sporadically funny,
      it falls short of satirizing the army, which Waugh uses as a macro-
      cosm of the private school and the Church Militant.

2     ANON.  "Apoplexy."  New York Times Book Review, 25 September,
      p. 8.
          An account of the invasion of Piers Court, Waugh's country
      estate, by Nancy Spain of the London Daily Express and Lord Noel-
      Buxton, and of the controversy which resulted.  See 1955.B34.

3     ANON.  "Books:  Briefly Noted."  NY 31 (9 July):75.
          Officers and Gentlemen does not complete Men at Arms; its
      loose ends bewilder the reader.  Waugh forsakes comedy for dogged
      exposition.

4     ANON.  "Crouchback's Crete."  Newsweek 46 (11 July):83.
          Denies that Waugh lacks compassion; his cruel humor may lack
      tolerance, but it brilliantly balances comedy and tragedy in
      Officers and Gentlemen.

5     ANON.  "Into Battle."  TLS, 8 July, p. 377.
          Officers and Gentlemen traces Guy's progressive disillusion-
      ment, but too many questions are left unanswered.  While Guy pur-
      sues his individual pilgrimage, Waugh consistently maintains his
      satiric viewpoint; but for all its confusion the army is affection-
      ately presented.

6     ANON.  "Literary Style in England and America."  Catholic
      Messenger, 13 October, p. 15.
          An account of Waugh's article in Books on Trial (October)
      comparing British and American literary styles.

7    ANON. "Philosopher Warns Against Grave Moral Implications
     Current in Catholic Novels." Catholic Messenger, 3 November,
     p. 17.
        Dietrich von Hildebrand of Fordham University criticizes
modern Catholic novelists for their inversion of spiritual values
and their "sin mystique."

8    ANON. "Profile: Evelyn Waugh." Observer (London), 31 July,
     p. 2.
        Identifies Waugh as a private personality with a literary
persona, and notes the eccentricity of his social attitudes and
his nostalgia for the past.

9    ANON. "Series End." Christian Century 72 (24 August):973-74.
        Officers and Gentlemen applies Waugh's characteristic wit to
the modern military machine, but his snobbery and Catholicism are
also evident. Despite disclaimers, a third novel will appear, in
which Guy will discover the values of his religious, gentlemanly
father.

10   BRADFORD, CURTIS. "On Extended Active Duty." New Republic 33
     (11 July):19-20.
        Waugh's war novels fuse the tragedy and comedy of war into
remarkable realism. In Officers and Gentlemen he presents the retreat from Crete with classical allusions which raise it to universality.

11   CHASTAING, MAXIME. "Ein Satiriker in Stichworten." Wort und
     Wahrheit 10 (May):340-55.
        Translation of 1954.B5, with transposition of some of the
items to make their headings follow alphabetically in German.

12   CONNOLLY, CYRIL. "The Officers' Mess." Sunday Times (London),
     3 July, p. 5.
        Officers and Gentlemen does not complete the saga begun in
Men at Arms. Except for the Cretan segment, the novel suffers from
"benign lethargy" and inadequately drawn human relationships.
Waugh's new mellowness destroys his satire.

13   COOPERMAN, STANLEY. Review of Officers and Gentlemen. Nation
     181 (10 September):230.
        In Officers and Gentlemen, Waugh's acid talents have vanished;
his aristocratic heroes seem no better than their antagonists.

14   CORKE, HILARY. "At Last--the Truth." Encounter 5 (August):
     82-87.
        Officers and Gentlemen disproves the contention that Waugh's
powers have declined because of seriousness and Catholicism. His
work shows firm and logical development.

15   CUNEO, PAUL K. "Fiction." Books on Trial 14 (August-September):
     11.

In Officers and Gentlemen, the hero is an appealing figure.
The novel cannot be read without Men at Arms.

*16    DESCHNER, KARLHEINZ. "Evelyn Waugh." In Christliche Dichter
       der Gegenwart: Beiträge zur europaischen Literatur. Edited by
       Hermann Friedmann and Otto Mann. Heidelberg: Rothe, pp. 224-37.
       Source: Checklist, no. 944; 1972.A1. Revised: 1968.17.

17     DOOLEY, D.J. "Evelyn Waugh." In "The Impact of Satire on
       Fiction:  Studies in Norman Douglas, Sinclair Lewis, Aldous
       Huxley, Evelyn Waugh, and George Orwell." Ph.D. dissertation,
       State University of Iowa, pp. 245-383.
       Notes that it is the fashion to regret the passing of an
amusing entertainer whose early fantasies were delightfully cynical,
and the emergence of a writer of religious parables full of prosely-
tizing zeal.  Contends that Waugh's later ideas are implied in his
early works, and that in later works he has not ceased to be an
amusing and sharp-witted critic of the contemporary scene.  His
satires are more profound comments on the world than many readers
suspect; he may appear as "an embittered old schoolmaster" in
Scott-King's Modern Europe, but in many other works an ironic detachment produces satire of the highest rank.

18     FITZGERALD, DESMOND. "The Upper Class War." Tablet 206
       (2 July):14.
       Waugh's war writings are not novels, but social and military
history built around acutely observed characters. Officers and
Gentlemen is threatened by sentimentality, but Waugh's Catholicism
is less obtrusive.

19     FYTTON, FRANCIS. "Waugh-Fare." CathW 166 (December):349-55.
       Defends Waugh against Donat O'Donnell's imputation of a blend
of snobbery and religion.  Waugh's conversion was unfashionable and
counteraristocratic in the 1930s in Britain.  Also, Waugh satirizes
aristocrats who abdicate their traditional responsibilities; he defends a lost ideal against the ravages of twentieth-century decay.

20     GARDINER, HAROLD C. "Wit--But Compassion More." America 93
       (13 August):1475.
       Beyond Waugh's satiric wit, Officers and Gentlemen shows his
compassion and reverence for the fighting man.

21     GRAY, JAMES. "Man's Soul under Fire." SatR 38 (9 July):10.
       Officers and Gentlemen provides the fulfilment of Waugh's
distinguished if sometimes flighty talent; he takes a higher place
than he previously seemed to occupy.  He shows war as nothing but
a squalid offense against decency; he strikes a different note from
Dos Passos or Hemingway--that of contemptuous reproach.  The two
war novels constitute a story of one man's patient journey toward
despair.

22   HAMNETT, NINA.  Is She a Lady?  A Problem in Autobiography.
     London:  Allan Wingate, p. 58.
          Memoirs of bohemian life in London, Ireland, and Paris,
     1926 to 1948.  Describes a river party of the Bright Young People,
     including Waugh.

23   HORCHLER, R.J.  "The Mellowing of Mr. Waugh's Art."  Commonweal
     62 (August):476.
          Since the outrageously comic but chilling early novels,
     Waugh's ferocious imagination and negative attitude have modulated
     to compassion and tolerance, especially in Officers and Gentlemen,
     a study of man's search for value in a dying civilization.

24   IGOE, W.J.  "Virtuous Rake's Progress."  Duckett's Register 10
     (August):151-52.
          Officers and Gentlemen is "elaborately lucid" in structure,
     the ironic epic of a potential hero.  Waugh blends comedy, implied
     moral criticism, and compassion.

25   LINDLEY, ROBERT.  "End of a Saga."  Month 200 (September):182-83.
          Discusses Waugh's reputation, described as in flux since
     Brideshead.  He blends White's Club and the Catholic Church, neither
     of which is spared his wit; Officers and Gentlemen is comic, satir-
     ic, and tragic by turns.

26   Maclaren-ROSS, J.  "New Novels."  Listener 54 (14 July):75.
          If Officers and Gentlemen completes Waugh's planned war saga,
     he must have abandoned his initial concept; the novel shows Guy
     Crouchback disillusioned by the decline of the aristocracy and the
     death of tradition.

27   MILLAR, RUBY.  "Novels."  National and English Review 145
     (August):118-21.
          Waugh's assurance, worldliness, and satiric wit blend to
     create Officers and Gentlemen, in which the author enters "the
     dramatic world of conscience."

28   MOORE, GEOFFREY.  "Crouchback Carries On."  New York Herald
     Tribune Book Review, 10 July, pp. 1, 16.
          Waugh has evolved from satiric comedy to serious realism.
     Officers and Gentlemen reveals the mixture, though Waugh's meaning
     is unclear.  Guy Crouchback must be more than a picaresque charac-
     ter.  Mingling snobbery and sentimental nostalgia, the novel is
     loose-ended; it is also lacking in perspective and humanity.

29   OAKES, PHILIP.  "One Man's Waugh."  Truth, 15 July, p. 903.
          Ranging in mood from the comic to despair, Officers and
     Gentlemen illustrates Waugh's retreat into romantic sentimentality
     and ancestor worship.  Having accepted his snobbery, his readers
     miss his irascibility.

30    POORE, CHARLES. "Books of the Times." <u>New York Times</u>, 7 July, p. 25.

      Waugh is a first-rate military satirist; his precise, economical style contributes largely to the success of <u>Officers and Gentlemen</u>.

31    RICHARDSON, MAURICE. "New Novels." <u>New Statesman and Nation</u> 50 (9 July):50.

      Though not entirely successful as a novel, <u>Officers and Gentlemen</u> demonstrates Waugh's impeccable style and immense readability--but also the difficulties of transforming deeply felt experiences into fiction.

32    ROLO, CHARLES J. "Gentlemen at War." <u>Atlantic</u> 196 (August):84.

      Polished, controlled, and felicitous in observation, Waugh's <u>Officers and Gentlemen</u> is still animated by silly ideas of snobbery and nostalgia for medievalism.

33    SHRAPNEL, NORMAN. "Mr. Waugh's War." <u>Manchester Guardian</u>, 1 July, p. 4.

      <u>Officers and Gentlemen</u> disproves accusations of snobbery, for Waugh angrily deplores the physical and moral confusion of war.

34    SPAIN, NANCY. "My Pilgrimage to See Mr. Waugh." <u>Daily Express</u> (London), 23 June, p. 6.

      Describes the attempt of Nancy Spain and Lord Noel-Buxton to visit Waugh at Piers Court, and Waugh's brusque dismissal of them. This article resulted in a correspondence between Waugh and Lord Noel-Buxton in the <u>Spectator</u> (July). See also 1955.B2.

35    SULLIVAN, RICHARD. Review of <u>Officers and Gentlemen</u>. <u>New York Herald Tribune Book Review</u>, 10 July, pp. 1, 9.

      <u>Officers and Gentlemen</u> has immediacy, grace, sharpness, and conviction; beyond its satiric mockery lie new insight and sympathy. Since war is a succession of fiascos, Guy is no longer the potential crusader.

36    SYKES, CHRISTOPHER. "Forward to Victory." <u>Time and Tide</u> 36 (2 July):871-72.

      Discusses Waugh's surprising versatility, so disconcerting to the critics. <u>Officers and Gentlemen</u> is a wild extravaganza on the fantasy side of military life, blended with tragicomedy. Only the Halberdiers escape Waugh's ridicule.

37    WYNDHAM, FRANCIS. Review of <u>Officers and Gentlemen</u>. <u>London Magazine</u> 2 (August):78-79.

      <u>Officers and Gentlemen</u> shows Guy Crouchback doubly deceived by political and personal values, but this serious theme is presented without spontaneity and conviction. The separation of the comic and the serious weakens the novel.

1956

A.  BOOKS

1   DeVITIS, A.A.  Roman Holiday:  The Catholic Novels of Evelyn
    Waugh.  New York:  Bookman Associates, 88 pp.  Reprint.  London:
    Vision Press, 1958.
        Puts Waugh in the context of modern God-denying and God-
    seeking literature; though his Catholicism became explicit only
    with Brideshead Revisited, his moral stance informs his entire
    corpus.  Deals with Waugh's developing literary skill and critical
    reputation, as well as a gradual decline in artistic detachment
    culminating in Brideshead.  Defends both Brideshead and Men at Arms
    as efforts to trace the influence of the supernatural on the phe-
    nomenal world:  it is religion that provides an answer to the ills
    of the wasteland.

B.  SHORTER WRITINGS

1   ALBÈRES, R.M.  "Evelyn Waugh, ou de l'humour à l'essentialisme."
    Revue de Paris 63 (April):83-94.
        Waugh presents a disconcerting world, whose law is humor and
    inconsequentiality, not clarity or verisimilitude.  There is not
    the least spirituality in this world, but at least it is exempt
    from everything in the Babbitt or commercial world, which kills
    spirituality in our day.  His originality consists in his showing,
    through irony, the importance of moments in which we do glimpse
    the essential life of the spirit.

2   ANON.  "Officer and Gentleman."  TLS, 2 March, p. 129.
        Compares a successful novel about Commando life, Robert
    Henriques's Red over Green, to Waugh's treatment of similar mater-
    ial in his war trilogy.  Finds considerable similarities in the
    mockery of army types and in the discovery that apparently aimless
    characters can make courageous soldiers.  Notes, however, that
    Henriques is less of a satirist than Waugh, and not so careful a
    craftsman.

*3  BRANDER, DONALD M.  "Die Romane von Evelyn Waugh:  Charaktere
    als algebraische Figuren in einer irrealen Welt."  Deutsche
    Universitätszeitung 11, no. 4:13-15.
        Source:  Checklist, no. 883; 1972.A1.

4   BRAYBROOKE, NEVILLE.  "Evelyn Waugh en uniforme."  La vie
    intellectuelle 27 (27 April):135-40.
        Briefly relates Men at Arms and Officers and Gentlemen to
    works which anticipate them, such as Vile Bodies and Helena, and
    shows that the years since the war have enabled Waugh to see mili-
    tary affairs in perspective:  war is an image of the nature of man,
    in which good and evil are in perpetual combat.

5    COSMAN, MAX.  "The Nature and Work of Evelyn Waugh."  ColQ 4
     (Spring):428-41.
         In surveying his career, states that Waugh has had limited
     success because of his romantic idealism and penchant for the Middle
     Ages; these underlie his religious and social attitudes, and stulti-
     fy his point of view.  Feudal Catholicism, not fascism, is his fixed
     principle.

*6   ENGELBORGHS, MAURITS.  "Het laatste werk van Evelyn Waugh
     (Officers and Gentlemen)."  Dietsche Warande en Belfort 3
     (Autumn):167-77.
         Source:  Checklist, no. 2090; 1972.A1.

*7   GÖTZ, KARL-AUGUST.  "Die Romane von Evelyn Waugh."  Die Anregung
     8 (Beilage):40-43.
         Source:  Checklist, no. 1007; 1972.A1.

8    HERN, ANTHONY.  "Rebecca West Attacks Evelyn Waugh and Graham
     Greene."  Daily Express (London), 16 October, p. 6.
         In The Meaning of Treason, Rebecca West attacks Waugh and
     Greene for producing an intellectual climate conducive to intellec-
     tual treachery.  They confuse the moral with the aesthetic and make
     the aesthetic seem more important.

9    MARCUS, STEVEN.  "Evelyn Waugh and the Art of Entertainment."
     PR 23 (Summer):348-57.
         Explains critical hostility to Waugh as a reaction against
     an "entertainer" who rejects life's complexities, avoids serious
     moral judgments, and lacks a mature intelligence.  A clever observer
     and impeccable stylist, Waugh is interested only in life's surfaces;
     snobbish, bilious, uncompassionate and delightful, he is a comedian,
     not a satirist.  Reprinted:  1975.B21.

10   O'FAOLAIN, SEAN.  "Huxley and Waugh:  or I Do Not Think,
     Therefore I Am."  In The Vanishing Hero:  Studies in the
     Novelists of the Twenties.  Boston:  Atlantic, Little, Brown,
     pp. 31-69.  Reprint.  London:  Eyre & Spottiswoode, 1957.
         Waugh's detachment from his characters is ambiguous; it blends
     hardness of heart with compassion.  His "cruelty" is either the hor-
     rible cathartic laughter of the scapegoat or the technique of
     scourging, scornful laughter.  Despite his religious and social
     views, he is a destroyer of masks, a moral critic of his generation
     for its negative rebellion.  With Brideshead, he changed from a
     moral satirist to a romance writer; he lost his universality and
     detachment through excess of loyalty to class and religion.

11   RUSSELL, LEONARD.  "Editor's Note."  In The Russell Reader.
     London:  Cassell, pp. 334-35.
         Introduction to Scott-King's Modern Europe.  Calls it a sa-
     tire, but one without the ruthlessness of The Loved One.  It con-
     tains great draughts of the comic spirit, it mingles wit and warmth

and pathos, and in it Waugh's technical accomplishments are daz-
zling.

12   SPAIN, NANCY. "Does a Good Word from Me Sell a Good Book?"
     Daily Express (London), 19 March, p. 6.
         Angrily refutes Waugh's denial of her influence on the book-
     buying public by belittling his sales and suggesting that he is
     jealous of his brother Alec's popular success. Waugh successfully
     sued the Daily Express on the basis of these comments.

13   STOPP, FREDERICK J. "Waugh: End of an Illusion." Renascence 9
     (Winter):59-67, 76.
         Discusses Officers and Gentlemen as closely linked to and
     aptly concluding Men at Arms. The illusions about war and the
     military life in the first volume are gradually deflated in the
     second.

14   TINDALL, WILLIAM YORK. Forces in Modern British Literature,
     1885-1956. New York: Vintage, pp. 62-63, 104-6.
         A revision of 1947.11, bringing in later novels. Says
     Brideshead, a subtle study of imperfect Catholics and of Catholicism
     triumphant, is Waugh's most open treatment of his faith. Calls The
     Loved One an Englishman's idea of America. Says his two novels of
     the Second World War "have enough eccentrics and boobies to embody
     the old disgust."


                                  1957

1    AMIS, KINGSLEY. "Laughter's To Be Taken Seriously." New York
     Times Book Review, 7 July, pp. 1, 13.
         Satire, essential to any culture, is beginning a new golden
     age:  it is now marked by humor and realism. The cruel and snob-
     bish satire of Evelyn Waugh, now rejected by him in favor of laments
     for a dying aristocracy, is definitely passé.

2    ANON. "Evelyn Waugh and the Daily Express." Daily Express
     (London), 5 April.
         Discusses the settlement in Waugh's favor of a libel suit
     against the Daily Express for Anthony Hern's review of Rebecca
     West's book attacking Waugh and Greene for creating a climate fav-
     orable to treason. See 1956.8.

3    ANON. "A Question of Psychology." Times Weekly Review (London),

     The Ordeal of Gilbert Pinfold provides an instructive and
     entertaining portrait of the author, but the hero's ordeal is too
     frightening to be comic, and the other characters are too unreal
     to be taken seriously.

4    ANON. Review of The Ordeal of Gilbert Pinfold. National Review

4 (12 October):335.
Traces the change in Waugh's reputation as he evolved from jester to romantic poet. The Ordeal of Gilbert Pinfold is a grotesquely humorous account of the hallucinatory result of romantic longings clashing with outside pressures.

5    ANON. "Sardonic Squire." Books and Bookmen 2 (July):5.
Profile of Waugh, in which he defines Catholicism as the fundamental norm. His "snobbery" appears as belligerent romanticism.

6    ANON. "Self-Inflicted Satire." Time 70 (12 August):72.
In The Ordeal of Gilbert Pinfold, Waugh turns his sharp satiric eye upon himself, blending reality and fantasy with his usual skill.

7    ANON. "Self-Portrait?" TLS, 19 July, p. 437.
A "fantasticated autobiography," The Ordeal of Gilbert Pinfold exemplifies Waugh's status as a minor writer and illuminates his "freak talent" as an immensely successful comic novelist.

8    ANON. "Tweedledum and Tweedledee." Times (London), 14 September, p. 7.
Notes the Waugh-J.B. Priestley battle over The Ordeal of Gilbert Pinfold, and warns that entertaining writers should avoid politics and sociology. See 1957.26.

9    ANON. "War of the Writers." Newsweek 49 (11 March):108.
Discusses Waugh's battles with Nancy Spain of the Daily Express. See 1956.B12.

10   BREIT, HARVEY. "W. Somerset Maugham and Evelyn Waugh." In The Writer Observed. Cleveland: World; London: Redman, pp. 147-49. Reprint. New York: Collier Books, 1961, pp. 34-36, 101-2.
Maugham and Waugh comment on their writing. Waugh's pride in Helena rests in its varied themes, its broad and hidden jokes, and the pleasure of writing it. Revision of 1949.5.

11   BRYDEN, R. "New Novels." Listener 58 (1 August):178.
The Ordeal of Gilbert Pinfold presents in more subjective terms Waugh's familiar fascination with nightmare visions. A "panic Lewis Carroll," he takes the whole modern age as his wonderland of disaster and hysteria.

12   CASEY, GENEVIEVE. Review of The Ordeal of Gilbert Pinfold. Critic 16 (August-September):35-36.
Stresses Pinfold's boredom and modesty as the cause of his ordeal. Discusses the difficulty in assessing Waugh's degree of seriousness.

13   COSMAN, MAX. Review of The Ordeal of Gilbert Pinfold. Carolina

Quarterly 10 (Fall):69-72.
   The Ordeal of Gilbert Pinfold is a parable of England's reaction to postwar pressures. Folly projected into the world will
always return seven-fold upon the projector.

14   CRONIN, ANTHONY. "Portrait of the Artist." Sunday Times
     (London), 21 July, p. 6.
        The Ordeal of Gilbert Pinfold celebrates the author's triumph
over malevolent spirits by means of courage, stubbornness and adroit-
ness, and presents an attractive self-portrait.

15   DOYLE, PAUL A. "Evelyn Waugh: A Bibliography (1926-1956)." BB
     22 (May-August):57-62.
        A pioneering bibliography of Waugh's own work, and of critical
studies of it. Briefly outlines peculiar difficulties facing Waugh's
bibliographers.

*16  ELSEN, CLAUDE. Preface to the French translation of The Ordeal
     of Gilbert Pinfold. Paris: Stock.
        Source:  Checklist, no. 1865; 1972.A1.

17   LAPICQUE, F. "La satire dans l'oeuvre d'Evelyn Waugh." EA 10
     (July-September):193-215.
        Says Waugh's humor is never disinterested: a satirist, even
a moralist, he mounts a massive attack against his age, and even
his earliest works are linked to certain controlling ideas. In a
survey of his novels, demonstrates the variety of his satire, but
contends that the satire in Brideshead and Helena would have been
more effective if not so narrowly based. A comparison with three
other critics of contemporary society--D.H. Lawrence, Aldous Huxley,
and Graham Greene--brings out the originality and value of Waugh's
satiric position.

18   LEHMANN, JOHN. "Foreword." London Magazine 4 (September):9,
     11.
        The Ordeal of Gilbert Pinfold reveals Waugh's attitude to
himself as fastidious literary stylist; Pinfold's hallucinations
reveal that since Brideshead Waugh has worked against the grain of
his own comic genius.

19   MADDOCKS, MELVIN. "Waugh's 'Brief Bout of Hallucination.'"
     Christian Science Monitor, 15 August, p. 7.
        Lacking Waugh's usual ironic double perspective and morally
interesting viewpoint, The Ordeal of Gilbert Pinfold is all hallucination and no vision.

20   McCORMICK, JOHN. Catastrophe and Imagination: An Interpreta-
     tion of the Recent English and American Novel. London:
     Longmans, pp. 286-89.
        Laments Waugh's decline from satiric toughness and implicit
moral vision to Catholicism, snobbery, and sentimentality.

21   McEWAN, R.L.    "Mr. Pinfold's Hallucinations."  Month 204
     (October):247-49.
          In The Ordeal of Gilbert Pinfold, Waugh turns his irony on
     his own critics.

22   NEMEROV, HOWARD.  Review of The Ordeal of Gilbert Pinfold.  PR
     24 (Fall):602-4.
          Based on hallucinations, The Ordeal of Gilbert Pinfold cannot
     be taken seriously, but Waugh's crisp style gives much reading
     pleasure.

23   O'BRIEN, CONOR CRUISE [Donat O'Donnell].  "The Loved One."
     Spectator 199 (19 July):112.
          The Ordeal of Gilbert Pinfold is unfunny and embarrassing,
     except for Waugh's self-portrait.  Waugh excels at the comic treat-
     ment of the grimmest themes, except when writing about himself.

24   PRESCOTT, ORVILLE.  "Books of the Times."  New York Times, 12
     August, p. 17.
          Dull and depressing, The Ordeal of Gilbert Pinfold entirely
     lacks Waugh's malicious wit and comic exuberance.  Only the opening
     self-portrait offers interest.

25   PRICE, MARTIN.  Review of The Ordeal of Gilbert Pinfold.  YR 47
     (Autumn):150.
          Although they have the force of vicarious nightmare, Pinfold's
     delusions never achieve an interesting order.  Characterized in
     terms of the spectral accusing voices, Pinfold is a baffling per-
     sonality.

26   PRIESTLEY, J.B.  "What Was Wrong with Pinfold."  New Statesman
     and Nation 54 (31 August):244.
          Accuses Waugh-Pinfold of drowning his self-awareness that he
     is a fake, only to be tormented by subconscious self-accusations.
     The lifestyle of the Catholic landed gentry is incompatible with
     the function of the artist, and indeed smothers it.  Waugh responded
     [Spectator 199 (13 September):328-29] with a characteristic counter-
     attack on Priestley's own disappointed hopes.

27   RAYMOND, JOHN.  "Mr. Waugh on Deck."  New Statesman and Nation
     54 (20 July):88.
          Both satirist and romantic, Waugh possesses a unique moral
     vision which permeates all his various "manners" of writing.  The
     Ordeal of Gilbert Pinfold is "a near-perfect farce of bromide,
     chloral and champagne."

28   ROLO, CHARLES.  "Contemporary Masters."  Atlantic 200 (November):
     244-46.
          A disturbing image of isolation and boredom emerges from
     Waugh's self-portrait in The Ordeal of Gilbert Pinfold.  The novel
     lacks suspense, and Pinfold appears to learn nothing from his ex-
     perience.

29 RYAN, THOMAS C. "A Talk with Evelyn Waugh." Sign 37 (August): 41-43.
   An interview in which Waugh discusses his Catholicism, his writing, and his fellow novelist converts, together with the difference between American and British Catholic writers.

30 SARTON, MAY. "A Bottle of Pop." Nation 185 (31 August):96-97.
   Waugh excels in using savage humor, irony, and schoolboy hilarity to attack simple targets. But The Ordeal of Gilbert Pinfold fails as an exploration of his idiosyncratic personality, for Pinfold never confronts his hallucinations.

31 SINGER, BURNS. "Fantasies and Sobrieties." Encounter 9 (October):78-80.
   The hero of The Ordeal of Gilbert Pinfold survives by clinging stubbornly to reality; but, from a fascinating beginning, his tale becomes a bore. Perhaps Waugh takes himself too seriously.

32 STOPP, FREDERICK J. "Apology and Explanation." Renascence 10 (Winter):94-99.
   In The Ordeal of Gilbert Pinfold, Waugh raises up the negative aspects of his creative personality in order to conquer them. The internal action traces the disintegration and re-integration of the personality by means of the masks. Also reviews A.A. De Vitis's Roman Holiday (1956.A1), criticizing some aspects of the argument and bibliography.

33 SYKES, GERALD. "Some Sinister Voices and an Author at Bay." New York Times Book Review, 11 August, p. 4.
   As Waugh's novelistic powers decline, his talents as a polemicist increase. The Ordeal of Gilbert Pinfold lacks suspense and excitement; it is a vain attempt by the author to escape himself.

*34 SZALA, ALINA. "Brideshead Revisited Evelyna Waugh." Roczniki Humanistyczne 6, no. 6:95-105; English summary, 156-57.
   Source: Checklist, no. 1626; 1972.A1.

35 TOYNBEE, PHILIP. "Mr. Waugh Shifts Gear." Observer (London), 21 July, p. 13.
   The Ordeal of Gilbert Pinfold is a tour de force, somewhat marred by the precision of Waugh's writing. His ironic detachment is remarkable, for the persecuting voices come from the classes he most admires.

36 VREDENBURGH, JOSEPH. "The Character of the Incest Object: A Study of Alternation Between Narcissism and Object Choice." AI 14 (Spring):45-52.
   Discusses the relationships of Charles Ryder with Sebastian and Julia Flyte in Brideshead in terms of Freudian theory.

37    WEALES, GERALD.  "Mr. Waugh's Bad Dream."  Reporter 17 (5
      September):42-43.
          Calls The Ordeal of Gilbert Pinfold slim and only intermit-
      tently funny, but finds it fascinating because of its revelations
      of Waugh's personality.

38    W[OODRUFF], D[OUGLAS].  "While the Going was Bad."  Tablet 210
      (20 July):60.
          Waugh's self-portrait in The Ordeal of Gilbert Pinfold is
      remarkably objective yet self-contained; this sturdy, sympathetic
      character dominates the book.  Asks why Pinfold's hallucinations
      regarding himself are not more searching and profound.


                                    1958


A.  BOOKS

1     HOLLIS, CHRISTOPHER.  Evelyn Waugh.  Writers and Their Work,
      no. 46.  London:  Longmans, Green, 40 pp.
          Revision of 1954.A1, adding two novels to previous discussion.
      Revised:  1966.A2; 1971.A3.

2     STOPP, FREDERICK J.  Evelyn Waugh:  Portrait of an Artist.
      London:  Chapman & Hall, 254 pp.
          A pioneering work; the first general study of Waugh.  Gives
      biographical details in the first part; goes systematically through
      the novels in the second; in the third, "The Artist," stresses the
      importance of comedy, fantasy, and myth in Waugh's writings; con-
      cludes with a portrait of the artist in middle age.  States that
      distrust of the comic impulse and Waugh's provocative opinions pre-
      vent sufficient attention being given to the novels; this is a pity,
      because they are so subtle in technique and structure, so right in
      allusion, that there is no end to the fascinating task of exploring
      them.  Claims that Waugh's is a world of fantasy which has its own
      laws; satire is endemic, but sometimes absent, whereas fantasy is
      never absent.  Revision of 1954.A1.


B.  SHORTER WRITINGS

1     ALLSOP, KENNETH.  The Angry Decade:  A Survey of the Cultural
      Revolt of the Nineteen-Fifties.  London:  Peter Owen, pp. 12,
      25-26.
          Discussing The Ordeal of Gilbert Pinfold, describes Waugh as
      symbolic of the castaways on the rugged rocks of the fifties; the
      torment of Pinfold's mental illness is really no more hallucinatory
      than his squirearchal life.

2     ANON.  "Antic Antiques."  Times (London) 71 (21 April):83-84.

Compares Waugh to Aldous Huxley, calling them both dated.
Charles J. Rolo's anthology (The World of Evelyn Waugh) shows the
writer's blend of comedian and commando. As a firm moralist, he
satirizes the aristocracy for what it fails to do.

3   DOYLE, PAUL A. "The Church, History, and Evelyn Waugh." ABR 9
    (Autumn-Winter):202-8.
        Defends Waugh against attacks on his "feudal" Catholicism and
rejection of modernity by examining his view of the continuity and
stability of the Church in time past, present, and future.

4   _____. "The Persecution of Evelyn Waugh." America 99 (3 May):
    165, 168-69.
        Defends Waugh against accusations that Catholicism has marred
his work, and comments on doubts about Waugh's good faith coming
from his coreligionists.

5   GREENFIELD, MEG. "Half-People in a double World." Reporter 18
    (26 June):38-39.
        Reviewing Charles Rolo's The World of Evelyn Waugh, describes
Waugh's achievement as highest before Brideshead, in which he lost
comic detachment. His characters have moved from the world of satire to that of romance. When he asks the reader to accept the reality of his comic world, and then condemns it, he sacrifices his
comic genius.

6   HEPPENSTALL, RAYNER. "Elders & Betters." Observer (London),
    16 November, p. 20.
        Reviewing Frederick J. Stopp's Evelyn Waugh (1958.A2) along
with David Hughes's J.B. Priestley, says Priestley complains about
the age, while Waugh turns his back on it. Wonders what Waugh will
do next; the contemporary world may be irredeemable, but he could
brighten it a little. Complains that Stopp has caught none of the
felicities of Waugh's style and takes too Jungian an approach--all
those animas cannot be much to Waugh's taste.

7   HOLLIS, CHIRSTOPHER. Along the Road to Frome. London:
    Harrap, pp. 58, 61.
        Mentions Waugh in discussion of the Hypocrites' and Offal
Clubs at Oxford.

8   POORE, CHARLES. "Books of the Times." New York Times, 12 April,
    p. 17.
        Reviews Charles Rolo's anthology (The World of Evelyn Waugh)
as a panorama of England's Bright Young Things in peace and war.
Waugh's wild humor is combined with an extreme conservatism.

9   [RAYMOND, JOHN.] "'Industria Ditat.'" TLS, 19 December, p.
    726.
        Review of Frederick J. Stopp's Evelyn Waugh (1958.A2), prais-
ing its balanced, lucid and thorough interpretation, and predicting

that it will alter Waugh's public image and literary reputation.
Notes Stopp's search for moral coherence in Waugh, the new insight
he provides into Brideshead, and his defence of Helena. Reprinted:
1960.29.

10    ROLO, CHARLES J. "Evelyn Waugh." Critic 16 (April-May):11-13,
      65-67.
          Reprint of 1958.B11, with minor omissions caused by adapta-
      tion from an introduction to an article. Revision of 1954.B12.

11    _____. "Introduction to The World of Evelyn Waugh. Boston:
      Little, Brown, pp. [v]-xvi.
          A revision of 1954.B12, expanding its defense of Waugh's
      literary consistency, defining his attitude toward the aristocracy,
      and enlarging the comments on individual novels. Calls Brideshead
      the turning point in Waugh's career, because of its loss of detach-
      ment and championing of romantic archaism. Adds comments on later
      novels, especially The Ordeal of Gilbert Pinfold and Officers and
      Gentlemen. Reprinted: 1958.10.

*12   ROOS, HANS-DIETER. "Die zwei Gesichter des Evelyn Waugh:
      Gespräch mit dem britischen Satiriker." Die Kultur 7 (15
      October):10.
          Source: Checklist, no. 1183; 1972.A1.

*13   SEIDLER, MANFRED. "Die ubergrossen und die kleinen Sunder:
      Über die Romane der englischen Konvertited Graham Greene und
      Evelyn Waugh." Werkhefte katholischer Laien 12:234-39, 258-62.
          Source: Checklist, no. 1202; 1972.A1.

14    SYKES, GERALD. "Basil, Evelyn, and Old Mr. Todd in an Over-
      Reasonable Society." New York Times Book Review, 13 April, p.
      5.
          Charles J. Rolo's anthology (The World of Evelyn Waugh) pro-
      vides a survey of Waugh's anarchic comic universe and proof of his
      precise, fertile imagination. His schoolboy jokes, ideological re-
      tardation, and inspired wit make him a carefree clown in an Eton
      collar.

15    VOORHEES, RICHARD J. "Evelyn Waugh's War Novels: A Toast to
      Lost Causes." QQ 65 (Winter):53-63.
          Argues for the consistency of Waugh's viewpoint, which is
      grounded in religious, political, and social conservatism and ro-
      mantic individualism. The war novels show his enthusiasm for mili-
      tary tradition; in fact his stance can be compared to Jacobitism.

<u>1959</u>

A. BOOKS

1   CARENS, JAMES F. "Evelyn Waugh: His Satire, His Ideas of Order, and His Relation to other Modern English Satiric Novelists." Ph.D. dissertation, University of California, 300 pp. [<u>DA</u> 20: 1362.]
    Source: <u>Checklist</u>, no. 1362; 1972.A1.
    Notes seriousness underlying the levity of the early novels, even though they are essentially negative and sometimes ambivalent. Puts Waugh among the romantic writers converted to Catholicism in this century; says that <u>Brideshead</u> confuses social with religious values and subordinates satire to sentiment. Discusses Waugh's relation to political rightism, endeavoring to correct common misapprehensions. Discusses his affinities with other satiric novelists, including Norman Douglas, Aldous Huxley, Ronald Firbank, Wyndham Lewis, and Anthony Powell; says his satiric poise, though often strained, gave him a staying power these others lacked.

B. SHORTER WRITINGS

1   ANON. "Out of Step?" <u>TLS</u>, 9 October, pp. 569-70.
    Review of <u>Ronald Knox</u>, suggesting that Waugh projects his own discontents onto his subject, and that the biography too often reminds the reader of Waugh's novels.

2   ANON. "Waugh Unmasked." <u>Jubilee</u> 7 (October):43-45.
    A photographic spread on Waugh and his family, with captions consisting of quotations from <u>The Ordeal of Gilbert Pinfold</u>.

3   ANON. "Wit . . . And the Popish Creed." <u>Times</u> (London), 8 October, p. 15.
    Criticizes Waugh's biography of Ronald Knox for its reticent, external treatment of Knox's complex and interesting life.

4   BARTON, JOHN M.J. "R.A. Knox." <u>Month</u> 208 (December):365-67.
    Praises Waugh's reticence and tact in his biography of Knox, but argues against the stress on Knox's sufferings and disappointments.

*5  BORY, JEAN-LOUISE. "Lorsque le diable pince sans rire: L'épreuve de Gilbert Pinfold." <u>L'Express</u> (Paris), 19 February, pp. 28-29.
    Source: <u>Checklist</u>, no. 1863; 1972.A1.

6   BOWRA, C.M. "Book Reviews." <u>London Magazine</u> 6 (December):63-65.
    Waugh's <u>Ronald Knox</u> adroitly portrays its subject's inner and outer life, though Waugh emphasizes Knox's sanctity and genius

without clear illustration of them.  Waugh's supremacy as a prose
stylist makes him an appropriate biographer.

7    BRENNAN, NEIL FRANCIS.  "The Aesthetic Tradition in the English
     Comic Novel."  Ph.D. dissertation, University of Illinois, 813
     pp.  [DA 20:1980-81.]
          Discusses the emergence of a new kind of comic novel within
     the last century, under the influence of Oscar Wilde, who wrote no
     comic novels himself.  Representative writers are E.F. Benson,
     Anthony Hope, and Max Beerbohm between 1890 and 1910; Saki, Ronald
     Firbank, and Norman Douglas in the next decade; and Aldous Huxley,
     Anthony Powell, and Waugh between the wars.  Says that the master-
     pieces were slow in coming, but with works like Vile Bodies and A
     Handful of Dust the tradition was at least as well established as
     Restoration comedy.

8    COOPER, DIANA.  The Light of Common Day.  Boston:  Houghton
     Mifflin Co., pp. 112, 114, 115.
          Contains brief accounts of treasure hunts in London and rides
     in Sussex with Waugh.

9    CORBISHLEY, THOMAS.  "Evelyn Waugh on Ronald Knox:  One Literary
     Artist to Another."  Catholic Herald (London), 9 October, p. 3.
          A laudatory review of Waugh's biography, denying that unin-
     tentional satiric malice has crept in, but admitting an overempha-
     sis on Knox's tribulations.

10   DOOLEY, D.J.  "The Strategy of the Catholic Novelist."  CathW
     189 (July):300-304.
          Suggests the importance to the Catholic novelist of shocking
     his audience with either the chaos of a valueless society or the
     unexpected presence of grace.  Waugh's career shows what he must
     avoid:  overt statement of belief, as in Brideshead, produces re-
     actions like that of Edmund Wilson.  Reviews other responses to
     Brideshead and to Waugh's religion.  Reprinted in 1969.A3.

11   DOYLE, PAUL A.  "The Politics of Waugh."  Renascence 11 (Summer):
     171-74, 221.
          Travel hardened Waugh's conservatism, especially his racial
     and colonial attitudes.  Attracted temporarily to fascism as an
     alternative to communism and a preserver of European civilization,
     Waugh satirizes both totalitarianism and socialism in Scott-King's
     Modern Europe and Love Among the Ruins.  He opposes democracy as
     the rule of the mob, but his political views do not mar his liter-
     ary achievement.

*12  FERRI, PAOLA.  "Evelyn Waugh e la narrativa cattolica inglese."
     Vita e pensiero 42:831-38.
          Source:  Checklist, no. 983; 1972.A1.

*13  GLANZ, LUZIA.  "Der Mensch und die Eschata:  Gedanken zu

Dichtungen von Evelyn Waugh, Clive Staples Lewis, Edzard
Schaper und Boris Pasternak." In Kaufet die Zeit aus: Beitrage
zurchristlichen Eschatologie: Festgabe für Theoderich Kampmann.
Edited by Hermann Kirchoff. Paderborn: Schöningh, pp. 113-32.
Source: Checklist, no. 1002; 1972.A1.

14   GREENE, GRAHAM. "Portrait of a Priest." Observer, 11 October,
     p. 23.
     Waugh's external treatment of his subject in Ronald Knox is
both appropriate and inevitable, for a priest's spiritual life is
always private. Waugh's talents here will hold the interest of
even the unsympathetic. Reprinted: 1969.B16a.

15   JOHNSON, PAUL. "Old Etonian Papist." New Statesman 58 (10
     October):482.
     Waugh's Ronald Knox is both a response to Knox's critics and
an intelligent effort to define his elusive and absorbing character.

16   LUNN, Sir ARNOLD. "A Vivid and Moving Portrait of Ronald Knox."
     Duckett's Register 14 (November):1-2.
     From personal knowledge of Knox, says that Waugh has made
too much of his tribulations. But no biographer could have been
more successful than Waugh in protecting Knox's achievements and
personality from the rusts of time.

17   NOTT, KATHLEEN. "Evelyn Waugh and the Religious Novel." In
     The Rationalist Annual, 1959. Edited by Hector Hawton. London:
     Watts, pp. 26-33.
     Though a brilliant writer, Waugh has marred his work and the
humanistic tradition of the novel with Catholicism, which incul-
cates a preference for the irrational, a formulaic view of human
conduct, militarism, and nostalgic romanticism. Waugh's view of
history is highly subjective.

18   RAYMOND, JOHN. "Ronald Knox's Road." Sunday Times (London),
     11 October, p. 16.
     Comments on Waugh's difficult task of separating the man from
the legend in his life of Knox, and compares the portrait of Knox
to those of Edmund Campion and St. Helena. The three figures form
a "heroic triptych" in Waugh's life.

19   STÜRZL, ERWIN. "Evelyn Waugh's Romanwerk: Makabre Farce oder
     'Menschliche Komödie?'" Neueren Sprachen 8 (Heft 7):314-26.
     Says that on one side Waugh seems to follow Aldous Huxley's
precept, "You can't write a good book without being malicious."
He begins with macabre farce; he is shocking and distressing. On
the other hand, he resembles Balzac in trying to write a "comédie
humaine"; broadening his scope through the use of traveler-adven-
turers, he brings in more aspects of the contemporary world than
people realize. He is at his best when he mingles farce and absurdity with the dance of death over an abyss.

20   WHEELER, Msgr. GORDON.  "Waugh on Knox:  An Appraisal."  Dublin
     Review 233 (Winter):346-52.
          Waugh's Ronald Knox brilliantly recaptures the spirit of
     Oxford, but fails in its explanation of Knox's relations with the
     Church hierarchy, in its stress on the frustrations of Knox's life,
     and in its exploration of Knox's spiritual life.


                                 1960


1    ANON.  "Evelyn Waugh's Jaunt."  Newsweek 56 (14 November):114-15.
          Review of A Tourist in Africa, complaining that Waugh's testy
     personality has now become tedious.

2    ANON.  "Life & Death of a Monsignor."  Time 75 (25 January):
     49-50.
          Reviewing Waugh's biography of Ronald Knox, says Waugh guards
     his friend's privacy like a medieval moat; whenever the book be-
     comes personal, it is full of private jokes.  Also says Waugh's
     portrait is curiously Graham Greene-like, with Knox's outward ur-
     banity masking his inner anguish.

3    ANON.  "Safari of a People Watcher."  Time 76 (28 November):92.
          Reviewing A Tourist in Africa, observes that Waugh has a col-
     lector's eye for the gaudier human specimens.  Calls this a novel-
     ist's notebook, describes some of the more bizarre episodes in it,
     says that it conveys the full Waugh personality, and comments that
     no man writes English better.

4    ANON.  "Self-Portrait of a Lady."  Time 76 (19 December):65.
          Reviewing Diana Cooper's Trumpets from the Steep, says that
     she has a curious way of making real people seem like Waugh char-
     acters, mentions a brief appearance of Waugh dressed as a Royal
     Marine, and suggests that Lady Diana was Waugh's Mrs. Stitch.

5    ANON.  "Successful Radio Play from a Waugh Novel."  Times
     (London), 8 June, p. 16.
          Praises the integrity of the radio adaptation of The Ordeal
     of Gilbert Pinfold.  Waugh's comic horrors are preserved intact.

6    ANON.  "Wintering Abroad."  TLS, 1 September, p. 603.
          A Tourist in Africa combines the familiar Waugh wit with
     political myopia.  With luck, Waugh will retire neither to a her-
     mit's cell nor too far within himself.

7    ANON.  "Yet Another Visit to Brideshead."  TLS, 16 September,
     p. 594.
          Waugh's public image is deceptive.  But the revisions to
     Brideshead show that he still confuses the social with the divine
     graces; grace and graciousness are not limited to a single social
     group.

8    BETJEMAN, JOHN. "Pilgrim's Progress." NY 36 (23 April):174-77.
          The perfection of Waugh's prose style, his sympathetic under-
     standing, and his charitable reticence combine to make his biography
     of Ronald Knox moving and authentic.

9    COLEMAN, JOHN. "No Room for Hooper." Spectator 205 (29 July):
     187.
          Comments on Waugh's public image, unfailing humor, and tech-
     nical adroitness. The early novels, regarded as his purest art,
     make a technique of detachment. With Brideshead, his serious pur-
     pose emerged, together with justification of his prejudices:
     Catholicism, snobbery, and romantic immaturity.

10   CONNOLLY, CYRIL. "Was This Journey Really Necessary?" Sunday
     Times (London), 25 September, p. 27.
          Discusses A Tourist in Africa in terms of Waugh's pose of
     elderly buffer. As a travel book, the work is trivial; as a pro-
     duct of Waugh's pen, it is noteworthy.

11   COOPER, DIANA. Trumpets from the Steep. London:  Rupert Hart-
     Davis, pp. 36, 55-56, 203, 205.
          Wartime anecdotes of Waugh, especially of her asking "the
     knight-at-arms what ailed him."

12   CORKE, HILARY. "The Listener's Book Chronicle." Listener 64
     (29 September):524.
          Comments on Waugh's odd public image and its distortion of
     his genuine civility. In A Tourist in Africa, he is reasonable
     about everything except religion.

13   CROZIER, MARY. "Interviewing Mr. Waugh." Tablet 214 (2 July):
     623.
          Discusses Waugh's B.B.C. interview with John Freeman
     (1960.B18), criticizing the interviewer's preconceived views of
     the author and of the literary profession in general.

14   DAVIDSON, BASIL. "Mr. Waugh's Africa." New Statesman 60
     (24 September):439-40.
          A Tourist in Africa demonstrates more melancholy than wit.
     Waugh's political opinions are often silly, his facts wrong; he
     combines superb irony with a Victorian persona.

15   DAVIES, ROBERTSON. "An Extraordinary Man." Kingston Whig-
     Standard (Ontario), 20 February, p. 17.
          Lengthy discussion of Ronald Knox, commenting that Waugh's
     biography is a model of its kind, and that Waugh brings special
     sympathy to his portrait because both he and Knox were converts
     to Catholicism who felt that they had experienced losses as well
     as gains by that step.

16   DOYLE, P.A. "Evelyn Waugh." CritQ 2 (Fall):269-70.

Response to Dyson (1960.17), arguing that Waugh's characterization adds to his satiric effectiveness, and that the eschatological purpose of Brideshead negates criticism of its failure "in
human terms." Waugh is undervalued as a social historian.

17    DYSON, A.E. "Evelyn Waugh and the Mysteriously Disappearing
      Hero." CritQ 2 (Spring):72-79.
         Waugh's urbane savagery modifies his civilized style; nostal-
      gia tempers his early satire. Yet his irony lacks a center: he
      attacks both ideals and their corruption, he deliberately withholds
      compassion, his irony results from moral withdrawal. Brideshead is
      his greatest success, and most regrettable failure. Reprinted:
      1965.12.

18    FREEMAN, JOHN, interviewer. "Evelyn Waugh: Face to Face."
      London: B.B.C. Television, 26 July. Unpublished.
         Discussion of Waugh's childhood, education, youthful atheism,
      Oxford experiences, decision to become a writer, and conversion.
      He states his preference for Helena, despite the critical hostility
      to it, and asserts that at the end of the war trilogy Crouchback
      will turn from public causes to private, spiritual ones. He de-
      scribes his life as one of absolute solitude, not that of a country
      squire; he admits to irritability, rudeness, and deafness, but de-
      nies snobbery. The Ordeal of Gilbert Pinfold is an "almost exact"
      record of his illness in 1954.

19    FREMANTLE, ANNE. "Waugh in America." Vogue 136 (15 November):
      54, 65-66.
         Anecdotes about Waugh's visit to America in 1949, recording
      his whimsical conversation, idiosyncratic attitudes, and uneventful
      meeting with Jacques Maritain.

20    JACOBSON, DAN. "Passing Order." Spectator 205 (23 September):
      448.
         Some of Waugh's conservative insights in A Tourist in Africa
      are a valuable counterbalance to liberal opinions. Most remarkably,
      he does not indulge in nostalgia for the glories of Empire, and
      shows a new charity and self-restraint.

21    KERMODE, FRANK. "Mr. Waugh's Cities." Encounter 15 (November):
      63-66, 68-70.
         Reviews the revised edition of Brideshead, noting that Waugh's
      conservative religion is logically linked to his defense of civi-
      lization and the aristocratic tradition--though he admits the at-
      traction of barbaric vitality. He characteristically balances
      truth and fantasy, partly in the symbol of the country house as
      the City of God. Reprinted: 1962.B18. Waugh replied to Kermode's
      comments (December, p. 83), defending his good faith as a Catholic.

*22   KRANZ, GISBERT. "Vier grobe Erzähler aus christlichem Geist:
      Sigrid Undset, Werner Bergengruen, Graham Greene, Evelyn Waugh."

Die Kirche in der Welt (Munich) 11:357-70.
Source: Checklist, no. 1973, 1972.A1.

23  LAMBOTTE, CHARLES. "Evelyn Waugh: Un humoriste." In Convertis
du XXe siècle. Edited by Fernand Lalotte. Vol. 2. Paris:
Casterman, pp. 71-86.
    The story of Waugh's conversion, with incidental comments on
his writing--emphasizing its variety and its steady movement towards
more explicit treatment of religious themes.

*24  LENNARTZ, FRANZ. Ausländische Dichter und Schrifsteller unserer
Zeit: Einzeldarstellungen zur Schönen Literatur in fremden
Sprachen. 3d ed. Stuttgart: Kroner, pp. 714-18.
    Source: Checklist, no. 1082a; 1972.A1.

25  MURPHY, JOHN P. "A Life Reconsidered." Tablet 214 (2 April):
328-29.
    Discusses Waugh's emphasis on the somber side of Ronald Knox
in his biography. Waugh set himself a limited objective that should
serve as a stimulus to other studies of Knox. Evaluates Knox's conversion to Catholicism and the joyous aspects of his personality.

26  O'DONOVAN, PATRICK. "Portrait of a Man from Oxford." New
Republic 142 (4 April):25-26.
    Using Ronald Knox as a springboard for an essay, notes the
similarities between Waugh and his subject, and comments on Waugh's
exaggerated public persona, designed to infuriate the Left.

27  POORE, CHARLES. "Books of the Times." New York Times, 3 March,
p. 27.
    When one notable sytlist writes about another, conflict is
inevitable. In Waugh's Ronald Knox, the biographer stresses his
subject's spiritual conflicts and ignores his secular literary
achievements, wit, and humor.

28  PRYCE-JONES, DAVID. "The Social Philistine." Time and Tide 41
(23 July):863-64.
    The revised Brideshead contains few substantial changes; the
novel is an epitome of Waugh's work. He admits no alternatives;
his snobbery, lack of compassion, racism, and melancholy are in-
tensified by his religious views.

29  RAYMOND, JOHN. "'Industria Ditat.'" The Doge of Dover.
London: MacGibbon & Kee, pp. 148-55.
    Reprint of 1958.B9.

30  RICHARDSON, MAURICE. "Curtain-Raiser to Eternity." Observer
(London), 3 July, p. 25.
    States that the eagerly awaited interview of Waugh by John
Freeman on "Face to Face" made excellent viewing. Waugh avoided
the traps set for him; he was at ease and very friendly. What

emerged was a reasonably balanced view, a profile extended in time, but there was nothing about his writing.

31    _____. "Evelyn Waugh Runs a Fair." Harper's 220 (January): 30-37.
        Reprint of 1960.B32.

32    SHEEHAN, EDWARD R.F.  "A Weekend with Waugh." Cornhill Magazine 171 (Summer):209-25.
        Memoir of a visit to the Waugh family by an American admirer; he helped at the Piers Court garden fete in aid of St. Dominic's Church.  Describes Waugh's family and household, records his conversation, and relates the details of the fete.  Reprinted: 1960.B31.

33    WAY, ROBIN.  "John Freeman Meets His Match in Evelyn Waugh." Universe (London), 1 July, p. 4.
        Discussing the "Face to Face" television interview, says John Freeman had carefully supplied himself with the right bait, but this fish refused to bite, and quietly enjoyed the game.  It was all cool, courteous, and reasonable, and Waugh gave a considered apologia for his faith.

34    WICKLOW, Earl of (WILLIAM CECIL JAMES HOWARD).  "Biography and Memoirs." Studies 49 (Spring):84-87.
        Comments on the controversy arising out of Waugh's biography of Ronald Knox, and on Knox's enigmatic personality.

35    WILSON, ANGUS.  "Waugh's Knox." Encounter 14 (January):78-80.
        The critical hostility to Waugh's productions since Brideshead and Helena may have hindered his development.  The melancholy tone of Ronald Knox is uncomfortably close to the mood of Waugh's war novels, suggesting that the author has identified his own disappointments too closely with those of his subject.


## 1961

1    AMIS, KINGSLEY.  "Crouchback's Regress." Spectator 207 (27 October):581-82.
        Waugh's consistent theme is social and moral disintegration; it is reflected in structural devices which are sometimes risky. Unconditional Surrender reveals the centrifugal tendency of the entire war trilogy; despite the continuity of Ludovic's character, it disappoints hopes of final coherence.  Crouchback is an unbearable hero, dull and snobbish.

2    ANON.  "New Fiction." Times Weekly Review (London), 2 November, p. 10.
        The modest, dull Guy Crouchback figures even less in Unconditional Surrender than in the previous two volumes of Waugh's

trilogy; the latter is primarily a nostalgic wartime photograph
album, without sympathy or optimism.

3    ANON.  "The New Waugh."  TLS, 27 October, p. 770.
     Readers mistook Officers and Gentlemen as a failed comedy,
not as the study of wartime society it actually was.  Waugh's saga
required Unconditional Surrender for completeness; Guy Crouchback
abandons his crusade against modernity in favor of individual action, and Waugh shows a new humanity.  The trilogy is the one book
about the war likely to survive.

4    ANON.  101 Great Books of Our Time.  London:  Sunday Times,
     pp. 9, 41, 60.
     Evelyn Waugh has two entries in this annotated list of the
outstanding books of the first half of the century.  One is Decline
and Fall ("As a farcical portrait of the seamier side of high and
medium life . . . it is unrivalled in our time") and the other is
Brideshead Revisited ("Mr. Waugh's most severely criticised book--
but it clearly grows in stature year by year").  In a brief introduction, John Braine writes that he admires Waugh immensely, but
the pleasure he gives is tinged with guilt, "because of his lack
of love, because of his deep underlying despair."

5    BALFOUR, PATRICK (LORD KINROSS).  "The Years with Kinross."
     Punch 241 (26 July):138-46; (2 August):174-75; (9 August):210-11;
     (16 August):246-47; (23 August):282-84.
     Autobiographical sketches of Kinross's childhood and youth.
Discusses the pleasures of Oxford, where he knew Waugh, his life
as a gossip-column writer in the era of the Bright Young Things
(which linked him with Waugh's Vile Bodies), and his coverage of
the Abyssinian War with Waugh in 1935.

6    BEATON, CECIL.  The Wandering Years:  Diaries 1922-39.  London:
     Weidenfeld & Nicolson, pp. 173-74.
     Recollection of terrifying experiences at Heath Mount day
school, where a small but fierce Evelyn Waugh led a pack of bullies
in attacking him.

7    BERGONZI, BERNARD.  "The Defeat of a Gentleman."  Manchester
     Guardian, 27 October, p. 7.
     Unconditional Surrender demonstrates Waugh's supberb style
and admirable plotting.  Guy Crouchback embodies Waugh's peculiar
myth of true value resting in the Catholic and aristocratic tra-
ditions--a creatively valuable myth, here defeated by modernity.

8    CHRISTIANSEN, ARTHUR.  Headlines All My Life.  New York:
     Harper, p. 154.
     Memoirs of a seasoned foreign correspondent, noting Waugh's
rich and witty satire on newspaper reporting in Scoop, but describing his weaknesses in news coverage.

9    CONNOLLY, CYRIL. "A Saga of Disillusion." Sunday Times
     (London), 29 October, p. 31.
         All three volumes of Waugh's war trilogy must be read together;
     it is the finest novel to come out of the war. It is a study in
     disillusionment; hero-worship is continually deflated, though Guy
     Crouchback recovers his faith in religion and the landed gentry.
     Waugh reveals his essential biliousness in his treatment of the
     minor characters.

10   COSMAN, MAX. "Notes of Refreshment." Commonweal 73 (6 January):
     392-93.
         Notes Waugh's John Bullishness and neofeudalism in A Tourist
     in Africa. He is a highly gifted, idiosyncratic writer.

11   DERRICK, CHRISTOPHER. "Swords about the Cross." Tablet 215
     (28 October):1024, 1026.
         The Sword of Stalingrad in Unconditional Surrender is linked
     to Sir Roger de Waybroke's sword in Men at Arms. Guy's pilgrimage
     involves mortifying his love of lineage and crusading idealism,
     and accepting sacrifice. Waugh has learned humanity.

12   FULLER, JOHN. "Disenchantment." Listener 66 (26 October):
     665-66.
         Unconditional Surrender completes Guy's disillusionment, but
     his rehabilitation to civilian life is patently false. Waugh shows
     his true comic genius by taking comedy seriously.

13   GREEN, MARTIN. "British Comedy and the British Sense of Humor:
     Shaw, Waugh, and Amis." TQ 4 (Autumn):217-26.
         A comparison of these three British writers clarifies the
     national sense of humor--class conscious, asexual, and reactionary.
     A serious, brilliant artist, Waugh rests his claim to genius on his
     early satires, in which social conventions and moral decency are
     outraged. Basil Seal (compared by Green to the young Winston
     Churchill) is the perfect Waugh hero. Waugh is snobbish, reaction-
     ary, and anti-intellectual.

14   GREEN, PETER. "Du côté de chez Waugh." Review of English
     Literature 2 (April):89-100.
         Reviews the critical response to A Handful of Dust. Here
     Waugh achieved a unique balance--never repeated--between the war-
     ring opposites that make up his creative impulse: Catholicism,
     and aristocratic tradition and romantic nostalgia.

15   HALL, JAMES. "The Other Post-War Rebellion: Evelyn Waugh
     Twenty-five Years After." ELH 28 (June):187-202.
         Discusses Waugh's "narrowed view of reality." He chronicles
     the sad history of the postwar rebellion in manners by testing its
     ideals from within. Revised: 1963.B11.

16   IGOE, W.J. "Mr. Waugh's 'Success and Failure.'" Catholic

Herald, 1 December, p. 9.

Reviews Unconditional Surrender as the completion of Guy Crouchback's crusade. Waugh's heroes are, typically, diffident and anachronistic, their values unappreciated by modern society. He has succeeded in diagnosing the nature of sanctity; tragedy becomes comedy in the Christian perspective.

17　LONG, RICHARD A., and IVA G. JONES. "Towards a Definition of the 'Decadent Novel.'" CB 22 (January):245-49.

Defines the "decadent novel" as focused on the more rarified aspects of life, with detailed analyses of emotion and themes of disintegration and alienation. Aristocratic and self-conscious in structure and style, the decadent novel rejects modern civilization for the medieval synthesis. Waugh's novels before 1945 fit into this category.

18　MacDONALD, EDWARD J. "A 'major' Waugh with the usual mesmeric prose." Universe (London), 29 December, p. 6.

In reviewing Unconditional Surrender, states that Waugh's trilogy ranks as one of his major works; it makes its points with economy and force. Guy stands for the good deed which is not allowed to shine in a naughty world.

19　MARTIN, GRAHAM. "Novelists of Three Decades: Evelyn Waugh, Graham Greene, C.P. Snow." In The Modern Age, The Pelican Guide to English Literature. Edited by Boris Ford. Vol. 7. Harmondsworth: Penguin Books, pp. 394-401.

Calls all of these minor novelists because none is fully in control of his material; describes Waugh as a prewar novelist, interest in whom is merely an exercise in nostalgia. Analyzes passages in Scoop and Vile Bodies to show that the world is disliked, but not understood, because Waugh has no alternative position, no criteria by which to judge.

20　McSHANE, FRANK. "Forest Lawn." Prairie Schooner 35 (2):137-148.

Criticizes Waugh and Aldous Huxley for presenting Forest Lawn as typical of California. Describes the reality of the cemetery in detail, noting its bogus view of Christianity and saccharine picture of life.

21　PITMAN, ROBERT. "Are They Unfair to Their Faith?" Sunday Express (London), 29 October, p. 6.

Asks whether Catholic writers such as Waugh, Graham Greene, and Muriel Spark do not lean over too far backwards in order to be fair. Having read Unconditional Surrender, would not like to meet Crouchback; not even all of Waugh's genius can make him warm to this dismal, unsmiling man.

22　PRITCHETT, V.S. "Vanities and Servitudes." New Statesman 62 (27 October):603-4.

Unconditional Surrender concludes Guy Crouchback's love

affair with the army with a paradoxical peace. Waugh's genius for specialized social effrontery is supreme. The trilogy is a memoir of personal experience from the moralist's viewpoint, humane and perfectly polished. Crouchback is a perfect focus for Waugh's attitude. Reprinted: 1980.B30.

23    QUINTON, ANTHONY. "Crouchback Unbound." Time and Tide 42 (26 December):1801-2.
     Unconditional Surrender provides coherent unity and completion to the first two war volumes; Guy sacrifices knightly idealism to the duty of charity imposed by his religion. The military narrative ends in disillusion, the personal in resigned contentment.

24    RAVEN, SIMON. "Crusader of our Time." London Magazine, n.s. 1 (November):72-75.
     Sees the war trilogy as a conflict between the dignity of tradition (the Halberdiers) and the amoral anarchy typified by Basil Seal. In Unconditional Surrender, Guy's journey takes him past idealism and despair to reconciliation through mercy and private dignity.

25    READY, WILLIAM B. "Current Interests." Critic 19 (January): 32-33.
     Review of A Tourist in Africa, discussing Waugh's literary self-revelation, and the way his travel experiences are transformed from dull fact to brilliant fiction. Notes Waugh's growing melancholy.

26    RUFF, LAWRENCE A. "Comments on the 'Decadent Novel.'" CE 23 (October):63-64.
     Responds to 1961.18, condemning the inclusion of Waugh among the decadent novelists. Argues that Waugh has a consistently moral purpose in his work.

27    TOYNBEE, PHILIP. "Evelyn Waugh: Mourner for a World That Never Was." Observer (London), 29 October, p. 21.
     It is difficult to decide when Waugh is satirist, farceur, or serious novelist; Unconditional Surrender illustrates the problem. A survey of his fiction shows that his opinions are inseparable from it. The end of the war saga shows his deep misanthropy, devoid of idealism. Snobbish patriotism prevails.

28    WASSON, RICHARD. "A Handful of Dust: Critique of Victorianism." MFS 7 (Winter):327-37.
     A Handful of Dust embodies Waugh's critique of English social and religious life, bankrupted by its separation from the source of ethical and religious values, the Roman Catholic Church. The Victorians tried to preserve the trappings of Christianity without its essential faith. The "picturesque" thus replaces the authentic, and masks its absence.

1962

A. BOOKS

1   LINCK, CHARLES EDWARD, Jr. "The Development of Evelyn Waugh's
    Career." Ph.D. dissertation, University of Kansas, 393 pp.
    [DA 24:747-48.]
       Relates Waugh's career as a novelist to biographical details,
    with considerable new information about his writing during his
    years at Oxford. States that because his novels were based upon
    his life and times, he was a more potent force and influence upon
    social thinking than his current reputation might indicate.


B. SHORTER WRITINGS

1   ANON. "A Class War." Time 79 (19 January):67.
       The End of the Battle completes Waugh's trilogy and estab-
    lishes him as the social historian of an obsolete world. Guy
    Crouchback accepts the grey world in which the only crusades are
    private ones.

2   ANON. "Evelyn Waugh." Books and Bookman 7 (March):3.
       Succinct comparison of "early" and "late" Waugh, the change
    occurring in response to World War II.

3   ANON. "Time's Laughing Stocks." TLS, 29 June, p. 476.
       Cites Waugh's article on Ronald Firbank (1929), and notes
    his influence on Waugh in the comic technique of indirection.
    Reviews Decline and Fall as a contrast to Waugh's post-Brideshead
    Revisited writing. Differentiates between Waugh and Anthony Powell.

4   BOATWRIGHT, TALIAFERRO. "Witty War-Time Trilogy: The Last
    Act." New York Herald Tribune Books, 7 January, p. 5.
       The End of the Battle unifies Waugh's vision of an individ-
    ual's struggle with the forces of evil. Crouchback, and Waugh,
    are world-weary, though personal faith is clarified and related
    to public acts.

*5  BURROWS, L.R. "Scènes de la vie militaire." Westerly, no. 1,
    pp. 3-6.
       Source: Checklist, no. 2086; 1972.A1.

6   COFFEY, WARREN. Review of The End of the Battle. Ramparts 1
    (May):94-95.
       Describes Waugh's literary career as divided by Brideshead
    Revisited into satire and lyric statements of the Catholic position.
    The completed trilogy is a mixed success, well handled on the re-
    ligious level but marred by a naive hero. Waugh surveys characters
    and social institutions with witty comedy and humanity.

7    CORBISHLEY, THOMAS. "Literary." Month 213 (March):186.
       Unconditional Surrender finally demonstrates Waugh's true
     sense of humane compassion.

8    CORR, PATRICIA. "Evelyn Waugh: Sanity and Catholicism."
       Studies 51 (Autumn):388-99.
       Discusses the serious undertones of Waugh's fiction. The
     humorist may conceal the moralist, but Waugh's concerns about
     science, progress, and lack of leadership in the modern world
     have always been present. Reviews Waugh's hostile critics, and
     defends his Catholicism. Reprinted: 1963.B7; in 1969.A3.

9    DIDION, JOAN. "Evelyn Waugh: Gentleman in Battle." National
       Review 12 (27 March):215-17.
       "Hardness of mind" separates Waugh from his American readers,
     who misread him as either reactionary or purely comic. The End of
     the Battle completes his elegiac study of declining civilization;
     the trilogy examines an individual, his God, and his society in
     perfect balance.

10   DOYLE, PAUL A. "Brideshead Rewritten." Catholic Book Reporter
       2 (May):9-10.
       Comments on the 1945 reaction to Brideshead Revisited, and
     notes Waugh's changes to the 1960 edition, aimed at stylistic,
     structural and thematic improvements.

11   GARDINER, HAROLD C. "Books." America 106 (27 January):564.
       Waugh's trilogy traces Guy's progressive disillusionment,
     and his defeat by the triumphant Modern Age. The Catholic landed
     gentry is eclipsed.

12   HELLER, JOSEPH. "Middle-Aged Innocence." Nation 194 (20
       January):62-63.
       Waugh is best understood by regarding his humorous novels
     seriously and his serious novels humorously. The End of the Battle
     must be seen as part of the larger trilogy; Waugh seems to regard
     his material as unimportant. Guy Crouchback is an insufferable
     bore.

13   HIGHET, GILBERT. "The Distorting Mirror." In The Anatomy of
       Satire. Princeton: Princeton University Press, pp. 193-95,
       199, 204-5.
       Takes a number of examples from Waugh, especially Decline
     and Fall and The Loved One.

14   HINES, LEO. "Waugh and His Critics." Commonweal 76 (13 April):
       60-63.
       Reviews Waugh's literary reputation, and the cliché concern-
     ing his post-Brideshead Revisited decline. Waugh marches counter
     to the intellectual forces dominating literary criticism. Yet his
     meaning is clearly embodied in his style, and the continuity is

seen in his religious seriousness embodied in the symbol of the
country house.

15    HYNES, SAM. "The Mournful End of Guy Crouchback's Crusade."
      Commonweal 75 (2 February):495-96.
            The trilogy deals with the idiocy of the military man, a
      rich field for comic-satiric inventiveness. The End of the Battle
      becomes a bitter denunciation of the entire Allied cause. The
      Modern Age has won, and Waugh abandons the wit, objectivity, and
      obliquity of true satire. His brilliant style remains.

16    JACOBSON, DAN. "How Waugh Ends the War." New Leader 45
      (14 May):10-11.
            The End of the Battle is the least successful volume of Waugh's
      trilogy. Guy's actions are wasted, he is weary and dissatisfied;
      Waugh is insufficiently detached from his hero to explore his mal-
      aise successfully.

17    KARL, FREDERICK R. "The World of Evelyn Waugh: The Normally
      Insane." In A Reader's Guide to the Contemporary English Novel.
      New York: Noonday Press, pp. 167-82. Reprint. London: Thames
      & Hudson, 1963.
            What Orwell attacked by rational argument, Waugh in his
      early novels makes farcical. He avoids issues, decisions, and con-
      troversy, for the world is the object of his farce. Therefore
      Brideshead falls flat; all of his doctrinaire works, in fact, are
      slight and unrewarding. At his hilarious best he would have thumbed
      his nose at his own Gilbert Pinfold.

18    KERMODE, FRANK. "Mr. Waugh's Cities." In Puzzles and Epiphanies.
      London: Routledge & Kegan Paul, pp. 164-75.
            Reprint of 1960.21.

19    _____. Review of Unconditional Surrender. PR 29 (Summer):
      468-71.
            Waugh's war trilogy presents the theme of the Catholic gentry
      as England's garrison; unclever, gentlemanly piety is the norm of
      conduct. Even a chaotic world has movements of grace, and Guy's
      total disillusionment is not despair. Waugh's vision is both self-
      subsistent and creatively valuable, however implausible.

20    KLEINE, DON W. "The Cosmic Comedies of Evelyn Waugh." SAQ 61
      (Autumn):533-39.
            Argues for the lasting value of Waugh's early satires; they
      chronicle "the vagaries of chance in a random universe." Waugh's
      secret subject is the doomed quest for value in the modern world.

21    LEO, JOHN. "Evelyn Waugh Versus the Ecumenical Council."
      Catholic Messenger, 27 December, p. 10.
            Deplores the reactionary attitude towards liturgical change
      and lay theologians expressed by Waugh in an article entitled "The
      Same Again Please" (National Review 13 [4 December 1962]:429-32).

22    LOWREY, BURLING. "Quest for the Grail, 1939-45." SatR 45
      (6 January):65-66.
          Waugh's war saga, now complete, focuses on Guy Crouchback,
      Catholic, romantic, aristocratic gentleman. From viewing the war
      as a regenerative crusade, Guy comes to almost total disillusion-
      ment, mitigated by two frustrated acts of mercy. Catholicism is
      admirably used on both a symbolic and a literal level.

23    LUNN, Sir ARNOLD. "The Genius of Evelyn Waugh." Duckett's
      Register, January, pp. 1-2.
          Unconditional Surrender is Waugh's greatest novel--and a
      statement of his religious faith in the face of worldly disillu-
      sionment.

24    MacKINNON, MURDO. "Waugh Mistrusts Wartime Values." Globe and
      Mail (Toronto), 10 February, p. 15.
          Calls Unconditional Surrender a novel of disillusionment or
      disenchantment, though not a gloomy book. Guy Crouchback can
      scarcely be called a hero; he is merely a man to whom things happen.

25    MADDOCKS, MELVIN. "New Novels: Waugh's Trilogy Completed."
      Christian Science Monitor, 11 January, p. 7.
          Discusses Waugh's development, and his creation of a world;
      he is the last of the Romantics. The End of the Battle completes
      Waugh's idiosyncratic view of the war as conflicting barbarians.
      Waugh values honor, bravery, and courtesy, but his snobbery is in-
      defensible.

26    McDONNELL, THOMAS P. "Book of the Month." CathW 194 (March):
      365-66.
          Refutes the cliché of Waugh's decline from early promise;
      his true theme is the problem of gentility amid modernity. The
      End of the Battle completes Guy's deflation with his acquisition
      of compassion and personal integrity.

27    NICHOLS, JAMES W. "Romantic and Realistic: The Tone of Evelyn
      Waugh's Early Novels." CE 24 (October) 46:51-56.
          Discusses the modern satirist's problem: the creation of an
      acceptable moral norm within each satire. By blending "realistic"
      and "romantic" elements, Waugh establishes a satiric tone to embody
      a standard of judgement and an adverse attitude to those who trans-
      gress it.

28    O'DONOVAN, PATRICK. "Evelyn Waugh's Opus of Disgust." New
      Republic 146 (12 February):21-22.
          The End of the Battle completes Waugh's war
      saga of the defeat of the West. Guy's military-spiritual Aeneid
      ends in total disillusion and a kind of peace. Uncharitable, snob-
      bish, and rigid, Waugh has still created a masterpiece.

29    PRESCOTT, ORVILLE. "Books of the Times." New York Times,
      8 January, p. 37.

Divides Waugh's career into the exuberant prewar comedies and the morose, postwar apologias. The End of the Battle, despite pleasant sections and Waugh's masterful style, fails in emotional and dramatic power.

30    READY, WILLIAM B. "Books." Critic 20 (March):70-71.
The End of the Battle is the crown of Waugh's career, blending compassion, humor and tragedy. The public cause of war fades into one man's involvement with Christ.

31    SALE, ROGER. Review of The End of the Battle. HudR 15 (Spring):141-42.
Waugh's completed war trilogy is a major achievement, similar in many ways to Ford's Parade's End. Waugh has polished his style with great precision.

32    STYAN, J.L. The Dark Comedy: The Development of Modern Comic Tragedy. Cambridge: Cambridge University Press, p. 293.
The simple disguises of satire, the imaginary worlds of Swift, of Waugh, and of Aldous Huxley, are mission-school parables compared with the hoaxes and snares of Chekhov, Pirandello, and their disciples.

33    TYSDAHL, BJØRN. "The Bright Young Things in the Early Novels of Evelyn Waugh." Edda 62, no. 3:326-34.
Waugh is comedian and farceur as well as satirist; the Bright Young Things are neither idealized nor attacked, but serve to contrast with the older generation in their vitality and romance. Fantasy tempers the satiric edge and blurs moral judgement.

34    VIDAL, GORE. "Evelyn Waugh." In Rocking the Boat. Boston: Little, Brown, pp. 235-43.
Reprint of 1962.B35.

35    _____. "The Satiric World of Evelyn Waugh." New York Times Book Review, 7 January, pp. 1, 28.
Defines the satirist as one who reacts rather than creates. Waugh is a Catholic, Tory traditionalist who seeks value in the past; when he turns from vice to virtue, the satirist disarms himself. The End of the Battle continues Waugh's romantic daydreams. He attacks communists, left-wing intellectuals, Americans, and the lower classes, but fails to embody his vision of good convincingly. Yet Waugh can satirize himself and Brideshead Revisited. Reprinted: 1962.B34.

36    WAUGH, ALEC. The Early Years of Alec Waugh. London: Cassell; New York: Farrar, Straus & Co., 308 pp., passim.
Autobiography of Evelyn Waugh's older brother, giving a family background and an account of the brothers' casual affection. Describes Waugh's transfer from Duckworth's to Chapman and Hall in 1928 and the 1926 publication of Waugh's story "The Balance."

Declines to comment on Evelyn at length, for he cannot enter into
the mind of a person for whom religion is the dominant force.

37    WILSON, COLIN. "Evelyn Waugh and Graham Greene." In The
      Strength to Dream: Literature and the Imagination. Boston:
      Houghton Mifflin Co., pp. 42-55. Also published as Literature
      and the Imagination. London: Gollancz, pp. 52-65.
      The method of Waugh's humour aims at the rejection of the
futility of modern life. Waugh's Catholic snobbery, sentimentality,
and respect for the aristocracy sometimes mar his work.


                                   1963


A.  BOOKS

1     CHURCHILL, THOMAS PAINE. "The House of Waugh: A Critical
      Study of Evelyn Waugh's Major Novels." Ph.D. dissertation,
      University of Washington, 183 pp. [DA 24:2906.]
      Deliberately avoiding the religious aspect of Waugh's novels,
takes the comic aspect as central. Examines three major issues:
how betrayal sets the problem for the comic reconciliation; how
eccentricity represents the civilizing element in a stylized world;
and how the theme of the country house develops. Analyzes Vile
Bodies in some detail, calls Brideshead cloudy and dubious, and
regrets that the war trilogy is not pure comedy: the comic characters are all killed off, and humor is abandoned for a thesis.


B.  SHORTER WRITINGS

1     ANON. "A Rake Raked Up." TLS, 13 November, p. 921.
      Basil Seal Rides Again is a nasty answer to Waugh fans clam-
oring for the "old Waugh manner." The protagonist is more Waugh
than youthful Basil Seal.

2     BARNETT, WILLIAM. "A Thought for the Interim." America 108
      (30 March):440-42.
      Waugh's objections to the liturgical reforms and ecumenical
spirit of Vatican II deserve serious consideration, for his wrong-
headedness demonstrates the paradox of the isolated Catholic. A
letter from Father Martin D'Arcy defending Waugh appeared 20 April,
p. 516.

3     BENEDICT, STEWART H. "The Candide Figure in the Novels of
      Evelyn Waugh." Papers of the Michigan Academy of Science, Arts,
      and Letters 48 (Annual Meeting):685-90.
      Voltaire created the comic archetype of the naive sheltered
young man, uprooted from his environment and thrust into the real
world. Waugh frequently used the Candide figure in his humorous

novels of 1928 to 1952; analysis shows he is at his best when he
does so.

4   BERGONZI, BERNARD.  "Evelyn Waugh's Gentlemen."  CritQ 5
    (Spring):23-36.
        Waugh's career was marked by an early shift from nihilistic
    fun to Tory romanticism, developing into a total myth in which the
    Catholic aristocracy guards traditional values against modern bar-
    barians.  The war trilogy transforms this myth:  Guy Crouchback is
    Waugh's ideal of the gentleman, progressively disillusioned but ul-
    timately at peace with the modern age.  Discusses A Handful of Dust
    in terms of the war trilogy, and reevaluates Brideshead, Helena,
    and Put Out More Flags.  Reprinted in 1969.A3.

5   CASEY, GEORGE.  "The Same Always, Please."  Commonweal 77
    (1 February):487-89.
        Criticizes Waugh's view on Vatican II (National Review 13
    [4 December 1962]:429-32) as reactionary and idiosyncratic.

6   CECCHIN, GIOVANNI.  "Echi di T.S. Eliot Nei Romanzi di Evelyn
    Waugh."  EM 14:239-75.
        Accuses critics of labeling Waugh too easily, without reading
    him as closely as he requires.  Finds echoes of T.S. Eliot's poetry
    not only in the obvious place, A Handful of Dust, but also in
    Brideshead and the war trilogy, and notably in Vile Bodies.  Re-
    pudiating the idea that Waugh is a "fantastic confuser of issues,"
    maintains that his works, like Eliot's, represent a gradual process
    of clarification, and that his art reflects exceptional discipline.

7   CORR, PATRICIA.  "Evelyn Waugh:  Sanity and Catholicism."
    Catholic Mind 61 (March):17-22.
        Reprint of 1962.B8.  Reprinted in 1969.A3.

8   CULLMAN, MARGUERITE.  "A Waugh-Time Memory."  Harper's Bazaar
    90 (February):109-10.
        Anecdotes dealing with a train trip from New York to Los
    Angeles in 1945, including an amusing incident in which Waugh (soon
    to describe the Happier Hunting Ground in The Loved One) munched
    happily but unconsciously on dog food.  Extract from her Occupation:
    Angel (New York:  Norton, 1963).

9   FEINBERG, LEONARD.  The Satirist:  His Temperament, Motivation,
    and Influence.  Ames:  Iowa State University Press, pp. 28, 64,
    67, 262, 283.
        Declares that it is not easy to accept morality as Waugh's
    motivation:  his is a negative morality, emphasising hatred and
    criticism of contemporary institutions instead of Christian love.

10  FLOOD, EDMUND.  "Jungman Revisited, or a Word to Mr. Waugh."
    Life of the Spirit 17 (March):383-87.
        Discusses the pastoral function of the liturgy, and how

liturgical reform should improve this function.  Criticizes Waugh
for arguing that authentic lay participation in the Mass is an un-
realizable ideal.

11    HALL, JAMES.  "Stylized Rebellion:  Evelyn Waugh."  In The
      Tragic Comedians:  Seven Modern British Novelists.  Bloomington:
      Indiana University Press, pp. 45-65.
          Revision of 1961.B15, with expanded comments on Waugh's lan-
      guage and characterization, and on A Handful of Dust and The Loved
      One.

12    JEBB, JULIAN, interviewer.  "The Art of Fiction XXX:  Evelyn
      Waugh."  Paris Review 8 (Summer-Fall):72-85.
          Counters the image of Waugh as arrogant, irritable, and re-
      actionary.  Waugh comments on his early writings, literary tech-
      niques, characterization, literary antecedents, and moral purpose,
      and also gives his opinions on contemporary reviewing and the
      artist's need to be reactionary.

13    KIELY, ROBERT.  "The Craft of Despondency--The Traditional
      Novelists."  Daedalus 92 (Spring):  Perspectives on the Novel,
      220-37.
          Waugh belongs to a group of novelists who sought to sustain
      and embellish rather than revolutionize the novel; he is comparable
      to Graham Greene and Katherine Anne Porter.  His world is called
      insane or absurd, but he achieves absurdity in a special way; the
      hero of his trilogy is a man burdened like Christian with an active
      mind and conscience.  There is a peculiar brilliance to all three
      of these writers; they are sophisticated and entertaining guides
      to hell.

14    LODGE, DAVID.  "The Modern, the Contemporary, and the Importance
      of Being Amis."  CritQ 5 (Winter):335-54.
          Compares Kingsley Amis's I Like It Here to Waugh's Ordeal of
      Gilbert Pinfold and Vladimir Nabokov's Pale Fire as a novel turned
      inward upon literary art and the artist himself.  States that the
      originators, the exuberant men, are extinct, and that the "modern"
      element is being submerged in contemporary writing.

15    POPE-HENNESSY, JAMES.  "Thirty years on."  Sunday Times (London),
      27 October, p. 39.
          Declares that Basil Seal Rides Again does not represent a
      successful return to Waugh's younger manner; it makes sad and un-
      inspired reading.

16    PRITCHETT, V.S.  "Time's Revenges."  New Statesman 66 (15
      November):706-7.
          Criticizes Basil Seal Rides Again for destroying the earlier
      fictional image of Waugh's arch-rogue.

17    WEST, PAUL.  The Modern Novel.  London:  Hutchinson, pp. 48,

60-61, 66-69, 80, 127-28.
Traces Waugh's type of comic novel to William Gerhardi, who
derived it from Chekhov. Says Waugh's exposure of insanity is more
blistering than Aldous Huxley's, more inventive and callous than
E.M. Forster's; there is no doubt that spiritual security gave him
extra licence for savagery. Complains that names like <u>Trimmer</u> in
the war trilogy testify to the parochialism of the English imagination. Revised: 1965.27.

1964

A. BOOKS

1    BRADBURY, MALCOLM. <u>Evelyn Waugh</u>. Writers and Critics Series.
     Edinburgh and London: Oliver & Boyd, p. 120.
     Particularly interested in kinds of comedy in Waugh, and his
use of a comic approach to establish a scale of values. In the
early novels, Waugh depicts an unredeemable and anarchistic universe. As his own values gradually come in, a compensating mechan-
sim builds up the opposition to them, so that those committed to
his beliefs are isolated and ripe for disaster. The world of disorder is never brought under control; Waugh is a totally modern
novelist, offering his own values with assertive prejudice, but in
a world where the really truthful statement is that of flux and
anarchy.

B. SHORTER WRITINGS

1    ALLEN, WALTER. <u>Tradition and Dream. The English and American</u>
     <u>Novel from the Twenties to Our Own Time</u>. London: Phoenix House,
     pp. 208-14. Also published as <u>The Modern Novel in Britain and</u>
     <u>the United States</u>. New York: Dutton, pp. 208-14.
     In most of Waugh's novels, the hero is an innocent caught up
in the machinations of a wicked world; but the nature of that world
changes from fantasy to reality. Seeing Guy Crouchback as the victim of fantastic actions in a real world, however, we may feel that
the world of the earlier novels was more true to life than we had
believed.

2    ANON. "Anatomy of a Dangerous Thing." <u>TLS</u>, 10 September, p.
     836.
     Comments on Waugh's self-portrait as an aged fossil in <u>A</u>
<u>Little Learning</u>. The autobiography traces the speed and degree
of change in recent history; Waugh feels exiled from the past in
the tragic process. He may unconsciously distort the facts.

3    ANON. "But Barnes Laughs." <u>Newsweek</u> 64 (9 November):104-5.
     In <u>A Little Learning</u>, Waugh describes his education as

preparing him only to be a writer of prose; the volume is a portrait
of the making of an artist.  His literary skills are as evident here
as in his fiction, though the Catholic traditional moralist and
aristocratic Tory casts a melancholy shade.

4    ANON.  "Lacuna."  TLS, 16 July, p. 631.
        Wonders about the lack of a novel or poem to express the ex-
perience of World War II and postwar feeling as The Waste Land did
for World War I.  Describes Waugh's trilogy as the most impressive
attempt by any English novelist to come to terms with the war, but
like Crouchback himself, the trilogy retreats wearily from war to
a half-parody of it.

5    ANON.  "Mid-Victorian in Exile."  Time 84 (13 November):92.
        Discusses Waugh's life-long hatred of modernity, as evident
in A Little Learning.  Waugh's fiction outshines his autobiography.

6    ANON.  "Mr. Waugh gives new life to old times."  Universe and
        Catholic Times (London), 30 October, p. 5.
        Reviewing A Little Learning, describes Waugh as one of the
fortunate few whose memories are not blurred in middle age; the
book deserves a careful reading because of the delight given by
its style.

7    ANON.  "Return of a Comic Writer to Childhood and Youth."  Times
        (London), 10 September, p. 15.
        After P.G. Wodehouse, Waugh is the most successful living
comic writer.  In A Little Learning, his glaring, sometimes nostalgic eye is turned on his own past.  The book reveals little of
his own transition from enfant terrible to Catholic Colonel Blimp.

8    ANON.  Review of A Handful of Dust.  TLS, 5 March, p. 201.
        Comments on Waugh's blended tones in the novel, showing the
narrow margin between the economical and the superficial.  Also
notes the alternative endings.

9    ANON.  "Tilbury and Copper."  TLS, 10 September, p. 837.
        Comparing Waugh's Scoop to P.G. Wodehouse's Frozen Assets,
comments how alike yet unalike the two humorists are.  Waugh's
targets are real ones, and his method is direct observation; Scoop
is uneven but a small classic.

10   ANON.  "Waugh World I."  Economist 212 (12 September):1031.
        Reviews A Little Learning, noting the paradox of Waugh's love
of privacy and the autobiographical streak in his fiction.  Waugh's
reticence and candor are equally sincere.

11   BELFORD, S.  "Loved and Loving."  New York Herald Tribune Book
        Week, 15 November, pp. 3, 25.
        A Little Learning is a modest, urbane, truthful autobiogra-
phy, polished and witty.  Waugh is self-effacing, charitable and
detached.

12   BERGONZI, BERNARD.  "Evelyn Waugh's The Sword of Honour."
     Listener 71 (20 February):306-7.
         The first two war novels reveal the familiar Waugh ethos of
     Tory romanticism, the cult of the gentleman doomed by modernity,
     and admiration for the Catholic upper class.  Unconditional Surrender
     clarifies its predecessors by completing the structure and theme and
     transforming Waugh's myth.

13   _____.  Review of A Handful of Dust.  Blackfriars 45 (July-
     August):349-50.
         Waugh's masterpiece blends farce, tragedy, and the macabre,
     and points to later treatments of the gentlemanly ideas in Brideshead
     and Sword of Honour.  Discusses the two endings.

14   BRADBURY, MALCOLM.  "Waugh Revisited."  Spectator 213 (11
     September):347.
         Waugh's reputation has declined because of his apparent snob-
     bery; he is oblique and ambiguous, however, both in fiction and
     personal statement.  His interest in comic anarchy makes his writ-
     ing consistent, significant, and influential.  A Little Learning
     clarifies his cultural background and his pose as dandy.

15   BROPHY, BRIGID.  "Mr. Waugh's Eschatology."  New Statesman 68
     (25 September):450.
         Divides Waugh's career sharply into pre- and post-1945 in
     terms of style, imagination, and sensibility.  Scoop is mere enter-
     tainment, but A Handful of Dust is a major work, tragic in inten-
     tion.  The fragmentary method helps establish Waugh's direction
     toward a Particular and a General Judgement.

16   BURGESS, ANTHONY.  "Waugh Begins."  Encounter 23 (December):64,
     66, 68.
         Comments on Waugh's stoic, self-mocking pose of Augustan
     champion.  His style is a kind of morality; his background explains
     his romanticism and sentimentality--A Little Learning shows that he
     derives naturally from his father.  Reprinted:  1968.B8.

17   COGLEY, JOHN.  "Revisiting Brideshead."  Commonweal 80 (17
     April):103-6.
         Comments on Waugh's mastery of language, and his unimagina-
     tive, formalistic theology, in Brideshead.  The remoteness of
     Waugh's Catholicity makes his novel an anachronism in the age of
     Pope John XXIII.

18   _____.  "A Suggestion for Mr. Waugh."  Commonweal 81 (23
     October):120-23.
         Laments Waugh's opposition to the liturgical reforms of
     Vatican II, suggesting that the author's role as stylist is to
     assist in translating the liturgy into English.  Waugh replied
     (4 December, pp. 352-53) defending his view of the meaninglessness
     of the vernacular.

19　　DAICHES, DAVID. "Ah, the Past, How Pleasantly Different."
　　　New York Times Book Review, 1 November, pp. 4, 18.
　　　　　A Little Learning verifies Waugh's nostalgia for the past and
resentment of modernity. With restrained precision and total acceptance, Waugh recreates his early life with convincing skill.
His love of the lifestyle discovered at Oxford caused him to attempt its perpetuation in his own life.

20　　DAVIS, ROBERT MURRAY. "The Externalist Method in the Novels
　　　of Ronald Firbank, Carl Van Vechten, and Evelyn Waugh." Ph.D.
　　　dissertation, University of Wisconsin, 236 pp. [DA 25:2509.]
　　　　　Finds similarities in detachment; in the use of a mixture of
narrative styles to secure economy and rapid pace; and in the use
of a subtle interweaving of minor plots, instead of traditional
framework of plot, which may be called the externalist method.
Shows influences of Firbank and the cinema on the early Waugh, and
points out that since the method cannot deal with deep emotions or
complex characters Waugh abandoned it as he dealt with more serious
moral conflicts. But the method is effective for comic and satiric
purposes, especially since it effaces the author while allowing him
to comment covertly.

21　　EIMERL, SAREL. "From Imp to Blimp." Reporter 31 (3 December):
　　　55-56.
　　　　　A Little Learning offers intriguing clues to the paradoxical
relationship between the sprightly early Waugh and the later, pomp-
ous one. Despite excellence of style and comic genius, Waugh's
reputation as a satirist is unjustified; his skills are those of
an observant gossip columnist.

22　　ELLIS, A.E. "Hetton Revisited." Spectator 212 (20 March):
　　　328-29.
　　　　　A Handful of Dust unfolds with classic inevitability. Waugh's
dialogue conveys all meaning, and his characterization is superb,
but snobbery is his blind spot.

23　　FIELDING, GABRIEL. "Evelyn Waugh: The Price of Satire."
　　　Listener 72 (8 October):541-42.
　　　　　Referring to his personal relations with Waugh, describes
him as the literary touchstone of a generation within the great
complex of the Church. His early satire concealed his pain and
anger; Brideshead revealed his romanticism. His war trilogy,
though ambitious and important, fails in the rendering of the hero
and his father; it is a Catholic declaration of an outmoded sort.
Gilbert Pinfold shows the price Waugh paid for his satire--the conflict between faith and despair. Revised: 1965.14.

24　　FRASER, G.S. The Modern Writer and his World. London: Andre
　　　Deutsch; Harmondsworth: Penguin, pp. 111, 133, 141-44, 169,
　　　394, 404-5.
　　　　　Revision of 1953.B9, with special emphasis on A Handful of
Dust and The Ordeal of Gilbert Pinfold.

25   FULLER, JOHN.  "Life Before the Works."  <u>Manchester Guardian</u>
     <u>Weekly</u>, 17 September, p. 11.
         Like all autobiography, <u>A Little Learning</u> reveals the myths
     its author spent a lifetime promulgating.  The book intrigues the
     critic, but disappoints the reader.  Waugh is too laconic and de-
     tached, though his observation and recording of incidents are pre-
     cise and entertaining.

26   GREENE, GEORGE.  "Scapegoat With Style:  The Status of Evelyn
     Waugh."  <u>QQ</u> 71 (Autumn):485-93.
         Defends Waugh's attitude to modernity.  Discussing the war
     trilogy, notes Waugh's probing of the reader's sensibility through
     a precise yet evocative style.  Language enhances his theme of
     threatened cultural discontinuity.  While his reputation is un-
     likely to shift radically, he is a true artist.

27   GROSS, JOHN.  "Waugh Revisited."  <u>New York Review of Books</u>,
     3 December, pp. 4-5.
         <u>A Little Learning</u> is reticent and mellow, punctuated with
     humor, and resolutely old-fashioned in style:  Waugh's Augustan
     pose hides a well-informed modern.  His mastery of language is
     dazzling, his portrait of his father impressive and revealing.  Be-
     hind the satirist is a wounded romantic.

28   HARDY, JOHN EDWARD.  "<u>Brideshead Revisited</u>:  God, Man, and
     Others."  In <u>Man in the Modern Novel</u>.  Seattle:  University of
     Washington Press, pp. 159-74.
         Though <u>Brideshead</u> is a book of nostalgia, Charles Ryder at-
     tempts to transcend that nostalgia through Catholicism--a part of
     the English tradition which brings past values into the present.
     Snobbery still remains a problem in the novel, which fails because
     Waugh tries to mingle romantic and satiric characters, and because
     Ryder's conversion is unrelated to his art.

29   HART, JEFFREY.  "The Seriousness of Evelyn Waugh."  <u>National</u>
     <u>Review</u> 16 (29 December):1152-53.
         Sees <u>A Little Learning</u> as moving from stability to disorder,
     personally and historically, revealing the private sources of
     Waugh's comic creation; incorporating disorder into art is Waugh's
     way of conquering it.  Notes the influence of T.S. Eliot on his
     vision.

30   HOWARD, ELIZABETH JANE, interviewer.  "An Aged Novelist:
     Evelyn Waugh at 60."  London:  B.B.C. Television, 16 February.
     Unpublished.
         Calling comic invention a function of youth, Waugh discusses
     the changes in his literary powers brought by age.  Commenting on
     his own career, says that there are a limited number of stories
     and characters in the world, that reality is too absurd for fic-
     tion, and that in a properly told story the feelings are communi-
     cated indirectly.  On contemporary writing, points to the perni-
     cious influence of Joyce and Gertrude Stein.  Also talks about

his own fears of old age and boredom, and says that writing his autobiography is difficult after age twenty-one, for most of his experience has been used in fiction.

31   IGOE, W.J.   "A Book You Close Wishing for More."  Catholic
     Herald, 2 October, p. 9.
         Waugh writes supremely well; his tragic vision is rendered comic by his gift for caricature.  A Little Learning reveals the impact of the modern world upon him.

32   JAMESON, PETER.  "The Youth of Evelyn Waugh."  Time and Tide 45
     (23 September):22.
         Waugh's elegant prose often conceals a sharp edge; in A Little Learning his fondness for the past colors his hatred for the present.

33   JONES, D.A.N.  "Waugh Revisited."  New York Review of Books,
     20 February, p. 3.
         The limited edition of Basil Seal Rides Again is a sharp, cool comedy with vulgar classiness.  Loyalty to his adopted class, not snobbery, marks Waugh's hostility to those who abdicate their social responsibilities, but he himself has aided the decline of aristocratic grandeur.

34   KERNAN, ALVIN B.  "The Wall and the Jungle:  The Early Novels
     of Evelyn Waugh."  YR 43 (Winter):199-220.
         Finds in Waugh's fiction a master image of the conflict be-tween civilization and barbarism:  the wall dividing order from anarchy is ineffective, the powers threatening traditional values have already infiltrated.  Representatives of the old order, how-ever, are treated as savagely as the new barbarians.  Waugh's ar-rangement of events reveals his indictment of modern society:  all the activity produces only a circular movement.  In fact, the circle-as-meaninglessness dominates Waugh's structures and themes. Revised:  1965.B21.  See also 1969.A3.

35   La FRANCE, MARSTON.  "Context and Structure of Evelyn Waugh's
     Brideshead Revisited."  TCL 10 (April-October):12-18.
         Considering that Brideshead has become the focus for Waugh criticism, examines it in the context of his first six novels, finding many similarities in thought and technique, image and character, but flaws in structure and tone.  Reprinted in 1969.A3.

36   LEJEUNE, ANTHONY.  "Child Waugh."  Books and Bookmen 10
     (October):37, 50.
         Waugh provokes ambiguous responses, even from admirers.  A Little Learning tells in perfect prose of a personal and general decline from happiness to harshness, but it is detached and reti-cent.

37   LINCK, CHARLES G., Jr.  "Works of Evelyn Waugh, 1910-1930."
     TCL 10 (April):19-26.

Offers most complete bibliography to date of Waugh's juvenilia and early writings, before his conversion to Catholicism.

*38    LORDA ALAIZ, F.M.  "De romanschrijver Evelyn Waugh."  Raam, no. 12, pp. 13-29.
       Source:  Checklist, no. 1098; 1972.A1.

39    MANDRAKE [pseud.].  "Words with Evelyn Waugh."  Sunday Telegraph (London), 23 August, p. 6.
      Anecdote of a visit to Waugh's home.  He denies living the life of a country gentleman; his motive for living in the country is a desire for peace and quiet.

40    MITFORD, JESSICA.  "Waugh is Hell--or Anyhow, He Was Once."  Life 57 (13 November):12-13.
      A Little Learning connects the Bright Young Waugh to the Cantankerous Old Gentleman.  Notes Waugh's nastiness in childhood and youth.  His autobiography laments the passing of those things he once sought to destroy.

41    MOORE, BRIAN.  "Melancholic Clown."  Harper's 229 (December): 130, 133-34.
      A Little Learning begins with the suggestion of a spoof on ponderous memoirs, but fades into the certainty that the author has become an elderly eccentric.  Compares Waugh's early years with Samuel Johnson's.

42    MORTIMER, RAYMOND.  "A Tale of Good Fortune."  Sunday Times (London), 13 September, p. 33.
      Says Waugh's admirers will be happy to read in A Little Learning how auspicious his start in life was; his childhood was sunny, and the acerbity of his satire remains unaccounted for.

43    MURRAY, JAMES G.  "'Till Tired He Sleeps . . .'"  America 111 (12 December):782.
      Present and future are distasteful to Waugh, but A Little Learning examines the past apathetically and pathetically.  Notes his current image as a curmudgeon.

*44    PAKENHAM, FRANK.  Five Lives.  London: Hutchinson, pp. 14-15, 16, 105, 196.
       Source:  Checklist, no. 1155; 1972.A1.

45    PLOMER, WILLIAM.  Review of A Little Learning.  Listener 72 (2 September):397.
      Waugh has good reasons for his pose as an anachronism.  A Little Learning reveals experience, wit, and a fine prose style, the tools of a brilliant social satirist.

46    PRESCOTT, ORVILLE.  "The Diverting Memories of Evelyn Waugh."  New York Times, 4 November, p. 37.

Waugh's early comic novels were savagely witty; after World War II his fiction became disillusioned and morose. A Little Learning may mark a third phase--one of detached, sophisticated amusement.

47    PRITCHETT, V.S.  "Mr. Waugh's Exile."  New Statesman 68
      (25 September):445-46.
      A Little Learning contains the melancholy of Sword of Honour, and displays Waugh's gifts as impersonator and his long-standing preoccupations.  Discusses Waugh's multiple literary personality, noting that his reticence suggests inner conflict.  Also discusses the sociable, masculine vein in English comedy.  Reprinted: 1980.B30.

48    PRYCE-JONES, ALAN.  "Evelyn Waugh."  Commonweal 81 (4 December):
      343-45.
      Comments on Waugh's sense of hierarchy and order, and on the contrast between his public image and the reality.  Compares A Little Learning to The Ordeal of Gilbert Pinfold.  Also analyzes Waugh's method of characterization.

49    RAVEN, SIMON.  "Waugh's Private Wars."  Spectator 212 (12 June):
      798.
      Reviews the Penguin edition of the war trilogy.  Raven's original admiration remains, but he objects to the "sheer silli- ness" of Waugh's reverence for old recusant families and contempt for the lower classes and modernity.  His satiric techniques are unsuited to a serious work, but Crouchback's pilgrimage legitimate- ly leads him to private salvation through private faith.

50    REED, JOHN R.  Old School Ties:  The Public Schools in British
      Literature.  Syracuse:  Syracuse University Press, pp. 85-93,
      195-201, et passim.
      Refers to Waugh's description of the commercialization of the public school, and also his comparison of it to army life. Says he does not criticize its concept of the gentleman as do many of his contemporaries.  Cites examples from Decline and Fall, Vile Bodies, Scott-King's Modern Europe, Love Among the Ruins, and Men at Arms in illustration of attitudes to the public schools.

51    WAUGH, AUBERON.  "And Father Came Too."  Books and Bookmen 9
      (January):9-11.
      Auberon Waugh, in an interview with Stephanie Nettell, dis- cusses the critical response to his second novel, and complains about reviewers.  Includes a comparison of the son with his father.

52    WHEELER, BISHOP GORDON.  "The Knox a Friend Knew."  Catholic
      Herald (London), 20 November, p. 6.
      Describes Father Thomas Corbishley's Ronald Knox the Priest as a corrective to Waugh.  The latter's biography is an incompar- able literary achievement, but not a complete assessment; it is

96

least successful concerning Knox's priesthood and his priestly
relations.

53   WOODRUFF, DOUGLAS.  "Mr. Waugh's Minority."  Tablet 218
     (12 September):218.
          Describes A Little Learning as a mellow retrospect, consider-
     ate to all the living and nearly all the dead; observes that at the
     end of it Waugh is only reaching maturity.  Notes that his early
     years show him warmhearted and almost indiscriminatingly sociable.


<u>1965</u>


1    ALEXANDER, SHANA.  "A Funny-Ugh Movie."  Life 59 (8 October):34.
          Most of the jokes in the film version of The Loved One are
     sick.  Its true queasy-making vulgarity lies in the fact that it
     mixes up jokes about our attitudes to death, which are often ab-
     surd, with death itself, which never is.

2    ALLSOP, KENNETH.  "Pinfold at Home."  In Scan.  London:  Hodder
     & Stoughton, pp. 90-101.
          Reviewing Waugh's career, discusses his image as Colonel
     Blimp.  Calls The Ordeal of Gilbert Pinfold a surprisingly reveal-
     ing book.  Describes a visit to Waugh's home and his comments on
     contemporary writing.

3    ANON.  Review of Vile Bodies and The Loved One.  TLS, 17 June,
     p. 489.
          Comments on the new uniform edition of Waugh's novels, and
     on the author's introductions, saying Waugh's books are as fresh
     as ever.

4    ATTICUS [pseud.].  "Scoop Scooped."  Sunday Times (London),
     21 February, p. 9.
          Describes plans by Basil Dearden and Michael Relph to make
     a film out of Waugh's Scoop.

5    AUDEN, W.H.  "Books:  As It Seemed to Us."  NY 41 (3 April):
     159-92.
          Reviews A Little Learning, comparing it to Leonard Woolf's
     Beginning Again.  Waugh's public image is Dickensian, but need
     not be taken seriously.  Auden interweaves his own life story with
     Waugh's and Woolf's.

6    BARRETT, MARVIN.  "At the Movies:  The Southern Way of Death."
     Reporter 33 (16 November):40-42.
          The film version of The Loved One promised much and delivered
     little.  Terry Southern, the scenarist, enjoys an undeservedly high
     reputation; this film script accentuates his faults.  Waugh's con-
     trolled world becomes Southern's frenzied one.

7   CAMERON, J.M. "A Post-Waugh Insight." Commonweal 83 (29
    October):114-15.
         In the controversy over liturgical changes, Waugh's stance
    is that an underground conspiracy exists to rob Catholics of their
    religious heritage. Attacks Waugh's "delusions" and misreadings
    of liturgical commentators.

8   CARROLL, JOHN. "A Waugh against Ugliness of Modern Age."
    Globe and Mail (Toronto), 27 February, p. 13.
         For admirers of Waugh's fiction, A Little Learning is a most
    desirable way of setting the engine slow astern and journeying in-
    to a world where cricket was a touchstone of character.

9   DAVIS, ROBERT MURRAY. "Evelyn Waugh's Early Work:  The Forma-
    tion of a Method." TSLL 7 (Winter):97-108.
         Analyzes "The Balance" (1926) to establish Waugh's discovery
    of an objective technique for rendering subjective reactions, par-
    ticularly through cinematic devices. Discusses the early fiction
    to show Waugh's development of detachment.

10  _____. Review of A Little Learning. MLJ 44 (November):458-59.
         As autobiography, A Little Learning is more emotional than
    factual. Waugh is coolly detached, but his book will tantalize
    students of his novels in revealing his attitude to the past.

11  DELASANTA, RODNEY, and MARIO L. D'AVANZO. "Truth and Beauty in
    Brideshead Revisited." MFS 11 (Winter):140-52.
         Analyzes the symbolic meanings of Brideshead to prove that
    its element of apologia is artistically conceived and integrally
    related to the theme.

12  DYSON, A.E. "Evelyn Waugh:  And the Mysteriously Disappearing
    Hero." In The Crazy Fabric:  Essays in Irony. London:
    Macmillan, pp. 187-96.
         Reprint of 1960.17.

13  EICHELBAUM, STANLEY. "Cinema:  The Loved One Revisited."
    Ramparts 3 (March):7-8, 10-11.
         Contrasts the film version of The Loved One with the novel,
    noting Waugh's objections to the screenplay. Describes sets and
    cast.

14  FIELDING, GABRIEL. "Evelyn Waugh and the Cross of Satire."
    Critic 23 (February-March):52-56.
         Reprint of 1964.B23, with minor changes that emphasize the
    Catholic content of the article.

15  GERSH, GABRIEL. Review of A Little Learning. SAQ 64 (Summer):
    425-26.
         Describes Waugh as an objective novelist in an age of sub-
    jective fiction. In A Little Learning, he blends both approaches.

16    GLEASON, JAMES.  "Evelyn Waugh and the Stylistics of Commitment."
      Wisconsin Studies in Literature, no. 2, pp. 70-74.
            Discusses critical hostility to Brideshead, and its position
      as the dividing line between early and late Waugh.  Argues that
      Waugh's commitment to the aristocratic tradition is present in
      earlier novels, especially in the symbol of the great house.

17    GREENBLATT, STEPHEN JAY.  "Evelyn Waugh."  In Three Modern
      Satirists:  Waugh, Orwell, and Huxley.  New Haven and London:
      Yale University Press, pp. 3-33.
            Considers Waugh's recording of the destruction of traditional
      values in the modern world; examines his early fiction for satiric
      devices and themes; and notes his growing pessimism and ironic
      double vision.

*18   HORTMANN, WILHELM.  Englische Literatur im 20. Jahrhundert.
      Bern and Munich:  Francke, pp. 115-18, 146-47.
            Source:  Checklist, no. 1048; 1972.A1.

19    ISAACS, NEIL D.  "Evelyn Waugh's Restoration Jesuit."  SNL 3
      (Spring):91-94.
            Analyzes Waugh's use of Father Rothschild, S.J., in Vile
      Bodies as a satire on the type character of historical fiction,
      especially by comparison with Father Holt, S.J., in Thackeray's
      Henry Esmond.

20    KAEL, PAULINE.  "Star-Studded Paste-Up for a Big Dirty Joke."
      Life, 29 October, p. 10.
            The Loved One became a Hollywood legend through the efforts
      of various writers to get a script out of material considered too
      daring and macabre.  A failure in almost all its serious intentions,
      this botched, patched-together movie is a triumphant disaster.

21    KERNAN, ALVIN B.  "Running in Circles:  The Early Novels of
      Evelyn Waugh."  In The Plot of Satire.  New Haven and London:
      Yale University Press, pp. 143-67.
            Revision of 1964.B34.  Reprinted in 1969.A3.

22    KOSOK, HEINZ.  "Brideshead Revisited."  In Der Moderne englische
      Roman:  Interpretationen.  Edited by Horst Oppel.  Berlin:
      Erich Schmidt Verlag, pp. 301-27.
            Through a very careful reading of Brideshead, strives to show
      that it has a place in the great tradition of the English novel.
      Calls attention to Waugh's artfulness in construction; in the use
      of thematic parallels and symbolic details; in the creation of
      characters varying from the merely functional to the fully devel-
      oped; in the evocation of an epoch; and in the subtle handling of
      theme.  For all the reservations expressed about it, it is a major
      novel.

23    MEHOKE, JAMES S.  "Sartre's Theory of Emotion and Three English
      Novelists:  Waugh, Greene and Amis."  Wisconsin Studies in

Literature, no. 3, pp. 105–13.
In Waugh, Greene, and Amis, the eighteenth-century picaro
has become the twentieth-century confidence man. Jean-Paul Sartre
defines emotion as "a transformation of the world" enacting "painful comedies." These two concepts can be applied to the Margot-
Paul relationship in Decline and Fall.

24   SHANAHAN, WILLIAM J.  Review of A Little Learning.  CathW 65
     (February):315–16.
     A Little Learning reveals Waugh's interest in analyzing his
life, free from the mask of fiction. His later novels draw author
and protagonist even closer together. Discusses his reputation.

25   SONNENFELD, ALBERT.  "Twentieth Century Gothic:  Reflections on
     the Catholic Novel." SoR, n.s. 1 (April):388–405.
     Discusses the reactionary conservatism of the Catholic novel
after the two World Wars; it displays a romantic, chivalric medi-
evalism in response to modernity. Waugh's heroes have their idealism destroyed in the modern world.

26   STRATFORD, PHILIP.  "Books in Review:  Back Home with the Waugh
     Boys." Saturday Night 80 (April):28–29.
     Their autobiographies reveal the sharp differences between
Alec and Evelyn Waugh. More chronicler than hero of his life,
Evelyn is too reticent in A Little Learning, particularly about
his imaginative life; however, the book is a good example of his
style, scrupulous to the point of pedantry.

27   WEST, PAUL.  The Modern Novel.  rev. ed.  Vol. 1.  London:
     Hutchinson University Library, pp. 66–68, et passim.
     Revision of 1963.17.

28   WOLFF, JOSEPH J.  "Evelyn Waugh's A Little Learning." Today 20
     (February):30–31.
     Reviews Waugh's career and his commitment to tradition, con-
tending that A Little Learning disproves the argument that his fiction is autobiographical.


1966


A.  BOOKS

1   CARENS, JAMES F.  The Satiric Art of Evelyn Waugh.  Seattle and
    London:  Washington University Press, 195 pp.
    Avoiding biographical and psychological speculation, attempts
to illuminate Waugh's central motifs, satiric techniques and attitudes, and development as an artist. Calls the total detachment
of the early novels a satiric mask, modelled on Firbank's. Describes the gradual emergence of Catholicism as a principle of

order in the novels, but sees it as mingled and confused with
Waugh's socio-political allegiances. Throughout his career, he
made no surrender to his age; but Sword of Honour reveals that,
though he was undiminished in satiric power, pity too was within
his range.

2   HOLLIS, CHRISTOPHER. Evelyn Waugh. Writers and Their Work,
    no. 46. London: Longmans, Green, 39 pp.
         Revision of 1958.A2, concluding with brief mention of Waugh's
first volume of autobiography, A Little Learning. Revised: 1971.A3.
See also 1954.A1.

3   JERVIS, STEVEN ALEXANDER. "The Novels of Evelyn Waugh: A
    Critical Study." Ph.D. dissertation, Stanford University, 263
    pp. [DA 27:1058A.]
         Considers the evolution of his art, the development of his
comic style, the growing prominence of his political and religious
convictions, and his changing methods of characterization. Calls
Brideshead his one extravagance, with its overwrought portrayal of
the conflict between worldly love and religious necessity. After
it he tried to return to his old mode in works like The Loved One,
but he produced only tired imitations. In the war trilogy, however,
he regained his fluency, and also showed a new depth of feeling.


B.  SHORTER WRITINGS

1   ACTON, HAROLD. "The Artist." Adam nos. 301-3, pp. 9-14.
         Discusses Waugh's literary achievement, humorous self-
portraits in fiction, and striking modernity of style. Calls him
a satirist of ruthless integrity, characterized by religion, romantic morality, and chivalrous conduct. His flair for absurdity
was a life-long gift.

2   ANON. "The Beauty of His Malice: Evelyn Waugh (1903-1966)."
    Time 87 (22 April):78.
         Obituary notice, stressing Waugh's fundamentally religious
but wickedly hilarious assault on the twentieth century. Reviews
his career, with stress on his conversion and the delusions and
melancholia of his later years. Calls the war trilogy his masterpiece.

3   ANON. "Evelyn Waugh." Christian Science Monitor, 12 April, p.
    2; "Never Apologize, Never Explain," 13 April, p. E1.
         Obituary describing Waugh as Britain's most successful satiri-
cal novelist--in his prewar fiction; conversion to Catholicism
markedly changed his writing. More than a critic and snob, he
warred on lack of conviction because of his concern for the values
of the past.

4   ANON. "Evelyn Waugh." New York Times, 16 April, p. 32.

Obituary, emphasizing Waugh's unique satiric stance, wild invention, deadpan attitude, and precise prose. His criticisms were just, but his solutions archaic.

5    ANON. "Evelyn Waugh is Dead at 62." San Francisco Chronicle, 11 April, p. 37.
Obituary defining Waugh's life and career in terms of his piety, courage, and nostalgia.

6    ANON. "Evelyn Waugh. R.I.P." America 114 (23 April):578.
Obituary commenting on Waugh's mordant satire, brilliant style, and stress on Catholic apologetics. His religious conservatism was not blameworthy.

7    ANON. "Evelyn Waugh, Satirical Novelist, Is Dead at 62." New York Times, 11 April, pp. 1, 35.
Describes Waugh as a major literary figure of modern Britain. Notes his prickly personality, commitment to the aristocratic tradition, and bizarre attitude toward modern life.

8    ANON. "Evelyn Waugh--Writer of Protest." Manchester Guardian Weekly, 14 April, p. 14.
Says that Waugh's ideals of honor and nobility unify his literary career; his middle-class origins and conversion to Catholicism are the central biographical facts. Compares him to George Bernard Shaw as a writer of protest.

9    ANON. "Lower the Flag." Newsweek 25 (25 April):92.
Waugh's role as arch-reactionary did not mar his fine satirical career or his founding of the modern comic novel. Without compassion, he specialized in sadistic humor.

10   ANON. "Mr. Evelyn Waugh: Artist in Satiric Prose." Times (London), 11 April, p. 10.
Reviews Waugh's life and career, calling attention to his perfection of style, deepening religious faith, and aversion to modernity. Reprinted: 1975.B1.

11   ANON. "Wartime Revisited." TLS, 17 March, p. 216.
Notes that the revisions to Sword of Honour have not corrected its flaws. The removal of Crouchback's children alters the tone of the ending, and many delightful passages have disappeared. The trilogy is as much about the servant question as an obituary of the Catholic Church in England, but it is a first-rate work of fiction. Reprinted: 1967.B1.

11a  BAKEWELL, MICHAEL. "Sword of Honour." Radio Times (London), 20 December, p. 19.
Quoting Cyril Connolly's "Unquestionably the finest novel to come out of the war," pays tribute to Giles Cooper, whose recent death had ended the career of a remarkable adapter, a searching

and relentless comic ironist, and therefore a man ideally suited
to prepare a television version of Sword of Honour.

12   BOWRA, C.M.  "The Next Generation."  In Memories 1898-1939.
     London:  Weidenfeld & Nicolson, pp. 154-87, 250.
     Describes the Harold Acton-Brian Howard generation at Oxford,
and gives portraits of Waugh's contemporaries.  His own friendship
with Waugh postdated Decline and Fall.  Comments on Waugh's real
character, talent for comic satire, moralist's stance, and social
life.

13   BRADY, CHARLES A.  "In Memoriam Arthur Evelyn St. John Waugh
     1903-1966."  America 114 (23 April):594-95.
     Obituary notice evaluating Waugh's achievement.  His conver-
sion to Catholicism, fathering a large family, and taking part in
World War II helped define his satiric focus.  A nostalgic romantic
and classical moralist, he had a long literary pedigree but in-
vented a special mode of comedy.

14   BRIEN, ALAN.  "Permission to Speak, Captain?"  Spectator 216
     (15 April):462-63.
     Condemns Waugh's method of dealing with attackers, hallucina-
tory or real.  Recounts his meeting with Waugh at White's Club with
Randolph Churchill in 1955.

15   BUCKLEY, WILLIAM F.  "Evelyn Waugh, R.I.P."  National Review 18
     (3 May):400, 402.
     Waugh was a great satirist, conservative, traditionalist,
passionately convinced Christian, and master stylist.  Discusses
his biography and double personality.

16   BURGESS, ANTHONY.  "The Comedy of Ultimate Truths."  Spectator
     216 (15 April):462.
     Obituary commenting on Waugh's later melancholy and his hun-
ger for order and stability on both worldly and spiritual planes.
His comedy is the medium for the expression of ultimate, sometimes
bitter truths.  Reprinted:  1968.B8.

*17  BUTCHER, MARYVONNE.  "Evelyn Waugh:  Er machte Kunst und
     Schlagzeilen."  Dokumente (Cologne) 22:236-38.
     Source:  Checklist, no. 897; 1972.A1.

18   CAMERON, J.M.  "Evelyn Waugh, R.I.P."  Commonweal 84 (29 April):
     167-68.
     Waugh's varied achievement made him the finest English novel-
ist, but his public and literary persona as champion of a dying
aristocratic culture and enemy of modern vulgarity obscured his
reputation.  The persona was assumed, however, for satirical and
self-protective purposes.

19   CARAMAN, PHILIP.  "Evelyn Waugh:  The Panegyric."  Tablet 220

(30 April):518.
Text of the panegyric preached at the Requiem Mass for Waugh.
Stresses his loyalty to friends, religion, and literary associates.

20  CHAMBERLAIN, C.L.  "In Memoriam."  Lancing College Magazine
    (Summer), pp. 58-61.
    Notes Waugh's life-long combination of the outrageous and
the outraged.  Describes his Lancing career, with reference to the
Corpse Club and the Dilettanti, and reprints two pieces of Lancing
juvenilia.

21  CLINTON, FARLEY.  "Evelyn Waugh, R.I.P."  National Review 18
    (3 May):416-17.
    Waugh's early work is irreplaceable, but vanished naturally
with his youth.  His later work bears constant rereading.  Recalls
his early travels, his conversion, and the deathbed repentance of
Hubert Duggan, which inspired Brideshead.

22  DAVIS, ROBERT MURRAY.  "Evelyn Waugh on the Art of Fiction."
    PLL 2 (Summer):243-52.
    Drawing out Waugh's views on fiction from reviews, essays,
travel books, and interviews, demonstrates his aesthetic consistency; his preference for an externalist approach to character and
narration; his stress on style and language; his distaste for ob-
scurity; his liking for a Firbankian noncausal, selective method;
and his concern for symmetry and order.

23  DOYLE, PAUL A.  "Waugh's Brideshead Revisited."  Explicator 24
    (March):item 57.
    Comments on the Chestertonian "twitch upon the thread" theme
in Brideshead, the multiple symbolism of the title, and the parallels between the deathbed repentances of Oscar Wilde and Lord
Marchmain.

24  FEATHERSTONE, JOSEPH.  "The Ordeal of Evelyn Waugh."  New
    Republic 155 (16 July):21-23.
    The Ordeal of Gilbert Pinfold is Waugh's last word about his
own literary stature.  Going beyond satire, he re-created his values in fictional settings; absurdly reactionary, he let his satiric
intensity decline as his compassion increased.  Brideshead, though
badly flawed, revealed his romanticism, adolescent nostalgia for a
vanished past, and snobbish Catholicism.  Sword of Honour and The
Ordeal of Gilbert Pinfold are his greatest achievements.

*25 FRICKER, ROBERT.  Der moderne englische Roman.  Rev. ed.
    Göttingen:  Bandenhoeck & Ruprecht, pp. 196-203.
        Source:  Checklist, no. 993; 1972.A1.

26  GADD, THOMAS W.  "Evelyn Waugh."  Spectator 216 (22 April):495.
    Letter to the editor refuting allegations of snobbery and
social opportunism on Waugh's part.  The following week (p. 524)
another correspondent testified to Waugh's courtesy and integrity.

27    GREENE, GRAHAM. Note to Waugh Obituary. <u>Times</u> (London),
      15 April, p. 15.
          Calls Waugh the greatest novelist of his generation, but de-
      scribes his virtues as a friend, despite differences of political
      opinion. Reprinted: 1967.B14.

28    GWYNN, DENIS. "Evelyn Waugh and Ronald Knox." <u>Irish</u>
      <u>Ecclesiastical Record</u> 105 (May):288-301.
          Reevaluates Waugh's biography of Knox, indicating his dis-
      regard for facts, especially concerning the revisions of the
      Westminster Hymnal and the Manual of Prayer. Argues against Waugh's
      view of Knox as frustrated, neglected, and discontented.

29    HART, JEFFREY. "The Roots of Honor." <u>National Review</u> 18
      (22 February):168-69.
          Describes <u>Sword of Honour</u> as a modern classic--the completion
      of <u>Brideshead</u> and the definitive novel of World War II. Combining
      oddity and outrage, Waugh's vision is congruent with reality. The
      trilogy proves that tradition and aristocracy are secondary to pri-
      vate order in Waugh's scale of values.

30    HINCHCLIFFE, PETER. "Fathers and Children in the Novels of
      Evelyn Waugh." <u>UTQ</u> 35 (April):293-310.
          All Waugh's major characters come from incomplete families,
      suggesting the decline of modern society. Notes Waugh's references
      to <u>King Lear</u> and Dickens. The broken family is healed only in the
      final volume of the war trilogy, <u>Unconditional Surrender</u>.

31    HOLLIS, CHRISTOPHER. Introduction to <u>Decline and Fall</u>.
      London: Heinemann, pp. ix-xx.
          Though in his later years Waugh was regarded as a symbol of
      reaction, in his first novel he was hailed as the spokesman for
      the rising generation. Hollis discusses Waugh's Oxford reputation,
      his youthful rebelliousness, his "snobbery," and the merits of this
      first novel.

32    KENNER, HUGH. "Evelyn Waugh:  In Memoriam." <u>National Review</u> 18
      (3 May):418, 435.
          Waugh's prose was the perfect vehicle for his vision; his
      constant structural device is the undergraduate practical joke.
      His attitudes were reactionary, his insight limited, yet he had
      the power to entertain and his fiction illuminates the twentieth
      century.

33    KOSOK, HEINZ. "Evelyn Waugh:  A Checklist of Criticism."
      <u>Twentieth Century Literature</u> 11 (January):211-15.
          Bibliography that continues 1957.15 and 1964.B37.

34    MEYER, HEINRICH. "Evelyn Waugh (1903-66)." <u>Books Abroad</u> 40
      (Autumn):410-11.
          Compares Waugh to P.G. Wodehouse in the invention of a

self-contained comic world, though Waugh's whimsical sense of
oddity is unique and his complexity elevates his humor.

35    MUGGERIDGE, MALCOLM. "Books." Esquire 66 (August):24, 26-27.
      Waugh's controversial social and political opinions are not
without nobility. His distaste for modernity led to delightful
social comedy; his restless melancholia led to the superb war trilogy; his conversion suggests identification with past glories, as in
Brideshead, which is both vulgar and romantic. Compares Waugh to
George Orwell.

36    _____. "Evelyn Waugh." Observer (London), 17 April, p. 26.
      Recalls brief encounters with Waugh and expresses regret at
his death. Discusses his public persona, contrasting him with
George Orwell; he was a snobbish antique, a frustrated mystic, a
failed saint. Brideshead reveals all that was most foolish in him,
but The Ordeal of Gilbert Pinfold is a near masterpiece. Reprinted:
1966.B37.

37    _____. "Evelyn Waugh, Esq." Critic 24 (June-July):56-58.
      Reprint of 1966.B36.

*38   _____. "Zum Tode des englischen Schriftstellers Evelyn Waugh."
      Die Zeit 21, no. 17:19.
      Source: Checklist, no. 1127; 1972.A1.

39    OSBORNE, JOHN. "Evelyn Waugh Faces Life and Vice Versa."
      Atlantic 218 (December):114-15.
      Anecdotes of Waugh's various involvements with Life magazine,
and of his country life and visit to America in 1947.

40    PARKER, KENNETH. "'Quantitative Judgements Don't Apply.'" ESA
      9 (September):192-201.
      Waugh's Tory romanticism, cult of the upper class, and view
of the gentleman as victim of modernity have colored his work since
1934. In the war trilogy these are infused with a tough-minded
satire on military life; and Guy's disillusionment involves a progress in self-knowledge.

41    POWELL, ANTHONY. "Hemingway: What Went Wrong?" Daily Telegraph
      (London), 22 September, p. 20.
      In reviewing a book on Hemingway, compares him to Waugh:
certain writers find the wear-and-tear of the world around them so
unsympathetic that they create personas for themselves, even though
this process may inhibit imaginative production. This was percep-
tible at times in Waugh, manifest in Hemingway.

42    _____. "A Memoir." Adam nos. 301-3:7-9.
      Anecdotes about Waugh's power to carry off any role he as-
sumed at Oxford, and about his carpentry efforts in London. Also
an analysis of Waugh's personality.

43   POWELL, DILYS.  "Death Sans Sting."  Sunday Times (London),
     3 April, p. 29.
         Parts of the film of The Loved One are pleasing, but the
     whole does not work.  Yet the novel still startles with its fero-
     cious elegance.

44   PRITCHETT, V.S.  "Evelyn Waugh."  New Statesman 71 (15 April):
     547.
         Obituary noting Waugh's mastery of the English tradition of
     satirical comedy, and his putting on a public personality.  His
     penchant for outrage and fantasy masked a gloomy moralist.  His
     excellence is based on his ear for idiom, concern for style, and
     respect for literary convention.

45   PROUSE, DEREK.  Interview with Tony Richardson (director of The
     Loved One).  Sunday Times (London), 13 February, p. 28.
         Richardson describes The Loved One as being about displaced
     values in a special society.  Admits to adding his own Hollywood
     experience to Waugh's.

46   QUENNELL, PETER.  "Speaking of Books:  Evelyn."  New York Times
     Book Review, 8 May, pp. 2, 33.
         Anecdotes of meetings with Waugh.  Argues that Waugh complete-
     ly transformed his character between 1924 and 1928 from gaiety to
     melancholy; the breakup of his first marriage deepened the melan-
     choly.  His persona was outrageous, forbidding, and bizarre, but
     the novels reveal a different man; his conflicts gave rise to great
     imaginative talent.

47   RAYMOND, JOHN.  "Waugh's Last Post."  New Statesman 71 (29
     April):608.
         Describes Waugh's Requiem Mass, and recalls Waugh at Ronald
     Knox's funeral.

*48  SERVOTTE, HERMAN.  "Evelyn Waugh 1903-1966:  Vlucht in de
     komiek."  Dietsche Warande en Belfort 111:334-46.
         Source:  Checklist, no. 1205; 1972.A1.

*49  SOBREIRA, ALBERTO.  "Evelyn Waugh."  Brotéria. Revista
     contemporanea de cultura (Lisbon) 82:838-40.
         Source:  Checklist, no. 1226; 1972.A1.

50   STALEY, THOMAS J.  "Waugh the Artist."  Commonweal 84 (27 May):
     280-82.
         Says Waugh's reputation rests largely on his early comic
     satires.  Abandoning satire, he made his moral vision explicit and
     lost his detachment in sentimentality.  Despite Tory and Catholic
     attitudes, the source of his art is romanticism.  A Handful of Dust
     is his masterpiece.

51   SUTRO, JOHN.  "The Friend."  Adam nos. 301-3:14-18.

Recalls a life-long friendship with Waugh, beginning at
Oxford; tells anecdotes revealing Waugh's wit, humor, and fantasy.

52   SYKES, CHRISTOPHER. "Evelyn." Sunday Times, 17 April, p. 12.
     Reminiscences about Waugh's contradictory personality and
endless comic sense, particularly in conversation. His literary
skills have been underestimated, for his comedy arose from serious
convictions.

53   Van ZELLER, DOM HUBERT. "An Appreciation of Evelyn Waugh."
     Downside Review 84 (July):285-87.
     Describes Waugh's integrity as an artist and friend. His
love of tradition, elegance, discipline, and good manners was genuine. Love of the order established in times of persecution led
to his distaste for liturgical reforms.

54   _____. "Evelyn Waugh." Month 222 (July-August):69-71.
     Defends Waugh's compassion, lack of hypocrisy, and love of
privacy; also explains his attitude to Vatican II. He never belittled ideals or virtues; rather, he was a romantic crusader for
Christian values, and his fiction reveals the sadness of wasted
opportunities.

55   WAGNER, LINDA WELSHIMER. "Satiric Masks: Huxley and Waugh."
     Satire Newsletter 3 (Spring):160-62.
     Compares After Many a Summer with The Loved One in the use
of the satirist's distancing persona. Defends Waugh's compassion
and characterization; his only inhumanity lay in his consistent
use of a mask and pose of disinterestedness.

56   WAUGH, AUBERON. "Death in the Family." Spectator 216 (6 May):
     562-63.
     Far-reaching attack on most of the writers of Waugh's obitu-
aries, who never knew or understood him. Defends him against
charges of Blimpishness, snobbery and social climbing, and describes
the serenity of his last years. Letters appeared in response (13
May, pp. 597-98), and Auberon Waugh replied (20 May, p. 630).

57   WICKLOW, Earl of (WILLIAM CECIL JAMES HOWARD). "Evelyn Waugh--
     An Appreciation." Irish Times, 21 April, p. 8.
     Discusses the real Waugh as opposed to the legendary one.
A romantic Tory rather than a snob, he was kindly, courageous,
sincerely religious, and loyal.

58   WILLETT, JOHN. "How Well Have They Worn?--10: Decline and
     Fall." Times (London), 10 March, p. 13.
     While Waugh's first novel is uneven, it is successful, and
it anticipates many of his later novels. Grimes has become part
of the English literary heritage.

59   WOODRUFF, DOUGLAS. "Evelyn Waugh: The Man Behind the Writer."

Tablet 220 (16 April):441-42.
Comments on Waugh's illness and melancholy in his later years, and his life-long ennui. Tells anecdotes of his early years, noting his romanticism, and of his military service. The Ordeal of Gilbert Pinfold reveals how the artist transforms his experience. Describes Waugh's progressive alienation from the contemporary world, including the Church. Notes his combination of moralist and outrageous wit.

1967

A.  BOOKS

1   DONALDSON, FRANCES. Evelyn Waugh: Portrait of a Country Neighbour. Philadelphia, New York, and London:  Chilton Book Company, 124 pp.
Describes the friendship between the Donaldsons and the Waughs, 1948-1966, particularly during Waugh's residence at Piers Court. Intended to redress the errors of the obituary writers, who described Waugh as a belligerent misanthrope, this anecdotal study illuminates the period of Waugh's life fictionalized in The Ordeal of Gilbert Pinfold.

2   WOOTON, CARL. "Responses to the Modern World. A Study of Evelyn Waugh's Novels." Ph.D. dissertation, University of Oregon, 277 pp.  [DA 28:2693A.]
Source:  Checklist, no. 3963A; 1972.A1.
Examines the comic and fragmented world depicted in Waugh's first six novels, and the variety of other worlds after the change which takes place in Brideshead. Finds two similarities in all the novels:  the presence of different angles of vision, and opposition to modernity. Says the distance between Paul Pennyfeather and Guy Crouchback represents a movement from a negative to a positive kind of withdrawal. It is a distance Waugh himself has traveled, and at the end he has discovered compassion for the modern world.

B.  SHORTER WRITINGS

1   ANON. "The Last of Evelyn Waugh." TLS 5. London:  Oxford, 123-27.
Reprint of 1966.B11.

2   ANON. "The Ordeal of Evelyn Waugh." TLS, 24 August, p. 759.
Reviews recent books on Waugh (Donaldson, 1967.A1, Carens, 1966.A1), noting that his dislocations in character were reflected in his books. On 14 September (p. 819), John Guenther responded by naming Nancy Cunard as the model for the "typical" heroines of Michael Arlen, Aldous Huxley, Ernest Hemingway, and Waugh.

3    BURGESS, ANTHONY. The Novel Now:  A Student's Guide to
     Contemporary Fiction. London:  Faber & Faber, pp. 18, 29, 54–
     58, 60, 94.
          Says Firbank taught writers like Waugh and Anthony Powell the
     use of ellipsis and dialogue.  Waugh's cool patrician craftsmanship
     is a world away from the Hemingway tradition; he likes to present
     purgatory in his novels.  The Sword of Honour trilogy did for World
     War II what F.M. Ford's Parade's End tetralogy did for World War I:
     it is the whole history of the European struggle itself, told with
     verve, humor, pathos, and sharp accuracy.

4    _____. "Television." Listener 77 (12 January):2.
          Reviews the first part of the television version of Sword of
     Honour.  The trilogy is essentially a literary experience, but
     Waugh's cinematic techniques assist the adaptation.

5    CARENS, JAMES F.  Review of Evelyn Waugh:  Portrait of a Country
     Neighbour, by Frances Donaldson. EWN 1 (Winter):6–7.
          States that it is not without charm, but light and personal,
     and does not contribute profoundly to our understanding of Waugh
     as a man or artist.  At her best when she assaults the false image
     of him built up by the media.  See 1967.A1.

6    CHURCHILL, THOMAS. "The Trouble with Brideshead Revisited."
     MLQ 28 (June):213–28.
          Recalls the critical hostility to Brideshead in 1945, and
     asks whether Waugh's 1960 revisions remove its flaws.  It is re-
     lated to Waugh's earlier novels, especially Work Suspended, in
     terms of the country house symbol, and to later works as well.
     The florid style, nostalgia, theological rigidity, and loss of
     ironic detachment mar the novel irretrievably.

7    CLAYTON, SYLVIA. "Crouchback's mixed fortunes." Daily Telegraph
     (London), 3 January, p. 15.
          Says the flavor of Sword of Honour, Waugh's masterpiece, was
     admirably caught in a television adaptation on BBC 2 the previous
     night.  The story has the finest array of comic characters of any
     postwar novel, and the late Giles Cooper, who adapted it, under-
     stood both the humor and the sense of chivalry betrayed which ani-
     mate the trilogy.

8    CLINTON, FARLEY. "Days of His Pilgramage--The Religion of
     Evelyn Waugh." Triumph 2 (April):31–34.
          Blames Waugh's Catholicism for his lack of recognition, using
     the example of Edmund Wilson.  Gives biographical background for
     Waugh's religious views, and examines the religious quality of his
     books.

9    DAVIS, ROBERT MURRAY. "The Mind and Art of Evelyn Waugh." PLL
     3 (Summer):270–87.
          Waugh's death makes a new critical perspective on him desir-
     able.  Neglected areas include his historical and intellectual

context, textual and bibliographical studies, the style and method
of individual novels, and evaluation of his strengths and weaknesses. Discusses his intellectual outlook, and provides an estimate
of his success in embodying his vision. Reprinted in 1969.A3.

10 _____. "Some Textual Variants in Scoop." EWN 1, no. 2
      (Autumn):1-3.
      Lists seventeen substantive variations between the first and
second uniform editions of Scoop, and comments on their effects.

11 DOYLE, PAUL A. "Decline and Fall: Two Versions." EWN 1, no.
      2 (Autumn):4-5.
      Comments on the differences between the standard 1928 edition
and the 1962 "original text"; quotes the Author's Note prefixed to
the 1928 edition beginning, "I hope that my publishers are wrong
when they say that this is a shocking novelette," and examines the
changes made at that time as a result of squeamishness.

12 ENGLISH, WILLIAM A. "Some Irish and English Waugh Bibliography."
      EWN 1 (Winter):5.
      A brief list of magazine and newspaper articles by and about
Waugh.

13 GERHARDIE, WILLIAM. "The Ordeal of Evelyn Waugh." Letter in
      TLS, 12 October, p. 961.
      An unusually valuable letter because, in addition to telling
anecdotes about Waugh, it pays tribute to him for his generosity
in acknowledging Gerhardie's influence on him.

14 GREENE, GRAHAM. "Graham Greene's Tribute." EWN 1 (Spring):1.
      Reprint of 1966.B27.

15 HARTY, E.R. "Brideshead Re-read--A discussion of Some of the
      Themes of Evelyn Waugh's Brideshead Revisited." Unisa English
      Studies 3 (September):66-74.
      Brideshead deals with the irrationality at the center of any
religious view of life. Its strength lies in its treatment of religious themes from an ironic perspective.

16 HEBBLETHWAITE, PETER. "How Catholic is the Catholic Novel?"
      TLS, 27 July, pp. 678-79.
      Asks whether a Catholic novelist is different from a non-
Catholic one. With Waugh and Greene there seemed to be a family
likeness, which sometimes seemed smug, but now the Catholic novelist is trying to discern patterns which emerge through characters
in situations instead of using a kind of moral Deus ex machina.

17 HEPPENSTALL, RAYNER. "A Friendly Sketch of Evelyn Waugh."
      Daily Telegraph (London), 11 May, p. 21.
      States that Frances Donaldson's book on Waugh (1967.A1) makes
pleasant if saddening reading, and its unpretentious factuality

will be useful to anyone who attempts a biography. Calls the
chapter on The Ordeal of Gilbert Pinfold particularly fascinating.

18    JERVIS, STEVEN A. "Evelyn Waugh, Vile Bodies, and the Younger
      Generation." SAQ 66 (Summer):440-48.
      Vile Bodies indicates Waugh's concern for the clash of genera-
tions, and constitutes a qualified vindication of the young--despite
disapproval of their behavior. Discusses Waugh's early years at
Oxford and his identification with the younger generation in conflict with the elder.

19    JOHNSON, ROBERT V. "The Early Novels of Evelyn Waugh." In
      Approaches to the Novel. Edited by John Colmer. Edinburgh and
      London: Oliver & Boyd, pp. 78-89.
      Analyzes Waugh's "phantasmagoric commentary" on English so-
ciety between the wars. Says his early novels have a serious purpose and consistent tone rarely achieved later. Catholicism provides him with a belief in ultimate order, despite the apparent
arbitrariness of fortune, but in his later fiction his opinions
obtrude too abruptly.

20    JOLLIFFE, JOHN. "Neighbours." Sunday Times (London), 14 May,
      p. 51.
      Attacks Frances Donaldson's Evelyn Waugh: Portrait of a
Country Neighbour (1967.A1) for being tedious and superficial and
for its style, which suffers from the faults that Waugh himself
avoided.

21    KINROSS, Lord (PATRICK BALFOUR). "Kinross on Waugh on Waugh."
      Envoy (London) 1 (November):7, 10, 65.
      Reviews of Alec Waugh's "My Brother Evelyn" (1967.B39), based
on personal friendship with both brothers. Distinguishes between
Evelyn's public image and private personality, and comments on his
first marriage, conversion, travels, and happy second marriage.

22    LINCK, CHARLES G., Jr. "Waugh Letters at the Texas Academic
      Center." EWN 1 (Winter):1-5.
      Descriptive bibliography of some of Waugh's correspondence
cataloged at the Humanities Research Center, University of Texas.

23    MITFORD, NANCY. "Nancy Mitford's Commentary." EWN 1 (Spring):
      1-2.
      Written in French, and originally appeared in Arts et loisirs.
Contains personal memories of Waugh dating back to 1928. Believes
that when his letters are published they will reveal a talent like
Voltaire's; the same kindness was hidden under the same irascibil-
ity. He took refuge from the ugliness of the modern world in the
Catholic Church, but the Council decrees wounded him: he died of
a broken heart.

24    OAKES, PHILIP [Atticus]. Comments on the "Waugh Industry."

Sunday Times (London), 8 October, p. 13.
Refers to the film versions of The Loved One and Decline and
Fall, the appearance of the Evelyn Waugh Newsletter, Paul Doyle's
comments on Waugh enthusiasts, and Alec Waugh's profile of his
brother.

25  RABINOVITZ, RUBIN. The Reaction against Experiment in the
English Novel, 1950-1960. New York and London: Columbia
University Press, pp. 5, 22, 46-47, 59, 115.
Refers to Kingsley Amis's qualified approval of Waugh, Aldous
Huxley, and Anthony Powell, but not of their views of class or so-
ciety; to Martin Green's assertion that Amis's comedy is more thor-
oughly moral than either Shaw's or Waugh's; and to C.P. Snow's de-
fense of writers who do not employ experimental techniques like
symbolism and stream-of-consciousness, such as Waugh and Graham
Greene.

26  RICHARDSON, MAURICE. "Waugh's Army Opens Fire." Observer
(London), 8 January, p. 23.
Finds Giles Cooper's television adaptation of Waugh's Men at
Arms very successful, especially in its military scenes.

27  STEVENSON, LIONEL. The History of the English Novel. Vol. 2.
New York: Barnes & Noble, pp. 351-62.
Placing Waugh in the context of the history of the English
novel, summarizes his literary career and his reputation, which
was damaged by the embarrassing revelations of The Ordeal of Gilbert
Pinfold.

*28  STONE, LINTON. Introduction to The Loved One. The Modern Novel
Series. London: Heinemann.
Source: Checklist, no. 1713; 1972.A1.

29  STRATFORD, PHILIP. "Man and Superman in the World of Waugh."
Parallel 1 (July-August):52, 54.
Divides Waugh's characters into the Immortals and the Mortals,
with the narrator dancing in between. Notes the classical touch to
the author's characteristic stance, and predicts that his reputation will suffer because his books are misunderstood.

30  SYKES, CHRISTOPHER. "Evelyn Waugh--A Brief Life." Listener 78
(24 August):225-29.
An account of Waugh's life, with comments by Tom Driberg,
John Sutro, Christopher Hollis, Harold Acton, and other friends
on Waugh's school years, first marriage, conversion, writings, and
military service.

31  SYKES, CHRISTOPHER, CYRIL CONNOLLY, RAYMOND MORTIMER, and
GORONWY REES. "A Critique of Waugh." Listener 71 (31 August):
267-69.
Discussion of Waugh's fiction from Work Suspended (1942) to

Sword of Honour (1965-66), exploring his literary methods and his strengths and limitations as a writer.

32    TOYNBEE, PHILIP. "Oh What a Lovely Waugh." Observer (London), 14 May, p. 26.
         Calls Frances Donaldson's book on Waugh (1967.A1) a skillful and moving tribute, but also giving a clear view of Waugh's eccentricities. Tells how Waugh has haunted his own imagination, as a powerful and impressive figure whom he has failed to please.

33    WAUGH, ALEC. "My Brother Evelyn." Atlantic 219 (June):53-60.
         A portrait of Waugh's early years--childhood, youth, Oxford and after--up to his conversion. Anecdotes and description of the brothers' relationship.

33a   _____. My Brother Evelyn and Other Profiles. London: Cassell; New York: Farrar, Straus & Giroux, pp. 162-98.
         Reprint of 1967.B33.

34    WELLS, JOEL. "The Three Little Pigs by *V*L*N W**GH." In Grim Fairy Tales for Adults. New York: Macmillan, pp. 31-35.
         A parody of Waugh's style and characters.


                                    1968


A.  BOOKS

1    COOK, WILLIAM JESSE, Jr. "The Personae Technique of Evelyn Waugh." Ph.D. dissertation, Auburn University, 388 pp. [DA 29:2704A.]
         Close examination of Waugh's technique shows that the later realistic novels are in direct succession from the early satires, and that there is artistic and thematic unity. The technique is based on a uniquely contrived relationship between the narrator-persona and a special character-persona. This allows almost complete detachment of the narrator in the first three works, his cautious identification with the hero beginning with A Handful of Dust, and complete identity in Brideshead. Viewed collectively, Waugh's novels form a single earnest attempt to solve within the novel a moral dilemma of universal proportions; their success in doing so is astonishing.

2    PAUL, MARTIN THOMAS. "The Comic-Romantic Hero in Eight Novels of Evelyn Waugh." Ph.D. dissertation, University of Wisconsin, 164 pp. [DA 30:288A.]
         Discusses the movement from the ingénu hero of the early novels to the rogue hero in Black Mischief and Put Out More Flags and the more fully developed hero in Sword of Honour. States that, in the role of a modern-day King Lear, Guy learns first that


                                    114

traditional values have no place in the present, second that his
real source of unhappiness is himself, and third that personal
redemption depends upon an active involvement in life.

*3    WALLIS, DAVID HUDSON, II.  "A Reading of Evelyn Waugh's
      Brideshead Revisited:  A Critical Survey and Thematic Analysis."
      Ph.D. dissertation, Tulsa University.
          The first part of this study shows the development of criti-
      cal opinion on the novel, and its centrality in the development of
      Waugh's artistry.   The second traces the symbolism of the Arcadian
      theme, which gives shape and direction to the novel and the develop-
      ment of its central character, but also illuminates Waugh's world
      view and animates his creative process.  Source:  EWN 2 (Winter):7.


B.  SHORTER WRITINGS

1    ANON.  "Commentary."  TLS, 1 February, p. 113.
         An account of Waugh's 1924 film, The Scarlet Woman, acquired
     by the British Film Institute in 1968.  Describes Waugh's writing,
     directing, and acting in laudatory terms.

2    ANON.  "Talking Points."  TLS, 24 October, p. 1201.
         Lengthy leading article discussing Derwent May's anthology
     of radio talks, Good Talk, and describing the impressionistic word-
     sketch of Waugh by a number of voices as the best thing in it.

3    BENDER, ELAINE.  "Sour Grapes."  EWN 2 (Autumn):4-6.
         Amusing essay listing the many references to foxes and chases
     in Decline and Fall and deciding that it is a novel about foxhunt-
     ing.

4    BENSTOCK, BERNARD.  "The Present Recaptured:  D.H. Lawrence and
     Others."  SR 4 (July):802-16.
         Argues that "the present is over," examining criticisms of
     four novelists to define its essential qualities.  Reviews James
     F. Carens's treatment of Waugh's wasteland concept and his satiric
     anger (1966.A1); says that Carens's apology for Waugh's fascism is
     unsuccessful.

*5   BODELSEN, C.A.  "Evelyn Waugh."  In Fremmede digtere i det 20.
     arhundrede.  Edited by Sven M. Kristensen.  Vol. 3.  Copenhagen:
     [?], pp. 185-98.
         Source:  Checklist, no. 875; 1972.A1.

6    BORRELLO, ALFRED W.  "A Visit to Combe Florey:  Evelyn Waugh's
     Home."  EWN 2 (Winter):1-3.
         Describes the house and gives an account of conversations
     with Mrs. Waugh about his writing.

7    BURGESS, ANTHONY.  "The Twenties revisited."  Sunday Times

(London), 14 January, p. 51.

Reviewing Marie-Jacqueline Lancaster's Brian Howard--Portrait of a Failure (1968.B30), says that Howard was the model for at least three of Waugh's characters, and acted out almost the whole of Vile Bodies himself.

8 _____. "Waugh Begins" and "The Comedy of Ultimate Truths." In Urgent Copy: Literary Studies. London: Cape, pp. 21-29. Reprint. New York: Norton, 1969.
Reprints of 1964.B16; 1966.B16.

9 CASSEN, BERNARD. "Evelyn Waugh: La nostalgie d'un ordre qui n'a jamais été." Le Monde (Paris), supplement to no. 7244 (27 April):iv-v.

Introduction to a special section occasioned by the appearance of the French translation of A Little Learning; contains an extract from the book, as well as the translation of an extract from Alec Waugh's My Brother Evelyn and Other Profiles headed "Un dévot intransigeant." (See 1967.B33a.)

Emphasizes Waugh's literary reputation in England, but points out that he was not personally popular; in fact, he thought of himself as an exile in his own country. His earliest novels were the most diverting, but as Sylvère Monod shows (1968.B35) his satire is only relative, because he has no remedy for the ills of civilization. His true values are those of the past--a past which never existed. The thinker may be dismissed, but the tale-teller, chronicler, and stylist endures.

10 CHURCHILL, RANDOLPH. "Evelyn Waugh: Letters (and Post-Cards) to Randolph Churchill." Encounter 31 (July):3-19.

Reproduces twenty-five years of Waugh's correspondence, beginning in 1941, and revealing his sometimes prickly idiosyncracies as a friend. Includes biographical information, Waugh's comments on Churchill's books, and some discussion of Waugh's own work.

11 CRAFT, ROBERT. "Stravinsky and Some Writers." Harper's 237 (December):101-2, 105-6, 108.

Anecdotes of Waugh's 1947 visit to America, and his meeting with Igor Stravinsky.

12 D'ARCY, Rev. MARTIN, S.J. "Father Martin D'Arcy, who will be 80 this year, talks to Quintin Hogg." Listener 79 (18 January): 74-75.

Brief comment that toward the end of his life Waugh got the sense that God had given him a job to do in life, and that he would not die until it was finished.

13 DAVIS, ROBERT MURRAY. "Notes Toward a Variorum Brideshead." EWN 2 (Winter):4-6.

Says that the textual history of Brideshead is probably the most complex for the bibliographer and the most rewarding for any student of Waugh, for the novel exists in at least five variant states. Outlines the problems and the kind of information that textual study can provide.

14    _____. Review of Alec Waugh's My Brother Evelyn and Other Profiles. EWN 2 (Spring):6-8.
    Remarks that one could have hoped for a more thorough account of Evelyn, but that hints and undeveloped leads are what we are likely to get for some time. Comments on the significance of Waugh's family relationships for his novels. He clearly distanced himself from his material, but he did not remove himself from it entirely. See 1967.B33a.

15    _____. "Textual Problems in the Novels of Evelyn Waugh." PBSA 62 (2d quarter):259-63.
    Notes that as Waugh has provoked more critical attention the need for a more thorough bibliography than Doyle's (1957.15) has become apparent. Taking examples from the publication histories of Brideshead, Work Suspended, Decline and Fall, and The Ordeal of Gilbert Pinfold, shows the need for precise bibliographic information to help the critic understand Waugh's intentions and his accomplishment.

16    _____. "The Year's Work in Waugh Studies." EWN 2, no. 1 (Spring):3-5.
    Finds that 1967 provided slender fare; the biographical material and critical articles tended to go over old ground with the support of new material. Singles out Thomas Churchill's "The Trouble with Brideshead Revisited" (1967.B6) for special comment.

17    DESCHNER, KARLHEINZ. "Evelyn Waugh." In Christliche Dichter der Gegenwart: Beiträge zur europaischen Literatur. Edited by Hermann Friedmann and Otto Mann. Bern and Munich: Francke, pp. 240-52.
    Revision of 1955.B16.

18    DOOLEY, D.J. "Waugh and Black Humor." EWN 2 (Autumn):1-3.
    Taking C.P. Snow's comment on the transmission of a particular vein of comedy from Russian to English fiction through William Gerhardi as a clear example of literary ancestry, argues that English progenitors such as Saki, Forster, and Firbank cannot be ignored. Questions whether this type of humor should be called black humor, if André Breton's definition of the latter as an essentially scandalous protest against an ordered world is accepted. Describing disorder, Waugh implied rather than ridiculed order.

19    DOYLE, PAUL A., and CHARLES E. LINCK, Jr. "Some Unpublished Waugh Correspondence." EWN 2 (Spring):6 (pt. 1); EWN 2 (Winter):3-4 (pt. 2).
    Descriptive bibliography of some Waugh letters to Linck; to Larned A. Bradford of Little, Brown, Waugh's American publishers; and to various other correspondents.

20    EDWARDS, JOHN D.  "Fleurs blanches et ours en peluche."  Le
      Monde (Paris), supp. to no. 7244 (27 April):iv-v.
          States that Waugh is everywhere present in his works, espe-
      cially through his scarcely veiled melancholy, snobbery, and the
      scorn for the contemporary world clearly expressed in Brideshead.
      His religion is in fact so little of this world that it requires
      some sleight of hand, a little too visible, for the artist to in-
      tegrate it at all.

21    EIMERL, SAREL.  "The Why of Waugh."  Reporter 38 (2 May):28, 40.
          Reviewing books by Alec Waugh and Frances Donaldson, describes
      Waugh as a baffling figure who lost his original brilliance and de-
      generated into a Blimp.  These memoirs are brief, limited, and un-
      satisfactory, and they fail to explain him.  Finds the key to his
      behavior in his need for sanctuary from his anguish and terror; he
      turned away from the realities of human society and sought the
      forms instead, whether in the shape of the Catholic Church or at-
      tachment to England's Tory past.

22    ENGLISH, WILLIAM A.  "Some Irish and English Waugh Bibliography
      II."  EWN 2 (Autumn):3-4.
          Continues 1967.B12, listing articles on Waugh, obituaries on
      his death, film reviews of The Loved One, and reviews of books by
      and about Waugh.

23    HILLIER, BEVIS.  "When Evelyn Waugh Joked With His Publisher."
      Times (London), 15 July, p. 8.
          Notes the upcoming sale of twenty-two letters and ten post-
      cards from Waugh to Tom Balston of Duckworth and Co., dating be-
      tween 1928 and 1930.  The letters deal with the collapse of his
      first marriage, travel, and family matters.  Waugh's exuberant
      comic vein is most evident.

24    HOWARTH, HERBERT.  "Quelling the Riot:  Evelyn Waugh's Progress."
      In The Shapeless God:  Essays on Modern Fiction.  Edited by
      Harry J. Mooney, Jr. and Thomas F. Staley.  Pittsburgh:
      University of Pittsburgh Press, pp. 67-88.
          Readers of Waugh's early novels expected a rake's progress;
      he gave them a pilgrim's.  Describes the place of religion in his
      novels, and relates it to the stance of the retrograde, observing
      that feudal England has been the habitat of a number of good writ-
      ers ever since Disraeli's Coningsby.  Notes that the ending of
      Sword of Honour is Waugh's unconditional surrender as well as
      Guy's.  Says Graham Greene learned from him that comedy represents
      and begets courage and sparkles with consolation.

25    KEARFUL, FRANK J.  "Tony Last and Ike McCaslin:  The Loss of a
      Usable Past."  University of Windsor Review 3, no. 2:45-52.
          Sees the central figures in Waugh's Handful of Dust and
      William Faulkner's Go Down, Moses as standing in comparable rela-
      tion to their society and their ancestral past.  Neither succeeds

in making traditional values operable, and both withdraw from the historical encounter, becoming paradoxical models of integrity and of failure. Both are viewed ambivalently by their authors; Tony does not embody the values Waugh wishes to emphasize, but in fact the very force of the ethical appeal comes from the fact that it is unstated.

26　KITCHIN, LAURENCE. "Snobs' Wars." Listener 80 (21 November): 679-81.
　　　Discusses the British army as it appears in fiction, and its relation to the social code of the landed gentry. Calls Waugh's trilogy parochial, appealing to nostalgic Edwardian illusions: he is too concerned with the erosion of a caste.

27　KNOX, OLIVER. "A Desperate Conversation with Evelyn." Cornhill nos. 1057-58 (Autumn-Winter):181-84.
　　　Ronald Knox's nephew recalls an embarrassing encounter with Waugh at Boodles' Club. Describes Waugh's formidable public personality. Reprinted: 1969.B20.

28　KOSOK, HEINZ. "Evelyn Waugh: A Supplementary Checklist of Criticism." EWN 2, no. 1 (Spring):1-3.
　　　Intended as a supplement to his bibliography in Twentieth Century Literature (1966.B33), and includes items to the end of 1966.

*29　KRANZ, GISBERT. Europas christliche Literatur. Paderborn: Schöningh, pp. 492-95.
　　　Source: Checklist, no. 1074; 1972.A1.

30　LANCASTER, MARIE-JACQUELINE, ed. Brian Howard: Portrait of a Failure. London: Anthony Blond, pp. 195-99, 375-77.
　　　Discusses Waugh's dislike of Howard, his use of Howard as a model for Ambrose Silk and Anthony Blanche, and Howard's anger at these portraits.

31　LEHMANN, JOHN. A Nest of Tigers: The Sitwells in Their Times. Boston: Little, Brown, pp. 5, 81, 114-15, 252-56, 275.
　　　Describes Waugh's involvement with the Sitwells from 1928 on, with special attention to his glowing appreciation of Osbert Sitwell on the latter's sixtieth birthday in 1952. Waugh pointed out that the Sitwells had declared war on dullness, and noted that paradoxically they had attracted considerable attention but had scarcely any imitators.

*31　LODGE, DAVID. "David Lodge Interviewed by Bernard Bergonzi." Alta: University of Birmingham Review, no. 7 (Winter).
　　　Believes that the Catholic novel is largely a thing of the past, first because Catholicism itself has become much more confused than it was, and second because the Church no longer presents the uniform view of life that it once did. Discussed by Bernard Bergonzi in 1980.B2, p. 48.

119

33   LUNN, ARNOLD.  "Evelyn Waugh Revisited."  National Review 20
     (27 February):189-90, 205.
         Anecdotes about Waugh's wit concerning devout egalitarians.
     Waugh played the supersnob role for fun, enjoying what society of-
     fered.  Describes Waugh's melancholy, and the supreme importance
     of his religion to him.

34   MATTINGLY, JOSEPH F.  "Guy Crouchback's Children."  ELN 6
     (March):200-201.
         Points out differences regarding the children of Guy
     Crouchback's marriage at the end of Unconditional Surrender and of
     Sword of Honour.  Says it is essential to Waugh's theme of social
     decline that Guy be childless.  See 1969.B7 for a reply.

35   MONOD, SYLVÈRE.  "Satire ou invective."  Le Monde (Paris), supp.
     to no. 7244 (27 April):iv-v.
         Notes that Waugh has the satirist's temperament, but criti-
     cizes his selection of easy subjects like the school and the army,
     his mixing of genres and uncertainty of tone, and his preference
     for the aristocracy and obsession with Catholicism.  Concluding
     that he cannot be a satirist because he lacks a firm standard, de-
     cides he must be a writer of invective.

*36  NEMOIANU, VIRGIL.  "Negatie si afirmat io La Evelyn Waugh
     (Negation and Assertion with Evelyn Waugh)."  In Roumanian
     translation of Decline and Fall, Declin şi prabuşire, 1968,
     pp. 7-20.

37   RATCLIFFE, MICHAEL.  The Novel Today.  London:  Longmans,
     Green, pp. 1-5.
         Begins this brief survey with Waugh, whom he describes as
     still impossible to place, though he says that Sword of Honour is
     increasingly regarded as the finest piece of fiction to come out
     of the Second World War.

38   RICHARDSON, MAURICE, narrator.  "Portrait of Brian Howard."
     Listener 79 (18 January):69-73.
         Describes the "Wild Party" period at the end of the 1920s
     and identifies Howard as the model for Ambrose Silk in Put Out
     More Flags and Anthony Blanche in Brideshead Revisited.

39   RUBIN, DONALD STUART.  "The Recusant Myth in Modern Fiction."
     Ph.D. dissertation, University of Toronto.  [DA 30:4462A.]
         Tries to demonstrate the existence of a private myth held
     by English Catholics concerning their historical sufferings and
     disabilities and to show how the myth has been used by twentieth-
     century Catholic novelists, including Ford Madox Ford, Waugh, and
     Muriel Spark.  On Waugh, says the theme of the early novels is the
     attempts of young aristocrats to impose order; calls Edmund Campion
     violently polemical, but pays particular attention to Brideshead
     and the novels which followed it.  Sees the recusant myth, with

its strong emphasis on spies and traitors, as coloring the Sword
of Honour trilogy.

40   RUTHERFORD, ANDREW. "Waugh's Sword of Honour." In Imagined
     Worlds: Essays on Some English Novels and Novelists in Honour
     of John Butt. London: Methuen, pp. 441-60.
          In the war trilogy, style is meaning: a source of delight,
     illumination, and discovery. The saga's grand design transforms
     experience into art; the final volume perfects the structure and
     thematic development, though the Sword of Honour recension obscures
     this. Discusses Waugh as moralist, his fusion of comic and tragic
     visions, and his peculiar prejudices.

41   SEMPLE, H.E. "Evelyn Waugh's Modern Crusade." ESA 11, no. 1
     (March):47-59.
          Toryism and Catholicism provided Waugh with a viewpoint from
     which to analyze society's sterility. Under the illusion that
     sacred and secular can still unite, Guy begins a crusade. Gradual-
     ly he learns that the war is neither just nor honorable, but his
     Catholic values remain, personal and applicable. Similarly, how-
     ever threatened and betrayed, the aristocratic tradition is still
     valuable.

42   TRACY, HONOR. "Evelyn Revisited." New Republic 158 (23 March):
     39-41.
          Calls Alec Waugh's My Brother Evelyn and Other Portraits
     (1967.B33a) chatty and unequal, and says its main interest lies in
     the part devoted to Evelyn. In searching for clues to Evelyn's
     brilliant, complex character, lights upon Evelyn's identification
     of himself with the go-getting, vulgar Lupin in The Diary of a
     Nobody; his melancholy may not have been due to resentment of so-
     cial change or loss of privilege, but the despair of one who sees
     Caliban when he looks in the mirror.

43   WEINTRAUB, STANLEY. The Last Great Cause: The Intellectuals
     and the Spanish Civil War. New York: Weybright & Talley, pp.
     173-75, 306, 323.
          Referring to Waugh's statement in Authors Take Sides on the
     Spanish Civil War in July 1937, describes this as an extreme right-
     ist position into which romantic toryism had led him. Notes that
     Officers and Gentlemen is one of the rare novels in which the
     Francoist point of view comes up.

44   WILEY, PAUL. "Evelyn Waugh." ConL 9, no. 2 (Spring):261-64.
          In The Satiric Art of Evelyn Waugh by James L. Carens
     (1966.A1)--the coolest of Waugh's critics--provides a useful survey
     of Waugh's accomplishments as an artist, but fails to find a per-
     spective behind the satirist's mask. Writers of Waugh's type may
     perform a special function, not in proposing norms, but in drama-
     tizing the intellectual and ethical conflicts of a transitional
     period. Waugh's equipment is clearly modern, yet we do not really
     know what to make of it.

1969

A.  BOOKS

1    BOGAARDS, WINIFRED MARY.  "Ideas and Values in the Work of
     Evelyn Waugh."  Ph.D. dissertation, University of Saskatchewan,
     428 pp.  [DA 31:4151A.]
         Because his views have been a crucial factor in judgment of
his fiction, examines them and explains why he holds them.  Makes
three main points:  he is hostile to most developments of the cen-
tury--social, political, religious, and aesthetic--because they
endanger order and morality and also individual freedom; he was
impelled to express his disgust more categorically after World War
II; and he was less dogmatic and conservative in his novels than
in his travel books and essays.  In the novels, he has never been
a champion of the political Right, the upper classes, or religious
bigotry.

*2   COSTELLO, HARRY PATRICK.  "The Mature Novels of Evelyn Waugh:
     A Study in Structure, Imagery, and Theme."  Ph.D. dissertation,
     Loyola University of Chicago, 196 pp.

3    DAVIS, ROBERT MURRAY.  Evelyn Waugh.  The Christian Critic
     Series.  St. Louis:  B. Herder Book Co., 116 pp.
         A collection of previously published essays, with an intro-
duction discussing Waugh's current reputation and stressing his
function of satirist, depicting "the world of wild aberration without theological significance."  Contains reprints of 1959.10;
1962.B3; 1963.B4, B7; 1964.35; 1965.21; 1967.B9.

4    DOYLE, PAUL A.  Evelyn Waugh:  A Critical Essay.  Grand Rapids,
     Mich.:  William B. Eerdmans, 48 pp.
         Begins by analyzing Decline and Fall, a novel which does not
sermonize but is outrageous, audacious, and generally casual; its
proclamation of social disintegration was not new, its manner of
showing it was.  Waugh characteristically shows life as a tragicomedy; his ironic vision works best when it intermingles the
tragic and the comic, rather than when he becomes earnest, as in
Helena.  A clearly defined pattern in his career emerges:  the
early satire evolved through his conversion into a serious probing
of the limits of humanism.  In effect he produced a sequence which
might be entitled "The Divine Tragicomedy of Existence."

5    LOWE, KEITH DELROY.  "Evelyn Waugh:  Man against History."
     Ph.D. dissertation, Stanford University, 283 pp.  [DA 30:1142A.]
         Countering a trend in modern fiction, where the hero becomes
an antihero, Waugh shows his protagonists becoming less and less
creatures of their environment.  Out of the decadent tradition
comes a negative example, the rogue hero like Basil Seal; out of
the old Catholic aristocracy comes a positive hero, Guy Crouchback.

But Guy retreats out of history; in the end he becomes as ahistori-
cal as the antihero.

6   MANNING, GERALD FREDERICK. "Continuity and Change:  The Pattern
    of Development in Evelyn Waugh's Fiction."  Ph.D. dissertation,
    Queen's University.
        Surveys Waugh's novels, showing how they illustrate the dis-
    eased condition of modern civilization, but also stressing Waugh
    as craftsman.  Sees a loss of consistency of tone and authorial
    detachment in Brideshead, even though in many ways it is a develop-
    ment from earlier novels.  Describes Sword of Honour as his magnum
    opus, an effective and complex fusion of Christian idealism and
    cultural pessimism.


B.  SHORTER WRITINGS

1   BOGAARDS, WINIFRED M. "Waugh's Letters to The Times:  1936-
    1964."  EWN 3 (Winter):5-6.
        Gives a complete list of these letters.

2   CALDER, ANGUS. The People's War:  Britain 1939-1945.  London:
    Jonathan Cape, pp. 51, 170, 393, 513-14, 560.
        Says that Put Out More Flags is still the funniest book about
    the phoney war.  Also writes that Waugh and Graham Greene had the
    advantage that their Catholicism remained valid, whereas the leaders
    of the literary "movement" of the 1930s had espoused a Communist
    faith which the Nazi-Soviet pact quickly subverted.

3   CAMERON, J.M. "The Catholic Novelist and European Culture."
    Twentieth Century Studies 1 (March):79-94.
        Examines four Catholic novelists--Georges Bernanos, François
    Mauriac, Graham Greene, and Waugh--in order to establish whether
    Catholicism presents only a European face.  Says no cradle Catholic
    would romanticize the recusants as Waugh does in Brideshead, his
    most ambitious attempt to use Catholicism as a central point of
    reference; finds the deathbed scene of Lord Marchmain objectionable
    in this novel.  Notes that in the war trilogy Catholicism is treated
    more lightly and ironically, and there is a moment where Waugh takes
    his attention away from the eccentricities of minorities and becomes
    a European writer.

4   CLODD, ALAN. "Some Textual Variants in Brideshead." EWN 3
    (Spring):5-6.
        Calls attention to an additional printed state of Brideshead,
    "the Author's edition," which is not discussed by R.M. Davis in
    1968.B13, and notes some variants between it and the first Little,
    Brown printing.

5   COHEN, NATHAN, narrator and interviewer. "A Profile of Evelyn
    Waugh."  Toronto:  CBC Radio (28 October).  Unpublished.

A series of comments and interviews. Anthony Powell describes Waugh's writing methods, Christopher Sykes describes his faults (open to view) and his virtues (hidden); Angus Wilson, Nigel Dennis, Peter de Vries, and Joseph Heller stress the debt other satirists owe him; Mordecai Richler says he was a snob and an anti-Semite, but the most original novelist of our time. Robertson Davies says he did not drag God into his novels (God was there all the time), and speculates that he may have outlived his soul. In a 1956 interview, Cohen asks about the man of integrity in the modern world, and Waugh replies that we are called to do individual acts of charity, not make the whole world over.

6    COSTELLO, PATRICK. "An Idea of Comedy and Waugh's Sword of Honour." KanQ 1 (Summer):41-50.
    Defines comedy as the celebration of an immediate sense of life, and laughter as a surge of vital feeling. Religion guarantees this vitality by acknowledging man's imperfection. This idea of comedy most commonly takes the structure of the pilgrimage. Examines Sword of Honour in illustration.

7    DAVIS, ROBERT MURRAY. "Guy Crouchback's Children--A Reply." ELN 7 (December):127-29.
    Answering 1968.B34, argues that Waugh changed his mind regarding Crouchback's children; moreover, the real theme of the war trilogy is not social decline but the acceptance of moral responsibility in the face of disillusionment.

8    ____. "Harper's Bazaar and A Handful of Dust." PQ 48 (October): 506-16.
    Finds that the "fear in a handful of dust" was removed literally and figuratively from Waugh's novel in order to suit it for serialization in Harper's Bazaar. Points to modifications in the tone, and restrictions on the range of reference. Also notes that Waugh's novels do not depend on plot for their major effects; very few changes were necessary in the body of the serial in order to accommodate a new ending.

9    ____. "The Serial Version of Brideshead Revisited." Twentieth Century Literature 15 (April-October):35-43.
    Compares the serial version and first edition of Brideshead. The serial version suggests a new way of regarding the structure, style and characterization, and indicates Waugh's literary intention and technical methods of achieving it.

10    ____. "The Shrinking Garden and New Exits: The Comic-Satiric Novel in the Twentieth Century." KanQ 1 (Summer):5-16.
    Defines the comic-satiric novel in terms of its refuge from the dominant "bad" society represented and reader sympathy for the protagonist. Since Norman Douglas, this novel has developed into the novel of ideas, the externalist novel, and absurdist comedy and satire; examines each type in detail.

11   DELBAERE-GARANT, J.   "'Who Shall Inherit England?'   A Comparison
     between Howards End, Parade's End, and Unconditional Surrender."
     ES 50 (Fall):101-5.
          All three novels end with an illegitimate child who inherits
     a family property symbolizing England, but the significance of the
     inheritance is different in each, revealing different responses to
     social transformation.  Waugh's contempt for democracy is evident;
     honor and pride abdicate before vulgarity.

12   DOYLE, PAUL A.   "Waugh Correspondence in the Fales Collection,
     NYU."   EWN 3 (Autumn):7-9.
          Description of Waugh letters, 1947-1959, at New York
     University.

13   _____.   "The Year's Work in Waugh Studies."   EWN 3 (Spring):6-8.
          Calls Andrew Rutherford's essay on Sword of Honour (1968.B40)
     the highlight among the biographical and critical studies in what
     seems to have been a slim year.

14   DOYLE, PAUL A., and ALAN CLODD.   "A British Pinfold and an
     American Pinfold."   EWN 3 (Winter):1-5.
          Notes that there are over two hundred variants between the
     American and British versions of The Ordeal of Gilbert Pinfold.
     Describes the more important of these, and confirms that a copy-
     editor at Little, Brown "Americanized" the novel by substituting
     American phrases and idioms for British ones.  Also notes changes
     in the Penguin edition.

15   FARR, D. PAUL.   "Evelyn Waugh:  A Supplemental Bibliography."
     BB 26 (July-Sept.):67-68, 87.
          Continues the work of 1957.B15, 1964.B37 and 1966.B33.  Gives
     only primary material, stressing Waugh's book reviews.

16   _____.   "Evelyn Waugh:  Tradition and a Modern Talent."   SAQ
     68 (Autumn):506-19.
          Essentially biographical, with reference made to Waugh's fic-
     tion.  His rebellion against his father's tradition expressed it-
     self in an early admiration for everything modern, and a later use
     of that tradition as a measuring standard for modern civilization.
     He used an essentially modern theme to make a conservative attack
     on modernism; at the same time he revealed the dichotomies in his
     own personality.

16a  GREENE, GRAHAM.   "Three Priests.  I, The Oxford Chaplain."   In
     Collected Essays.  London:  Bodley Head; New York:  Viking, pp.
     376-79.  Reprint.  Harmondsworth:  Penguin Books, 1970, 1977.
          Reprint of 1959.B14.

17   HODGART, MATTHEW.   Satire.  London:  World University Library,
     pp. 221, 227.
          Calls Waugh the most elegant and lucid picaresque satirist

of the twentieth century. Decline and Fall has a perfect circular
form, the ideal embodiment of the stoic resignation of the picaresque satirist.

18    HOLMAN-HUNT, DIANA. My Grandfather, His Wives and Loves.
      London:  Hamish Hamilton, pp. 13-28, 79, 233, 292-95.
         She became interested in the pre-Raphaelite painter's work
      because Waugh showed her that it was still possible to be enthusi-
      astic about it.  Her book My Grandmother and I became a bestseller
      partly because of a favorable review by Evelyn in the Spectator
      (she reprints this as an appendix).  Also says Waugh planned to
      write a life of Holman Hunt himself, but apparently never began it.
      Describes Waugh's eccentric behavior during a visit she made to
      Combe Florey.

19    HOSKINS, KATHERINE BAIL. Today the Struggle:  Literature and
      Politics in England During the Spanish Civil War.  Austin and
      London:  University of Texas Press, pp. 31-40.
         Gives a context for Waugh's minority political stance, call-
      ing Scoop and Put Out More Flags satires on leftist politics and
      demonstrations of Waugh's distrust of all politics.

20    KNOX, OLIVER. "No . . . er Creme de Menthe:  A Desperate
      Conversation with Evelyn Waugh." In The Compleat Imbiber 10.
      Edited by Cyril Ray. London:  Hutchinson, pp. 26-29.
         Reprint of 1968.B27.

21    KOSOK, HEINZ. "Evelyn Waugh:  A Supplementary Checklist of
      Criticism." EWN 3 (Spring):4-5.
         Intended as a supplement to 1966.B33 and 1968.B22, B28; in-
      cludes books and articles published since 1967, as well as some
      items omitted from the earlier lists.

22    LINCK, CHARLES E., Jr. "The Public View of Waugh's Conversion."
      In Evelyn Waugh. Edited by Robert Murray Davis. The Christian
      Critic Series. St. Louis:  B. Herder Book Co., pp. 25-32.
         Discusses Waugh's reticence regarding his conversion and
      assesses his 1930 Daily Express apologia as both public and private
      statement.  See 1969.A3.

23    _____. Review of Evelyn Waugh, by Paul A. Doyle. EWN 3
      (Winter):6-8.
         Finds the "Christian Tragi-Comic" view pursued too insistent-
      ly, in spite of thought-provoking discussion.

24    _____. "Waugh-Greenidge Film--The Scarlet Woman." EWN 3
      (Autumn):1-7.
         Provides the history and the screenplay of Waugh's 1924
      film, which involved John Sutro, Alec Waugh and other Oxford
      friends, as well as Elsa Lanchester.

25   LINCK, CHARLES E., Jr., and ROBERT MURRAY DAVIS.  "The Bright
     Young People in Vile Bodies."  PLL 5 (Winter):80-90.
         Discusses the social phenomenon of the Bright Young People
     in the summer of 1929, and Waugh's membership in this set, which
     made him their spokesman and interpreter.  He satirized a set of
     attitudes and a process of social change, and made them into a
     structural principle in Vile Bodies.

26   NICHOLS, BEVERLY.  "Interlude with Evelyn Waugh."  In The Sun
     in My Eyes.  London:  Jonathan Cape, pp. 265-74.
         Describing meetings with Waugh at a hotel on Dartmoor and
     aboard ship, shows how Waugh kept up a running satiric attack upon
     him, exploiting every possible weakness "in the congenial task of
     composing his satirical portrait of myself."  Calls Waugh a human
     paradox--the pretended patrician who was squat and paunchy and
     plebian, more ridiculous than any of his own caricatures.

27   REINHARDT, KURT F.  "Evelyn Waugh:  Christian Gentleman."  In
     The Theological Novel of Modern Europe:  An Analysis of Master-
     pieces by Eight Authors.  New York:  Frederick Ungar, pp. 203-16.
         In contrast to Graham Greene, who was preoccupied with the
     dialectic of good and evil, Waugh was intrigued by the dialectic
     of order and disorder.  In developing this theme in his mature
     works, he went far beyond social satire.  In the huge panorama of
     Brideshead, the decadence of upper-class society unfolds; what
     possibilities remain?  The answer, given with great psychological
     dexterity, is in theological terms.  It was Waugh's greatest
     achievement as a novelist.

28   St. JOHN, JOHN.  "Temporary Officers and Gentlemen (Including
     2nd Lt. E. Waugh)."  Sunday Times (London), 7 September, p. 10.
         Joined the Royal Marines on the same day as Waugh; discusses
     experiences of the first months of World War II, reminiscent of
     Men at Arms.  Says that Waugh's snobbery was an ironic pose.

29   SCHLÜTER, KARL.  Kuriose Welt im modernen englischen Roman,
     Dargestellt an ausgewählten Werken von Evelyn Waugh und Angus
     Wilson.  Berlin:  Erich Schmidt Verlag, 247 pp.
         Attempts to establish that the eccentric is an aesthetic
     category midway between the beautiful and the grotesque.  Employing
     close textual analysis, examines six Waugh novels, with especially
     detailed discussion of Brideshead, to illustrate the use of eccen-
     tric effects, characters, settings, and ways of life.

30   THÉRÈSE, Sister M.  "Waugh's Letters to Thomas Merton."  EWN 3
     (Spring):1-4.
         Transcription of five Waugh letters to Thomas Merton, dis-
     cussing religious and literary topics.

31   WALL, BERNARD.  Headlong into Change:  An Autobiography and a
     Memoir of Ideas Since the Thirties.  London:  Harvill Press,

pp. 138-43, et passim.
Reminiscences of an English Catholic who says his religious
views were very different from Waugh's; yet he admired Waugh and
thought him the most gifted story-teller of his time.  If art is
intuition, he was a superb artist.  He touched the nerve of all
that is darkest and most shady in our civilization.  The influence
on him of Hilaire Belloc and his disciples ought to be recognized.

32    WOOTON, CARL.  "Evelyn Waugh's Brideshead Revisited:  War and
      Limited Hope."  MQ 10 (July):359-75.
      Beginning with Brideshead, Waugh's fiction reflects his
responses to changes accelerated by World War II.  Catholicism
unifies the novel's double structure:  what Ryder remembers, and
Ryder remembering.  Ultimately, Ryder discovers limited hope for
the world in religious faith.


                              1970


A.  BOOKS

1    DUER, HARRIET WHITNEY.  "All of Us Exiles:  The Novels of
     Evelyn Waugh."  Ph.D. dissertation, University of Connecticut,
         258 pp.  [DAI 31:1269A.]
         Says that the division between "early" and "late" Waugh novels
is misleading.  Though each novel is different from the rest, there
is a recurring motif of the explorer or traveller.  From 1945 on,
he is in a newly ravaged and frightening wasteland; but in the war
trilogy, Waugh's last explorer returns to a limited world in which
it is possible to live.

2    PHILLIPS, GENE DANIEL, S.J.  "The Christian Vision of Evelyn
     Waugh."  Ph.D. dissertation, Fordham University, 268 pp.  [DAI
     31:6068A.]
         Waugh did accomplish in large measure his task of presenting
man in relation to God, without making his fiction parochial in
tone.  We must distinguish the fiction from the essays; critics
tend to find in the novels polemical views which are not really
there.  Because he was an artist, Waugh transcends his personal
beliefs to deal with the human condition in thought-provoking ways.


B.  SHORTER WRITINGS

1    ACTON, HAROLD.  More Memoirs of an Aesthete.  London:  Methuen,
     pp. 224-27, 318-19.
         Tells anecdotes of Waugh in Hollywood, observing that Los
Angeles and its purlieus offered rich pablum for the satirist;
believes that Waugh was more compassionate than satirists are
supposed to be; and calls attention to his drollery--his complete
ability to take in people unfamiliar with Wavian comedy.

2    BERGONZI, BERNARD. The Situation of the Novel. London:
      Macmillan; Pittsburgh: University of Pittsburgh Press, 1971,
      pp. 104-18, et passim. 2d ed. London and New York: Macmillan,
      1979.
          Shows how the myth of the English Christian gentleman who is
      a victim of the modern world came increasingly to dominate Waugh's
      fiction. But, as The Ordeal of Gilbert Pinfold made clear, an un-
      expected degree of detachment, an ability not to surrender wholly
      to the demands of his personal myth, existed in him; and this
      helped make him a major novelist. The total pattern of his work
      reveals a consciousness dedicated to looking backward but ultimate-
      ly unable to resist the pressures of modernity, though it never
      willingly surrenders to them.

3    BOGAARDS, WINIFRED M. "The Conclusion of Waugh's Trilogy:
      Three Variants." EWN 4 (Autumn):6-7.
          Discusses especially the effect of a small change on the last
      page, giving Guy Crouchback and his wife two boys of their own as
      well as the child of Virginia and Trimmer. But when he pointedly
      shows Trimmer's child as a providential gift, he suggests that com-
      passion should end the battle of the classes.

4    BORRELLO, ALFRED. "Evelyn Waugh and Erle Stanley Gardner."
      EWN 4 (Winter):1-3.
          Produces evidence that Waugh was not being facetious when he
      wrote to Gardner as "one of your keenest admirers"; he had read
      everything Gardner wrote, apparently with the respect of one crafts-
      man for another.

5    BURBRIDGE, ROGER T. "The Function of Gossip, Rumor, and Public
      Opinion in Evelyn Waugh's A Handful of Dust." EWN 4 (Autumn):
      3-5.
          Gossip, public opinion, and rumor are the instruments by
      which society establishes its standards of behavior; the London
      society in A Handful of Dust is a good example. Its chatter re-
      veals a specific set of values, turning on the ability to treat
      life as a game, so that its final effect is to satirize society
      by showing its superficiality.

6    CARENS, JAMES [F.]. Review of Evelyn Waugh, by Robert Murray
      Davis. EWN 4 (Spring):9.
          Calls the collection useful within its defined limits, de-
      scribing essays by Alvin Kernan and Bernard Bergonzi as exception-
      al.

7    _____. "The Year's Work in Waugh Studies." EWN 4 (Spring):3-6.
          Discusses memoirs of Waugh, investigations of textual prob-
      lems in his novels, and a variety of critical articles, especially
      essays by Robert Murray Davis (1969.B10) and Herbert Howarth
      (1968.B24).

8    DAVIS, ROBERT MURRAY.  "Evelyn Waugh and Brian Howard."  EWN
     4 (Autumn):4-5.
         With the publication of Marie-Jacqueline Lancaster's biogra-
     phy of Brian Howard, we can appreciate the extent to which Johnnie
     Hoop of Vile Bodies, Ambrose Silk of Put Out More Flags, and Anthony
     Blanche of Brideshead were caricatures or portraits of him.  The
     changes in Waugh's treatment of him should be noted, from minor
     fool to major character.

9    _____.  "Some Unidentified Works by Evelyn Waugh."  EWN 4
     (Winter):6-7.
         Derived from manuscript and clipping files in the Evelyn
     Waugh Collection, Humanities Research Center, University of Texas
     at Austin.

10   DOOLEY, D.J.  "The Council's First Victim."  Triumph 5 (June):
     33-35.
         Contends that Waugh's dismay at the reforms of Vatican II
     arose from his sense of the destruction of the community spirit
     among Catholics, and that the loss of this last bastion of security
     in an uncertain world brought him near despair.

11   DOYLE, PAUL A.  "Evelyn's Letters at Boston University."  EWN 4
     (Winter):5-6.
         A synopsis of thirteen Waugh letters held in the division of
     special collections in Boston University Library.

12   DOYLE, PAUL A., WINIFRED BOGAARDS, and ROBERT MURRAY DAVIS.
     "Works of Waugh 1940-1966:  A Supplementary Bibliography, Part
     I."  EWN 4 (Winter):7-10.
         A bibliography of primary works, including introductions to
     books and book reviews.

13   EAGLETON, TERRY.  "Evelyn Waugh and the Upper-Class Novel."
     In Exiles and Emigrés.  London:  Chatto & Windus, pp. 42-70.
         As in Aldous Huxley's Antic Hay, Waugh reveals a sense of
     disintegration which seems "metaphysical" and therefore does not
     impinge too closely on the established social order, and a satiric
     technique which is opportunistic rather than consistently angled.
     The novel can criticize its own environment without taking up an
     alternative standpoint; upper-class values are false, but they are
     all there is:  there is no effective appeal beyond them to wider
     social experience.  The blank neutrality of the early novels is
     really a way of concealing a deep-seated lack of control, an in-
     ability to interpret.

14   FARR, D. PAUL.  "The Edwardian Golden Age and Nostalgic Truth."
     DR 50 (Autumn):378-93.
         States that the view of the Edwardian period as a golden age
     appeared in the late 1920s; the symbol of an ordered society and
     the good life was the stately home.  Describes the "Souls," one of

the best-known of the groups which gathered in country houses, and the friends Waugh made from among their families, such as the Plunkett-Greenes, Lady Diana Cooper, and Ronald Knox. Knox and his generation came to represent for Waugh that civilization which had died with the War, a standard against which to measure decadence and chaos.

15  HART, JEFFREY. "A Touch of Chrism." Triumph 5 (June):28-30, 32-33.
    Waugh's tale of his attempted suicide blends the comic and tragic, the melancholic and the energetic. His despair was personal, historical and political; he attempted to defend civilization from the "cultural terrorism" of the modern age. Brideshead Revisited, particularly Marchmain's deathbed, is pivotal to Waugh's entire oeuvre, for there time and the timeless intersect.

16  KELLOGG, GENE. "The Catholic Novel in Convergence." Thought 45 (Summer):265-96.
    Waugh's satires of postwar decadents are the best example of that type of Catholic fiction which looks accusingly at the moral chaos of the secular environment. In his maturity, when he tried to write serious drama about the English Catholic community (in Brideshead), he failed.

17  _____. "Evelyn Waugh." In The Vital Tradition: The Catholic Novel in a Period of Convergence. Chicago: Loyola University Press, pp. 101-10.
    Waugh was the keenest satirist his era produced; with the adoption of Catholicism, he became harsher, and turned a rapier into a sledgehammer. A Handful of Dust is a depiction of an earthly hell, a supreme negation; when Waugh tried to set forth the positive side of his beliefs in Brideshead, the result was monstrous. Brideshead proves that sentimentality and the religious dimension cannot mix in the modern novel without destroying its impact and its art.

18  KOSOK, HEINZ. "Evelyn Waugh: A Supplementary Checklist of Criticism." EWN 4 (Spring) : 6-8.
    Includes books and articles published since 1968, together with some previously omitted.

19  _____. "The Film World of Vile Bodies." EWN 4 (Autumn):1-2.
    Waugh's interest in films is evident in the narrative technique of Vile Bodies, with its quick cuts, snatches of dialogue, and stress on visual aspects of the story. Beyond this, the film made in the novel, A Brand for the Burning, has an important structural function; it is, in fact, an epitome of the novel as a whole, and helps establish that the novel is not loving description of the world but bitter satire of it.

20  La FRANCE, MARSTON. "Charles G. Linck's Bibliography of Waugh's

Early Work, 1910-1930:   Some Additions and Corrections."  <u>EWN</u>
4 (Autumn):8-9.
Extends and corrects 1964.B37, with some notes on Waugh's
youthful "image."

21  LANE, CALVIN W.  "Waugh's Book Reviews for <u>Night and Day</u>."  <u>EWN</u>
4 (Spring):1-3.
Each week during <u>Night and Day</u>'s short run--from July to
December, 1937--Waugh reviewed several books; strong-minded and
illuminating, the reviews provide evidence of a clearly defined
critical taste.

22  MARKOVIC, VIDA.  "Tony Last."  In <u>The Changing Face:  Disintegration of Personality in the Twenteith-Century British Novel,
1900-1950</u>.  Carbondale, Illinois:  Southern Illinois University
Press, pp. 70-81.
Elsewhere the figures in Waugh's novels are almost invariably
comic caricatures, but in <u>A Handful of Dust</u> the spectacle takes on
a more general truthfulness.  Tony Last is the author's most sympathetic character, and he suggests the waste and futility, the impo-
tence and degeneration, of a whole era.  He suffers the greatest of
trials for no purpose whatever; he loses his identity.  When he re-
gains it at the end, life's little irony intervenes:  in the jungle
he comes to life, but he has missed his last chance.

23  NEW, MELVIN.  "Ad Nauseam:  A Satiric Device in Huxley, Orwell,
and Waugh."  <u>SNL</u> 8 (Fall):24-28.
Discusses images of physical illness as metaphor for moral
corruption, and the nausea of the satiric persona at the sight of
human folly.  Refers to <u>Vile Bodies</u>.

24  NEWNHAM, ANTHONY.  "Evelyn Waugh's Library."  <u>LCUT</u> n.s. 1
(March):25-29.
Describes Waugh's library, which came to Texas in 1967, noting some surprising omissions, and observing that the section of
his library which Waugh may be said to have collected rather than
accumulated is in the decorative arts, particularly of the eighteenth and nineteenth centuries.

25  PHILLIPS, GENE D.  "Waugh's <u>Sword of Honour</u> on BBC-TV."  <u>EWN</u>
4 (Winter):304.
Though some critics called it a glorious failure, the television version of <u>Sword of Honour</u> caught much of the flavor of the
original.  Giles Cooper's intelligent script, Donald McWhinnie's
thoughtful direction, and uniformly excellent acting made it a
fitting rendition of a brilliant novel.

25a  RUSSELL, JOHN.  <u>Anthony Powell:  A Quintet, Sextet, and War</u>.
Bloomington:  Indiana University Press, pp. 20, 39, 51, 157,
190-91, 215, 226.
Compares Powell and Waugh as novelists, noting Waugh's

statement that "path crossings" are an essentially English way of composing a novel, and contesting Bernard Bergonzi's view (1970.B2) that Powell's fiction is less clearly structured or patterned than Waugh's.

26   SCHLÜTER, KURT.  "Evelyn Waugh."  In Englische Literatur der
     Gegenwart.  Edited by Horst W. Drescher.  Stuttgart:  Alfred
     Kröner, pp. 23-46.
          A contribution to a series of thirty essays on contemporary
     English writers, this discussion focuses on Brideshead and Sword
     of Honour.  Describes the deepening of character in later Waugh
     novels, such as Brideshead, and the use of the great house as the
     representation of the summit of aesthetic and human values.  Views
     the war trilogy as a monumental work, the consummation of all as-
     pects of Waugh's art, and the only novel in English or perhaps any
     language to bring the whole war into perspective.

27   SHAW, VALERIE A.  "The Middle Age of Mrs. Eliot and Late Call:
     Angus Wilson's Traditionalism."  CritQ 12 (Spring):9-27.
          Beginning with Edmund Wilson's comparison of Waugh and Wilson,
     says that the latter has not inherited the cloak of satirical gai-
     ety which Waugh had seemed to drop from his shoulders in the for-
     ties; for there are important differences in the economic areas of
     society and moral attitudes they examine.  The endings of Late Call
     and Brideshead are not dissimilar; but Wilson's concentration on
     the present and its new social types involves no self-indulgent
     nostalgia for the twenties in the old institutions of Church and
     State.  He continues the Waugh wit with all its strengths, but
     without its weaknesses.

28   TOSSER, YVON.  "Bibliography of Waugh Criticism (French Area):
     Part I."  EWN 4 (Spring):8-9.
          A list of French critical articles and reviews of Waugh's
     work.

29   ULANOV, BARRY.  "The Ordeal of Evelyn Waugh."  In The Vision
     Obscured.  Edited by Melvin J. Friedman.  New York:  Fordham
     University Press, pp. 79-94.
          From Brideshead on, Waugh was accused of sentimentality.
     To find more than sentimentality or a passing joke in him, one
     must surrender to his world of the spirit, or see his own ordeal
     as a kind of spiritual exercise.  His work represents a complete
     oeuvre; working with the materials of a dying society, he found
     coherence and an underlying structure--the Catholic structure
     which still lies lightly buried beneath English life, and which
     could be explored through an allegory of irony.

30   WALL, STEPHEN.  "Aspects of the Novel 1930-1960."  In The
     Twentieth Century.  Edited by Bernard Bergonzi.  Sphere History
     of Literature in the English Language, vol. 7.  London:  Sphere
     Books, pp. 233-37.

In this survey of Waugh's career, the world of <u>Decline and Fall</u> is described as too fantastic and arbitrary to serve any coherent satirical purpose; <u>A Handful of Dust</u> as showing remarkable tension and economy of style; <u>Brideshead</u> as revealing similar dilemmas but less discipline; and <u>Sword of Honour</u> as having its large ambitions marred by narrow sympathies.

31    WEBSTER, HARVEY CURTIS.  "Evelyn Waugh:  Catholic Aristocrat."
      In <u>After the Trauma:  Representative British Novelists since
      1920</u>.  Lexington:  University of Kentucky Press, pp. 72-92.
          Rates Waugh very highly in his survey of recent British fiction.  Says <u>Decline and Fall</u> and <u>Vile Bodies</u> are more reminiscent of Voltaire or Swift than of Ronald Firbank or P.G. Wodehouse: flippancy is used mordantly.  Calls <u>Brideshead</u> his richest novel, and <u>Men at Arms</u> and <u>Officers and Gentlemen</u> the best dramatizations of modern war's essence yet published.  Concludes that he is a disconcerting writer, limited but suggesting truths in a distinctive manner.

<u>1971</u>

A.  BOOKS

1    COOK, WILLIAM J. Jr.  <u>Masks, Modes, and Morals:  The Art of
      Evelyn Waugh</u>.  Cranbury, N.J.:  Fairleigh Dickinson University
      Press, 352 pp.
          Surveys Waugh's entire career from the viewpoint of the narrator's relationship to the central character in each of the novels.  Summarizes critical opinion at various stages of the author's literary life in order to indicate misreadings of his work.

2    HEATH, JEFFREY MORTON.  "Evelyn Waugh and the Comic Macabre."
      Ph.D. dissertation, University of Toronto, 425 pp.  [<u>DAI</u> 32:
      6930A.]
          Maintains that Waugh's notorious fictional cruelties are functional from beginning to end.  Beyond the tonal neutrality we find certain touchstones and glimpses of norms or standards.  In the early episodic novels, the usual mode of resolution is through the comic macabre.  <u>Work Suspended</u> is an attempt at change, but in <u>Put Out More Flags</u> Waugh returns to an ironic mode, using the comic macabre to explode bureaucratic nonsense and wartime incongruities. <u>Brideshead</u> and <u>Sword of Honour</u> do not rely heavily on the comic macabre, but do use the image patterns associated with it; through them a mythology begins to resolve itself within Waugh's comic universe.  Ultimately the choice is between Brideshead and Godhead; Waugh's comedy of swift reprisals demonstrates the grisly fate of the human body devoid of grace.

3    HOLLIS, CHRISTOPHER.  <u>Evelyn Waugh</u>.  Writers and Their Work,

no. 46.  London:  Longmans, Green, 39 pp.
    Revision of 1966.A2 with an altered final paragraph and
changes in tense to take account of Waugh's death.  See also
1954.A1; 1958.A12.

4  LODGE, DAVID.  Evelyn Waugh.  Columbia Essays on Modern Writers.
    New York and London:  Columbia University Press, 48 pp.
    Concise survey of Waugh's career, tracing his version of the
"myth of decline" throughout his work.  Such a myth provided a
sliding scale of value by which everything may be found defective:
Waugh's consistent appeal to the ideal of Christian perfection
lies beyond the realm of his fiction.  Reprinted:  1974.B19.


B.  SHORTER WRITINGS

1  CHURCHILL, THOMAS.  "An Interview with Anthony Burgess."
    Malahat Review 17 (January):103-27.
    Admires Waugh, but with reservations:  he had horrible areas
of conservatism, and he hated Joyce.  Says people like Greene and
Waugh are converts using Catholicism for their own private ends--
Waugh because he wanted an endless aristocracy.  Likes Brideshead,
calling it one of his favorite books, and saying that Lord
Marchmain's death moves him to tears.

2  COHEN, MARTIN S.  "Allusive Conversation in A Handful of Dust
    and Brideshead Revisited."  EWN 5 (Autumn):1-6.
    In A Handful of Dust and Brideshead, often considered his
two best novels, Waugh has used the same technique of allusive
conversation (rarely employed in the other novels) to develop
character and enhance comic or dramatic effect.

3  CONNOLLY, CYRIL.  "Apotheosis in Austin."  Sunday Times (London),
    6 June, p. 31.
    Reveals that in the Humanities Research Center at the
University of Texas he "felt like Gray in his country churchyard
or Evelyn Waugh, discovering Forest Lawn."  Describes his emotions
on finding, in a copy of his own The Unquiet Grave, Waugh's un-
flattering assessment of him--a contemptuous description of himself as the typical man of his generation, the authentic inhabitant
of the wasteland.

4  DERRICK, CHRISTOPHER.  "Fact and Meaning in the Age of Aquarius."
    Triumph 6 (May):7-10.
    Uses Helena to define Waugh's vision of England's potential
contribution to the universal Church:  a hard, factual, objective
practicality.  Incarnation is the intersection of fact and meaning,
flesh and word.

5  DOYLE, PAUL A.  Review of Masks, Modes, and Morals:  The Art of
    Evelyn Waugh, by William J. Cook, Jr.  EWN 5 (Winter):8.

Calls Cook's discussion of Waugh's use of the persona and of
his change from satire to ironic realism a useful contribution to
Waugh studies, but says it has the look of a thesis about it and
fails to take account of important recent criticism.

6      _____. "Some Unpublished Waugh Correspondence III." EWN 5
       (Spring):3-4.
       Continues 1968.B19, with an annotated list of six Waugh
letters.

7      DOYLE, PAUL A., WINIFRED BOGAARDS, and ROBERT M. DAVIS. "Works
       of Waugh 1940-66: A Supplementary Bibliography, Part 2." EWN 5
       (Spring):8-13.
       Continuation of 1970.B11, with letters to the editor, reviews,
articles, and books by Waugh, including interviews with him.

8      FARR, D. PAUL. "The Success and Failure of Decline and Fall."
       EA 24 (April-June):257-70.
       Waugh finds in "the standards of civilization"--the sanity,
order, and discipline of a continuing tradition--a base for a unified and coherent attack on the madness of the modern world in
Decline and Fall. But he leaves unsettled the question of whether
Paul Pennyfeather ends as only a shadow, a satiric instrument, or
a real person, who has learned from experience and gained a perspective on the modern world. He seems to make an inadequate response to Peter Pastmaster's pathetic appeal; if he has become a
responsible churchman, he fails to perform his proper function of
helping modern youth achieve the standards of civilization.

9      FIRCHOW, PETER E. "In Search of A Handful of Dust: The
       Literary Background of Evelyn Waugh's Novel." JML 2 (Winter):
       406-16.
       Analyzes allusions to T.S. Eliot, Tennyson, Dickens and
Proust in A Handful of Dust, to indicate Waugh's indirect method
of presenting serious ideas and issues.

10     GALLAGHER, D.S. "Additional Waugh Bibliography." EWN 5
       (Autumn):6-7.
       Adds some book reviews between 1930 and 1940, and some cor-
rections to D. Paul Farr's "Evelyn Waugh: A Supplementary Bibliography" (1969.B15) and Paul A. Doyle's "Evelyn Waugh: A Bibliography (1926-1956)" (1957.B15).

11     _____. "Towards a Definitive Waugh Bibliography: Notations
       on the 1957 BB Checklist." EWN 5 (Spring):6-8.
       Additions and corrections to 1957.B15.

12     _____. "Waugh's Letters-to-the-Editor 1923-1966: A Supple-
       mentary Bibliography." EWN 5 (Winter):2-5.
       Annotated list of Waugh's letters, the items which provoked
his correspondence, and the consequences of his letters.

13   GORDON, GERALD T. "'Lake Isle of Innisfree': A Classical
     Allusion in Evelyn Waugh's The Loved One." EWN 5 (Winter):1-2.
        Calls Dennis Barlow a caricature of Virgil's Aeneas, and the
boatman who ferries him to the Lake Island of Innisfree a modern-
day Charon; the lovers who people the island are spiritually de-
funct, like the dead souls of the Greek and Roman underworld. Once
Dennis crosses to Innisfree there is no turning back for him; he
becomes like other plastic lovers, gratified only by sensual pleasures.

14   GRIBBLE, THOMAS. "Recent BBC Productions of Waugh Stories."
     EWN 5 (Spring):5-6.
        Describes adaptations of Vile Bodies and Put Out More Flags,
both in 1970, as well as of the short story "Winner Take All" in
1969. Says that the television versions of the two novels were
well worth watching but failed to give a sense of Waugh's use of
language for comic and ironic effect.

15   KOSOK, HEINZ. "Evelyn Waugh: A Supplementary Checklist of
     Criticism." EWN 5 (Spring):4-5.
        A continuation of earlier checklists, adding chiefly books
and articles published since 1969.

16   LINCK, CHARLES E., Jr. "The Year's Work in Waugh Studies."
     EWN 5 (Spring):1-3.
        A long list of items, all discussed briefly, justifies the
statement that it is a bullish Waugh market.

17   NICHOLS, JAMES W. Insinuation: The Tactics of English Satire.
     The Hague: Mouton, passim.
        Accounting for satire in terms of its techniques or tactics,
makes frequent reference to Waugh; turns to him for examples of
the use of a persona, use of an ingénu, use of two contrasting
scales of value, use of allusion, and other tactics of indirection.

18   NOVELLI, MARTIN A. "Witness to the Times: The War Novels of
     Ford Madox Ford and Evelyn Waugh." Ph.D. dissertation, Temple
     University, 419 pp. [DAI 32:3321A.]
        Says that Ford and Waugh shared a common moral and historical
vision and devoted their careers to an examination of the "Condition of England." In Parade's End and Sword of Honour, the heroes
are similar, both anachronisms fighting against modernity, both
nearly driven mad by their trials, both surviving not triumphantly
but with the ability to live in the modern world.

19   PEARSON, KENNETH. "Waugh's Scoop for Harry Worth." Sunday
     Times (London), 4 July, p. 19.
        Describes the seven-part BBC adaptation of Scoop for tele-
vision, and says Waugh's work is better served by television than
film, as Sword of Honour proved.

20  PHILLIPS, GENE D.  "The Page Proofs of Brideshead Revisited."
    EWN 5 (Autumn):7-8.
        A bound volume of the page proofs of Brideshead in the li-
    brary of Loyola College, Baltimore, reveals a surprising number of
    revisions considering that the proofs were gone over in Yugoslavia.
    Gives examples, and says that a full account of the emendations
    would be an interesting study.

21  _____.  Review of The Vital Tradition:  The Catholic Novel in a
    Period of Convergence, by Gene Kellogg.  EWN 5 (Autumn):9.
        Notes that only the Waugh chapter of this book is really in-
    adequate; it gives the impression that Waugh stopped writing in
    1945.

22  QUENNELL, PETER.  Casanova in London.  London:  Weidenfeld &
    Nicolson, pp. 113-68.
        Draws a contrast between the juvenile Waugh, "carefree, gay
    and affectionate," and the adult, somber and cross-grained, cut off
    from nine-tenths of the modern world.  Waugh was not an innovator;
    he was perfectly content with the situation of the English novel
    as he found it.  What he added were not fresh tricks of style but
    a far subtler originality.  The hidden conflicts that made him so
    strange a man may also have helped to shape an extraordinarily
    gifted writer.

*23 SEIDLER, MANFRED.  "Evelyn Waugh."  In Englische Dichter der
    Moderne:  Ihr Leben und Werk.  Edited by Rudolf Suhnel and
    Deiter Riesner.  Berlin:  Erich Schmidt.
        Source:  Checklist, no. 1203; 1972.A1.

24  WEINKAUF, MARY.  "The God Figure in Dystopian Fiction."  RQ 4
    (March):266-71.
        Stating that man can be just as humble under the control of
    an evil tyrant as under God, notes that the benediction in Waugh's
    Love Among the Ruins is "State Be With You."


                              1972


A.  BOOKS


1   DAVIS, ROBERT MURRAY, PAUL A. DOYLE, HEINZ KOSOK, and CHARLES
    E. LINCK, Jr.  Evelyn Waugh:  A Checklist of Primary and
    Secondary Material.  Troy, N.Y.:  Whitston Publishing Co., 211
    pp.
        The authors claim that this first comprehensive checklist of
    Waugh materials orders information currently available, and adds
    a good many items never before listed.  Still they stress that the
    problem of establishing a bibliography is a continuing one, and
    that there were many tantalizing leads they were not able to follow

up.  The bibliography lists Waugh's works chronologically according
to certain categories, and works about him alphabetically by author,
except that reviews and discussions of individual books are arranged according to the book's first date of publication.

2    DOLD, BERNARD.  Waugh Revisited.  Messina, Sicily:  Peloritana
     Editrice, 109 pp.
        A generalized, sometimes pejorative, survey of Waugh's fic-
     tion, concentrating largely on Sword of Honour.  Discusses the
     history of the British Army and English Catholicism.  Considers
     Waugh's treatment of marriage and architecture, his snobbery,
     racism, romantic nostalgia and style.

*3   PHILLIPS, KENNETH ALLAN.  "The Grace of God is in Courtesy:
     The Religious and Social Attitudes in the works of Evelyn
     Waugh."  Ph.D. dissertation, University of Alberta.


B.  SHORTER WRITINGS

1    BLAYAC, ALAIN.  "Technique and Meaning in Scoop:  Is Scoop a
     Modern Fairy-Tale?"  EWN 6 (Winter):1-8.
        Notes that Boot Magna is like the castle of Sleeping Beauty,
     where life stopped long ago.  Finds many elements of the fairy
     tale in Scoop; in it, the hero is presumably rewarded for his good-
     ness to disguised fairies.  But the fairy-tale types grow smoothly
     into spy-novel characters; and in the conclusion the hero falls
     back into the ineffectual man we met at the outset, so that the
     novel lacks coherence and Waugh's lesson remains unconvincing.

2    BOGAARDS, WINIFRED M.  Review of Evelyn Waugh:  A Checklist of
     Primary and Secondary Material, by Robert Murray Davis, Paul A.
     Doyle, Heinz Kosok, and Charles E. Linck, Jr.  EWN 6 (Winter):10.
     10.
        Says that this first comprehensive checklist of Waugh mater-
     ials (1972.A1) fulfils its compilers' claim that it reduces avail-
     able information to order and adds a good many items never before
     listed, but criticizes lack of a consistent policy in dealing with
     articles or parts of books published more than once.

3    BOWEN, JOHN.  "Literary Debts."  TLS, 4 August, p. 918.
        Letter describing an account in W. Graham Robertson's Life
     Was Worth Living of a story first told to Robertson by Oscar Wilde
     about the latter's imaginary Aunt Jane.  This was the story re-
     counted by Waugh in his "Bella Fleace Gave a Party."  Does not
     suggest that Waugh stole the story, but wonders about possible
     sources and other versions.

4    BRADBURY, MALCOLM.  "Muriel Spark's Fingernails."  CritQ 14
     (Autumn):241-50.
        Says that her aesthetics and her religion are closely

involved with each other, and that it is the Catholic novelists
like Greene and Waugh who have contributed self-conscious aesthe-
ics to the English literary tradition and given it a Jesuitical
streak. Considers M. Spark closer to the comic Waugh, who, de-
spairing of God's presence in modern history, feels free to represent it as chaos or vulgarized nonsense. The difference is that
he is a novelist of the contingent, whereas she sees a need for
wholeness and coherence.

5    CHAPMAN, ROBERT T. "'Parties . . . Parties . . . Parties':
     Some Images of the 'Gay Twenties.'" English 21 (Summer):93-97.
     Sets Waugh's description of parties in Vile Bodies against
Tom Driberg's account of a party given by the "gay young things"
of 1928: the reality was so fantastic that little imagination was
needed to turn it into fiction. Other accounts by Wyndham Lewis,
Noel Coward, Aldous Huxley, and others.

6    DAVIS, ROBERT MURRAY. "The Loved One: Text and Context." TQ
     15 (Winter):100-7.
     Discusses Waugh's dissatisfaction with postwar England and
his precarious literary position in it. During this transitional
period, travel and reading Henry James stimulated his writing.
Scott-King's Modern Europe shows his uncertainty. The Loved One
indicates his interest in distinguishing between art and morality,
and his delight in escaping Hollywood. Describes the process of
writing the novel, its publication, and its textual history.

7    _____. "Title and Theme in A Handful of Dust." EWN 6 (Autumn):
     1.
     Suggests, besides the lines from The Waste Land, appropriate-
ness of a passage in Ovid about the Cumaean Sybil's fate when she
forgot to specify eternal youth in asking Apollo for as many years
of life as the grains of dust she could hold in her hand.

8    DOBIE, ANN B., and CARL WOOTON. "Spark and Waugh: Similarities
     by Coincidence." MQ 13 (April):423-34.
     Compares M. Spark's The Comforters with Waugh's Ordeal of
Gilbert Pinfold, both published in 1957, and both novels about
novels and novelists. Both central characters have to choose
between sanity that looks like madness (the reality of humanly
inexplicable forces), and madness that masquerades as sanity (the
world of man as the ultimate reality). Both choose the former.
Their experiences lead them to discover form in chaos, meaning in
the unbelievable.

9    EDWARDS, A.S.G., and J.D. O'CONNELL. "Waugh's Letters to John
     Betjeman." EWN 6 (Autumn):2-3.
     Describes fifty-eight letters from Waugh to Betjeman over a
twenty-two-year period. Notes comments on art, architecture,
literary activities and religious conversion.

10    FARR, D. PAUL. "Waugh's Conservative Stance:  Defending 'The
      Standards of Civilization.'"  PQ 51 (April):471-84.
         Shows that Waugh acknowledged early on that something not
      easily regained was lost during World War I.  Distinguishes three
      periods in his nonfiction:  in early books like Labels and Remote
      People he shows a light satiric tolerance of the modern; in Waugh
      in Abyssinia and Robbery under Law he is a blind, bitter conserva-
      tive; in A Tourist in Africa his conservatism is calmer.  His
      stance is more complex than pejorative terms like snobbery, racism,
      and fascism suggest; he belongs in the tradition of humanism.

11    FRIEDMANN, THOMAS.  "Decline and Fall and the Satirist's
      Responsibility."  EWN 6 (Autumn):3-8.
         Contends satire is most effective when it observes enduring
      human nature rather than humanity at a particular moment.  When
      Decline and Fall depends on human types it is effective and devas-
      tating; when it depends on "history," it fails.  Historical ele-
      ments are beyond the reader's responsibility; the writer must
      establish an initial understanding with his audience.

12    GALLAGHER, D.S.  "Pinfold Unfolded."  EWN 6 (Spring):1-2.
         Reveals that Waugh wrote letters to the Catholic Herald under
      the pseudonym "Mrs. Teresa Pinfold," and quotes the only one of
      these he could find.  The name Pinfold was taken from the man who
      built Piers Court, the Waugh home.

13    GILL, RICHARD.  Happy Rural Seat.  New York and London:  Yale
      University Press, pp. 155-60, 211-22, et passim.
         Examines the country house as a recurring image in modern
      English fiction.  Waugh uses this symbolic setting to convey the
      continuity and decay of community values, in a blend of satire and
      elegy.  Brideshead suggests a more genial retrospection, balancing
      the earlier disintegration of Hetton in A Handful of Dust and the
      later Christian irony and measured hope of Broome in Sword of
      Honour.

14    GRIBBLE, THOMAS A.  "Some New Waugh Bibliography."  EWN 6
      (Autumn):8-10.
         Lists Waugh's articles, letters, reviews, and notes his
      B.B.C. radio and television appearances.

15    HOWARTH, HERBERT.  "Voices of the Past in Dickens and Others."
      UTQ 41 (Winter):151-62.
         Discusses Dickens's use of literary allusion, comparing him
      to Thackeray, Trollope, and Meredith; notes his influence on
      Firbank and Waugh.

16    HYNES, JOSEPH.  "Varieties of Death Wish:  Evelyn Waugh's
      Central Theme."  Criticism 14 (Winter):66-77.
         Gives an unusual interpretation to the notion that "all
      differences are theological differences."  The critic must grant

any novelist his subject matter, and then insist only that the
subject matter become one with form.  Reluctance to give oneself
to religious subject matter means neglecting Waugh's most substantial work and his thematic continuity.  Shows that the death wish
dominates his novels, while complete despair is rare:  something
usually sustains his figures, if only in a type of living death.
Pays special attention to Brideshead, in which the life associated
with the great house ultimately becomes secondary, and to the war
trilogy, in which Guy learns to live according to his father's
Christian values.

17   La FRANCE, MARSTON.  "The Year's Work in Waugh Studies."  EWN
     6 (Spring):3-6.
         Wittily dismisses essays by Barry Ulanov (1970.B29) and
     Terry Eagleton (1970.B13); finds Gene Kellogg's chapter on Waugh
     (1970.B17) brief but acceptable; calls David Lodge's short study
     very good of its kind; commends two essays by D. Paul Farr as
     genuine scholarship; and treats William J. Cook, Jr.'s, Masks,
     Modes and Morals with considerable severity.

18   LODGE, DAVID.  "The Arrogance of Evelyn Waugh."  Critic 30
     (May-June):63-70.
         Referring to Waugh's ogrish "public image" and self-portrait
     in The Ordeal of Gilbert Pinfold, argues that fantasy and role-
     playing underlay his toryism and snobbery.  He was sincere in
     opposing the reforms of Vatican II, and his pose was essential in
     concealing his despondency.  Revised:  1981.B18.

19   MAHON, JOHN W.  "Charles Ryder and Evelyn Waugh."  EWN 6
     (Spring):2-3.
         Calls attention to similarities in descriptions of Oxford in
     Waugh's A Little Learning and Brideshead Revisited; the biography
     reveals parallels in the lives of Waugh and his fictional character
     Charles Ryder.  The language and phrases of Brideshead survive
     twenty years after the novel was written.

20   MATTSON, FRANCIS O.  "Evelyn Waugh in the Berg Collection."
     EWN 6 (Autumn):2.
         Describes the New York Public Library collection of Waugh's
     books, particularly the limited editions, manuscripts and proof
     copies.

21   _____.  "Man the Exile."  EWN 6 (Winter):8-9.
         Describes and quotes from a letter from Waugh to John Kobler
     incorporating a brief essay entitled "Man the Exile," a proposed
     article for the "Adventures of the Mind" series in the Saturday
     Evening Post.

22   RUSSELL, JOHN.  "The War Trilogies of Anthony Powell and Evelyn
     Waugh."  Modern Age 15 (Summer):289-300.
         While Waugh and Powell reveal similar structures and time

spans in their respective war trilogies, they differ in political viewpoint, the temperaments of their protagonists, the relation of the individual to the army, and their focus on action or observation.

23   SISSMAN, L.E.  "Evelyn Waugh:  The Height of His Powers." Atlantic 229 (March):24, 26.
        Reviews Waugh's literary career, singling out Put Out More Flags as an undeservedly forgotten book, in which he fuses savage comedy with ominous seriousness, relating his characters directly to history.

24   THIEME, OTTO.  "Evelyn Waugh:  A Supplementary Checklist of Criticism."  EWN 6 (Spring):6-7.
        Continuation of earlier checklists, previously omitted items included, with books and articles published since 1970.

25   TOSSER, YVON.  "Bibliography of Waugh Criticism (French Area): Part II."  EWN 6 (Spring):7-8.
        Continues 1970.B28 noting new academic interest in Waugh at French universities.


1973


A.  BOOKS

1   PAZERESKIS, JOHN F.  "The Narrators of Evelyn Waugh:  A Study of Five Works of Fiction."  Ph.D. dissertation, Northwestern University, 195 pp.  [DAI 34:4463A.]
        Discusses the degree of involvement or detachment the narrator displays, and estimates his reliability.  Traces the use of narrators from early works in which the narrator is more important than the story, toward greater realism and (for Waugh) the blind alley of first-person narration, to his final successful adaptation of his conservative satiric vision to the conventional norms of the English novel.  Says that A Handful of Dust was his most successful; Waugh's genius lay in his unique manner of telling his story, and Sword of Honour was told in a conventional way.

2   PRYCE-JONES, DAVID, ed.  Evelyn Waugh and His World.  Toronto and Boston:  Little, Brown & Co., 248 pp.
        A collection of chronologically arranged essays and articles by Waugh's friends and acquaintances, dealing with his literary work, his education and religious views, his friendships and his literary ideals.

3   WYSS, KURT O.  Pikareske Thematik im Romanwerk Evelyn Waughs. Swiss Studies in English, vol. 77.  Bern:  Francke Verlag, 336 pp.

Says that comparison with the rogue tradition shows that
Waugh must have been under the influence of this type of novel.
In fact he uses both rogues and picaresque "saints," and thus introduces a new element into the picaresque: oscillation between
the innocent fool and the rogue. Amis, Wain, and Waterhouse are
thought to have brought about a renaissance of the picaresque in
the 1950s, but Waugh anticipated them in the 1930s.


B.  SHORTER WRITINGS

1   ANON. "Orgies among British Gentry Described in Waugh's
      Diaries." Globe and Mail (Toronto), 23 April, p. 3.
         An Associated Press story from London about the shocked re-
    actions to the revelations in Waugh's diaries, concluding with
    Auberon Waugh's comment that their publication could make a useful
    contribution to frankness and honesty in public life.

2   BEATON, CECIL. The Strenuous Years. Diaries 1948-55. London:
      Weidenfeld & Nicolson, pp. 66-71.
         In meeting Waugh at Diana Duff Cooper's in Paris, wonders
    how she puts up with his snobbery: "In our own way we were both
    snobs, and no snob welcomes another who has risen with him." Re-
    calls Waugh's persecution of him at Heath Mount preparatory school
    --"the bullies, led by a tiny, but fierce Evelyn Waugh." Wonders
    if Waugh ever really liked anybody.

3   BOGAARDS, WINIFRED M. "Evelyn Waugh, Oscar Wilde, and Irish
      Folklore." EWN (Spring):1-5.
         Referring to recent correspondence in the Times Literary
    Supplement compares Waugh's story "Bella Fleace Gave a Party" with
    Oscar Wilde's "Aunt Jane" anecdote, noting that there is a surface
    similarity but fundamental disparity. Waugh's main interest is in
    the decaying gentry, rather than the surprise ending.

4   BRADBURY, MALCOLM. Possibilities. Essays on the State of the
      Novel. London: Oxford, pp. 154-62, et passim.
         Links Waugh to Wyndham Lewis and Aldous Huxley in a discus-
    sion of the modern comic novel. His version of hsitory as a dis-
    integrating process releases Dionysian comedy and a self-ironizing
    but poised narrative posture. His achievement is a complete style,
    a modern comic form, despite his emphasis on tradition. His neu-
    tral method underlines the absence of a moral or psychological
    level of existence.

5   CLARK, JOHN R. "Verboten Passage: Strategy in the Early Waugh."
      EWN 7 (Autumn):5-9.
         Like most satirists, Waugh pushes impishly towards the limits
    of taste; he has something of his own Basil Seal in him.

6   COCKBURN, CLAUDE. "Evelyn Waugh's Lost Rabbit." Atlantic 232

(December):53-59.

Discusses extracts from Waugh's Diaries published in The
Observer. Comments on Waugh's insularity, love of fantasy in conversation, relations with his brother Alec, years at Oxford, and
the effects of World War I on him and a whole generation. Says he
idealized the England of his childhood, identifying it with religious values and civilization; describes his idiosyncratic snobbery. Gives a witty account of his role-playing. In the April
issue (p. 30), Alec Waugh complained that Cockburn had fabricated
his account of the brothers' relationship.

7        . "My Cousin Evelyn." Punch 264 (20 June):923.
Relates anecdotes concerning Waugh's insularity and snobbery.

8    DAVIE, MICHAEL. "The Diary of a Somebody." Observer (London),
25 March, p. 29.
Introduction, in the Observer Review section, to The Private
Diaries of Evelyn Waugh published in the Colour Magazine section
beginning on this date. Gives details about the diaries and the
people mentioned in them; also says that Waugh seems to have admired his own capacity for rudeness, and wished to raise it to a
minor art. Says that the diaries shed light on Waugh's strange
and vivid character. Gives a biographical summary, noting that
like Byron and Dickens he became famous overnight, and that his
last years were anything but serene; he disapproved profoundly of
Pope John, the Second Vatican Council, and Cardinal Heenan.

9        . "The Private Diaries of Evelyn Waugh." Observer
Magazine (London), 25 March, p. 18.
Introduces the diaries, which ran serially in the Observer
for eight issues until 13 May; the serial version is accompanied
by many photographs of Waugh and his contemporaries.

10   DAVIS, ROBERT MURRAY. "How Waugh Cut Merton." Month 234
(April):150-53.
Shows that Waugh's editing of Thomas Merton's The Seven
Storey Mountain under its English title of Elected Silence was intelligent and ruthless, following principles of clarity, economy,
and understatement. He held Merton to professional standards of
writing. When Merton dedicated his next book, The Waters of Siloe,
to him, he cut that too.

11   DOYLE, PAUL A. Review of To the War with Waugh, by John St.
John. EWN 7 (Autumn):11.
Notes there is interesting information about life in the
Royal Marines, and some interesting personal recollections of
Waugh, but much more of Evelyn is needed. See 1974.A2.

12   DRIBERG, TOM. "The Evelyn Waugh I Knew." Observer (London),
20 May, pp. 30-34.
Rounds off the serialization of Waugh's diaries with

recollections of him beginning with Lancing schooldays. Describes
his early development of sophisticated literary tastes, interest
in scandalous gossip, development of snobbery partly because of
association with the rich and titled at Oxford, taste for hoaxing
and mischief (with examples), and the slating of his masterpiece,
A Handful of Dust, by a Catholic journal, the Tablet. Contains
quotations from letters by Waugh.

13   GALLAGHER, D.S.   "'A Bald Story' (A Review of Alex Waugh's Card
     Castle signed 'E')."   EWN 7 (Autumn):10.
        Questions the attribution of a review in the Isis to Waugh
     by Charles E. Linck, Jr., on stylistic grounds.

14   GREENE, DONALD.   "The Wicked Marquess:  Disraeli to Thackeray
     to Waugh."   EWN 7 (Autumn):1-5.
        Believes the Flytes in Brideshead owe something to the Lygons,
     the family of the Lords Beauchamp, but by quotation of parallel
     passages, shows that a likely source for Lord Marchmain is
     Thackeray's Marquis of Steyne in Vanity Fair.

15   HEATH, JEFFREY M.   "Waugh and Rossetti."   EWN 7 (Winter):5-6.
        In his famous Times Literary Supplement review (1928.11)
     assigning Waugh's book on Rossetti to "a hitherto unknown spinster,"
     T. Sturge Moore referred to the author's mental eye as "slightly
     astigmatic."   Comments that Moore was right about this, if not
     about the author's sex, because of Waugh's idea that the Reformation
     was the beginning of cultural decadence in England.   He saw Rossetti's
     response to the past as not spiritual but picturesque and self-
     indulgent.

16   La FRANCE, MARSTON.   "The Year's Work in Waugh Studies."   EWN
     7 (Spring):5-7.
        Noting that 1972 was a vintage year in Waugh studies, calls
     special attention to the checklist by Robert Murray Davis and
     others.   Praises articles by Joseph Hynes and D. Paul Farr, re-
     mains unconvinced by Peter Firchow's ingenious discovery of echoes
     of T.S. Eliot and others in A Handful of Dust, and finds Davis's
     article "The Loved One:  Text and Context" a model of its kind.

17   LODGE, DAVID.   "Putting Out the Flags."   Tablet 227 (3 November):
     227, 1041-42.
        Reviews David Pryce-Jones's Evelyn Waugh and his World
     (1973.A2), John St. John's To the War with Waugh (1974.A3), Bernard
     E. Dold's Waugh Revisited (1972.A2), and Waugh's own A Little
     Learning.   Calls tracing the connections between Waugh's art and
     his life a fascinating exercise; remarks that he was something of
     a dandy, one who makes his own life style into a work of art; but
     concludes with Father Martin D'Arcy's statement:  "It has been
     said that his religious faith was a pose.  Nothing could be further
     from the truth."

18   McALEER, EDWARD C.   "Decline and Fall as Imitation."   EWN 7
     (Winter):1-4.
          Calls attention to Waugh's technique of imitation of passages
     from the Bible, Shakespeare, Pater, and other writers; as in T.S.
     Eliot, he summons up the past by allusion to a masterpiece, and
     uses the grand manner to clothe some shocking up-to-the-minute
     material. The device is especially appropriate in Decline and
     Fall, because it is a prose Waste Land.

19   MECKIER, JEROME.   "Evelyn Waugh:  Satire and Symbol."   GaR 27
     (Summer):166-74.
          An expert craftsman, Waugh exhibited a developed sense of
     form and style; what needs more attention is the symbolic aspect
     of his art. His ultimate symbol for twentieth-century disorder is
     the Second World War. Analyzes images of circularity, energy,
     feverish motion, and mechanical response, and points out that one
     of Waugh's major skills is his ability to fashion a satiric symbol,
     which summarizes the point being made by a stretch of narrative,
     perhaps an entire novel. Examples particularly from Vile Bodies
     and A Handful of Dust illustrate this symbolic condensation of a
     theme.

20   MIKES, GEORGE.   "Viewpoint."   TLS, 15 June, p. 670.
          Discusses diary-writing in general, with references to the
     Observer publication of selections from Waugh's Diaries. Notes
     Waugh's snobbery and development of a persona:  the diaries reflect
     the same image as the rest of his oeuvre.

21   MUGGERIDGE, MALCOLM.   Chronicles of Wasted Time. Vol. 2; The
     Infernal Grove.  London:  Collins, pp. 202-4, et passim.
          Discusses various meetings with Waugh, observing that there
     was always something strained in their relationship, and saying
     he greatly regrets that he made no serious attempt to overcome
     their mutual antagonism.

22   _____.  "A Waugh Memorial."  Observer (London), 14 October,
     p. 78.
          Reviewing David Pryce-Jones's Evelyn Waugh and His World
     (1973.A2), suggests that Waugh's cruel mockery concealed a failed
     saint:  his satire lacked Christian piety and love. His comic
     novels are unbearably tragic, and clearly reveal his desperation.

23   NICHOLS, BEVERLEY.   "Unholy Waugh."  Spectator 231 (27 October):
     546-47.
          Reviewing David Pryce-Jones's Evelyn Waugh and His World
     (1973.A2), quotes Noel Coward's remark that if Waugh had been
     offered the choice of being blackballed by White's Club or excom-
     municated by Rome he would have chosen excommunication. Says his
     snobbery moulded his conduct and shaped the pattern of his art.
     The attempt to reconcile his creed as a Christian with his conduct
     as a man is bound to fail.

In a fierce reply (10 November, p. 231) Graham Greene refers to the savage ritual of spitting upon a grave, stressing that Evelyn never waited until a man was dead to release his venom.

24    POWELL, ANTHONY. "Evelyn's Diary." London Magazine 13
      (August-September):67-72.
      Comments on excerpts from Diaries published serially in the Observer, noting the distortion inevitable in such publication methods, and arguing for the importance of Waugh as diarist.

25    PRITCHARD, WILLIAM. "Photo-Criticism." Listener 90 (1 November):
      603-4.
      Reviews David Pryce-Jones's Evelyn Waugh and His World (1973.A2) along with Stephen Spender's D.H. Lawrence: Novelist, Poet, Prophet. Recounts anecdotes dealing with Waugh's madcap follies, and also calls attention to the strong picture of his depressed nature.

26    RHODES, ANTHONY. The Vatican in the Age of the Dictators,
      1922-1945. London: Hodder & Stoughton, pp. 328-29, 333-35.
      Comments on a long report made by Waugh, then a captain in the army, on atrocities in Yugoslavia; he referred to a deliberate Communist policy of extermination of the Catholic Church, but also mentioned massacres of Orthodox Serbs and Jews.

27    RILEY, JOHN JAMES. "Gentlemen at Arms: A Comparison of the
      War Trilogies of Anthony Powell and Evelyn Waugh." Ph.D. dissertation, Tufts University, 209 pp. [DAI 34:5202A.]
      Finds close parallels in technique, style, and vision--in fact, a strong personal and private reciprocal tension, which became a generative principle of their art. Calls Waugh's war trilogy the culmination of his art--history fused with memory and imagination--and the most significant work concerning World War II in British fiction.

28    SHEED, WILFRED. "The Good Word: No Snob Like a Snubbed Snob."
      New York Times Book Review, 1 July, p. 2.
      Despite Waugh's faults, his diary excerpts in the Observer reveal him as likeable because of his self-mockery. Even his snobbery "has a certain grandeur."

29    SYKES, CHRISTOPHER. "Views." Listener 90 (26 July):105-6.
      Recollections of Nancy Mitford, saying that the main influence on her early novels was not Waugh but P.G. Wodehouse. Waugh's influence came later, particularly with The Pursuit of Love, the book which brought her fame; in fact Waugh made many suggestions during the writing of this novel, most of which she followed.

30    THIEME, HANS OTTO. "Evelyn Waugh: A Supplementary Checklist
      of Criticism." EWN 7 (Spring):8.
      Annual checklist of items published since 1971, and those previously omitted.

31   WAUGH, ALEC. <u>The Fatal Gift</u>. London and New York:  W.H. Allen,
     314 pp.
          In a foreword, says this is a work of fiction with one excep-
     tion:  "My brother Evelyn did in 1924 bring a girl to Oxford and
     take her, dressed as a man, to an undergraduate 'binge' which was
     raided by the proctor and his bulldogs."  The dust jacket says
     that around the life of Raymond Peronne, his protagonist, he has
     threaded the people and places he has known, such as his brother
     Evelyn, his cousin Claud Cockburn, Robin Maugham, and most of all
     himself.  The novel is about an imaginary contemporary of Evelyn's
     at Oxford, and from time to time Alec does introduce real people.

32   WAUGH, AUBERON.  "Father and Son." <u>Books and Bookmen</u> 19
     (October):10-12.
          Reviews Waugh's current "popularity," arising from serial
     publication of selections from the <u>Diaries</u>, and the contents of
     these selections.  Discusses Waugh's powerful personal presence;
     <u>The Ordeal of Gilbert Pinfold</u> is a "hopelessly inaccurate" portrait.
     Reviews contributions to <u>Evelyn Waugh and His World</u> (1973.A2), and
     <u>To the War with Waugh</u> (1974.A3).

33   _____.  "My Father's Diaries." <u>New Statesman</u> 85 (13 April):
     528-29.
          Commenting on the <u>Observer</u> publication of excerpts from
     Waugh's diaries, Waugh's son argues that the diaries are truthful,
     but give only a partial picture of his father.  Notes the benefits
     of indiscreet diaries.

34   _____.  "Waugh's World." <u>New York Times Magazine</u>, 7 October,
     pp. 20-21, 100-102, 106.
          Publication of excerpts from Waugh's diaries in the <u>Observer</u>
     proves that the author's world did in fact exist.  Comments on ob-
     jections to the publication, and discusses Waugh's class conscious-
     ness and taste for anarchy.


                              <u>1974</u>


A.  BOOKS

1    CAREW, DUDLEY. <u>A Fragment of Friendship:  A Memory of Evelyn
     Waugh When Young</u>.  London:  Everest Books, 96 pp.
          Says that the disastrous book <u>A Little Learning</u> showed that
     Waugh the man was fanatically determined to wipe away the memory
     of the marvellous creature, Waugh the boy.  Gives an entirely dif-
     ferent picture of Waugh at Lancing, quoting passages from a diary
     he himself kept at the time:  he was a perpetual inspiration and
     delight.  Also describes visits to the Waugh home, and the rich
     experience of having Evelyn read him the first fifty pages of
     <u>Decline and Fall</u>, roaring with laughter at his own comic invention.

*2   HANSARD, DAVID BOYD.  "Comic License:  The Art of Evelyn Waugh's
     Early Novels."  Ph.D. dissertation, University of Chicago.

3    St. JOHN, JOHN.  To the War with Waugh.  London:  Leo Cooper
     Ltd., 56 pp.  (Limited ed., London:  Whittington, 1973.)
        An account of Waugh's actual wartime experience from 1939 to
     the retreat from Crete, pointing out the factual basis of situations
     used in Sword of Honour.


B.  SHORTER WRITINGS

1    AMIS, KINGSLEY.  Introduction to Labels:  A Mediterranean
     Journey.  London:  Duckworth, pp. [5-7].
        The lapse of years has shown the sparkling freshness of
     Waugh's writings to be intrinsic, not a matter of their times.
     Commends Waugh's freedom from the Mediterranean mystique, his
     Englishman's suspicion of foreigners, and his honest response to
     the boredom and futility of sightseeing; also commends his beauti-
     ful prose.

2    ANON.  "Biffing."  TLS, 13 September, p. 976.
        Listeners to the radio adaptation of Waugh's Sword of Honour
     have so far been richly rewarded; Hugh Burden's reading as narrator
     provides fresh insights into the whole work, Jane Graham's neat
     production brings out the social niceties, and the characterization
     of Apthorpe is richly authentic.

3    ANON.  "A Farewell to Biffing."  TLS, 1 November, p. 1228.
        Makes judicious comments on the radio adaptation of Sword of
     Honour, commending most of the voices (Guy Crouchback's being an
     exception) and noting that, more than with any other modern novel-
     ist, close attention to Waugh's verbal precision is essential to
     a full appreciation of the text.

4    BELL, ALAN.  "General Cruttwell's Emporium."  Letter in TLS,
     25 October, p. 1197.
        Suggests that the store in which William Boot is fitted out
     for his journey to Ishmaelia in Scoop is not Harrod's or the Army
     and Navy Stores, but Lawn and Alder, "universal providers for
     colonial pioneers."

5    BLAYAC, ALAIN.  "The Evelyn Waugh-Dudley Carew Correspondence
     at the Humanities Research Center, University of Texas, Austin."
     EWN 8 (Autumn):1-6.
        Discusses the friendship began at Lancing, and describes
     the contents of forty-nine letters from Waugh to his friend written
     between 1921 and 1924.

6    _____.  "Evelyn Waugh's Drawings."  Library Chronicle of the
     University of Texas 7 (Spring):42-57.

Describes Waugh's gifts as a cartoonist and designer, at
Lancing and Oxford; evaluates and lists Waugh's 110 drawings, 1913-
1960, held in the Iconography Collection of the University of Texas,
Austin.

7    BROWNING, GORDON. "Silenus' Wheel: Static and Dynamic Charac-
     ters in the Satiric Fiction of Evelyn Waugh." Cithara 14
     (December):13-24.
         Contends that characterization in Waugh's fiction depends
heavily on the views expressed by Otto Silenus towards the end of
Decline and Fall: Waugh's code of survival is not based on conventional moral standards but on the individual's capacity for
finding his place on the wheel of life, for survival in an insane
world. Points out that in Black Mischief this theory applied to
the whole Azanian nation. Claims that Waugh delineates his late
satiric characters in the same way as his earlier ones; he shows
a consistency of technique not previously attributed to him.

8    DAVIS, ROBERT MURRAY. Review of Evelyn Waugh and His World,
     edited by David Pryce-Jones. EWN 9 (Spring):7-9.
         For the expert on Waugh, this collection is both essential
and disappointing: there are four really useful memoirs, but even
the critical essays by two able critics, Malcolm Bradbury and
David Lodge, do not show them to advantage. See 1972.A3.

9    DUER, HARRIET WHITNEY. "Pinfold's Pinfold." EWN 8 (Spring):
     3-4.
         Concludes that one of the meanings of pinfold, "pinner," is
important in The Ordeal of Gilbert Pinfold: the final lines show
Pinfold as pinner, asserting artistic control over events, placing
them within a framework--the book he begins.

10   FIRCHOW, PETER. The Writer's Place: Interviews on the Literary
     Situation in Contemporary Britain. Minneapolis: University of
     Minnesota Press, pp. 348-51.
         In an interview, Angus Wilson explains that the two writers
whom he admired most were Virginia Woolf and Waugh. Discusses
Waugh as a social satirist.

11   GALLAGHER, DONAT S. "Directory Enquiries." SoRA 7, no. 1:
     86-92.
         The Waugh Checklist (1972.A1) can be greeted in the spirit
with which one would greet a telephone directory if one had never
had one before; one finds, however, a considerable number of omissions and errors.

12   GIRAUDOUX, JEAN. Preface to the French edition of Black
     Mischief. Translated by Jeanne Desarmenien. EWN 8 (Spring):
     6-7.
         Marvels at man's giving up two weapons against stupidity and
pride, caricature and satire. Says there is no need to introduce

Waugh to French readers; simply wants to ensure that his characters
enter France with their pockets full of suspect qualities--his
cruelty, his acidity, and his new-found smile.

13    GREENE, DONALD.  "Sir Ralph Brompton--An Identification."  EWN
      8 (Winter):1-2.
           Comments on Waugh's use of real people as models for his
      characters, and says that Nigel Nicolson's Portrait of a Marriage
      confirms his surmise that Sir Harold Nicolson was the inspiration
      for Sir Ralph Brompton in Unconditional Surrender.

14    HEATH, JEFFREY M.  "Apthorpe Placatus?"  Ariel 5 (January):5-22.
           Noting Waugh's use of the double, the comic macabre, and the
      country-house setting, finds from his earliest writings the repeated
      paradigm of a dualism collapsing into a unity.  Describes Men at
      Arms as "a loose theological novel on the Augustinian model."  Dis-
      cusses Waugh's chronic depression and paranoia.

15    _____.  "Vile Bodies:  A Revolution in Film Art."  EWN 8
      (Winter):2-7.
           Part of the fun in Vile Bodies lies in watching Waugh in-
      corporate the resources of the cinema into his fictional technique;
      but the real force is metaphoric.  Vile Bodies is organized around
      a film of the life of John Wesley; Waugh draws an analogy between
      this film-life and the "film-life" of Adam Fenwick-Symes and the
      other Bright Young People.  The real attraction of the novel lies
      in the perfect relationship of its theme--conversion--to its opera-
      tive metaphor--cinematic inversion.  It is a decidedly accomplished
      modern novel.

16    JOHNSON, J.J.  "Counterparts:  the classic and the modern
      'Pervigilium Veneris.'"  EWN 8 (Winter):7-8.
           The central chapter of Decline and Fall, entitled "Pervigilium
      Veneris," is a satirical transformation of the classic truths and
      beauties of the anonymous Latin poem of this name.

17    La FRANCE, MARSTON.  "The Year's Work in Waugh Studies."  EWN
      8 (Spring):1-3.
           Viewing the publication of the diaries as the most important
      event of the year for Waugh scholars, calls the editing no small
      feat, describes some of the gaps as quite startling, and shows
      that the book provoked considerable discussion.  Describes a remi-
      niscence by Waugh's cousin Claude Cockburn as excellent, but David
      Pryce-Jones's Evelyn Waugh and His World (1973.A2) as a mixed,
      somewhat disappointing bag, and John St. John's To the War with
      Waugh (1974.A3) as woefully light.

18    LEVIDOVA, INNA.  "At an Englishman's Home."  Soviet Literature,
      no. 11, pp. 156-58.
           A very sympathetic introduction to Waugh's works, describing
      the scathing Swiftian satire of The Loved One, the heart-rending

bitterness of <u>A Handful of Dust</u>, and best of all the nostalgia of
Charles Ryder in <u>Brideshead</u>. Religion does not give his characters
peace, but provides only a sense of humbleness and obligation; a
sense of home, in the broadest meaning, is highly typical of him.

19  LODGE, DAVID. "Evelyn Waugh." In <u>Six Modern British Novelists</u>,
    edited by George Stade. New York:  Columbia University Press,
    pp. 43-86.
        Reprint of 1971.A4.

20  MECKIER, JEROME. "The Case for the Modern Satirical Novel:
    Huxley, Waugh, and Powell." <u>Studies in the Twentieth Century</u>
    14 (Fall):21-42.
        Contends that the modern satirical novel is a recognizable
    genre.  Giving illustrations from these three novelists, says it
    has six common characteristics:  1) it contains a profound but dis-
    comforting observation of reality; 2) it fashions a symbol embody-
    ing the observation and shaping the novel; 3) it makes the reader
    the ultimate target; 4) it has positive aspects, instead of being
    pure negation; 5) it employs extensive animal imagery; 6) it re-
    gards time as the ultimate weapon, for it provides an ironic, re-
    morseless judgment on the character.

21  NEWBY, ERIC. "The Most Unforgettable Character I Never Met."
    <u>Horizon</u> 16 (Summer):110-11.
        Amusing account of cordial correspondence with Waugh and of
    seeing him four times but being reluctant to meet him.

22  NYE, ROBERT. "Window onto a World that Never Was." <u>Christian
    Science Monitor</u>, 2 January, p. F7.
        Calls David Pryce-Jones's <u>Evelyn Waugh and His World</u> (1973.A2)
    a big, bright, depressing book.  Says that disgust was Waugh's pri-
    mary motivation, and that, like St. Augustine, he felt that the
    human condition is a state of exile from beginning to end.

23  ROSTEN, LEO. "How I Met Evelyn Waugh." <u>SatR</u>, 9 September, p.
    35 (pt. 1); 5 October, p. 39 (pt. 2).
        Describes what happened when the Rostens invited the Waughs
    to tea in London.  Waugh might have stepped out of Trollope; he
    was a pudgy, moon-faced figure in a heavy tweed suit who looked
    like a satanic cherub.  Records an Alice-in-Wonderland type of
    conversation:  when he tried to talk about Waugh's books, Waugh
    kept asking unnerving questions about Rosten's clothes and shoes.

24  SINCLAIR, STEPHEN GERARD. "Moralists and Mystics:  Religion in
    the Modern British Novel." Ph.D. dissertation, University of
    Michigan. [<u>DAI</u> 35:7328A.]
        Says the changing attitudes toward religion of Joyce, Waugh,
    Lawrence, Huxley, and Greene are reflected in their novels, and
    asks how well the novel can withstand the strain of religious dis-
    cussion.  Suggests that the novel cannot exist without realism;

propaganda destroys it.  Concludes that those novelists who are
most confident in their religious beliefs (like Waugh and Greene)
are also most likely to incorporate that religion successfully in
art.

25   THIEME, HANS OTTO.  "Evelyn Waugh:  A Supplementary Checklist
     of Criticism."  EWN 8 (Autumn):6-7.
        Annual checklist of items published since 1971, including
items omitted from preivous lists.

26   THOMAS, DENNIS.  "Making Waugh."  Listener 92 (15 August):215.
        In Jane Graham's production of Sword of Honour, running as
an eleven-part serial, there is plenty to enjoy, even though the
words just miss the feeling of absolute rightness which rises from
the printed page.

27   WALKER, RONALD GARY.  "Blood, Border and Barranca:  The Role of
     Mexico in the Modern English Novel."  Ph.D. dissertation,
     University of Maryland, 409 pp.  [DAI 36:913A.]
        As Catholics, Greene and Waugh saw in the religious persecu-
tion of the Mexican Revolution an ominous portrait of a world
abandoning its faith in favor of political dogma.  Waugh's exposure
to Mexico was meager, and he did not use his Mexican experience in
a novel.  His nonfiction book, Robbery under Law (1939), is little
more than political reportage, with no pretense of objectivity.

28   WILSON, B.W.  "Sword of Honour:  The Last Crusade."  English 23
     (Autumn):87-93.
        The war trilogy shows Waugh overcoming the limitation of his
early novels.  His extensive irony is based on the central metaphor
of the chivalrous crusader, which reflects historical allusion,
literary parody, and wry social comment.


                                 1975


A.  BOOKS

1    LANE, GEORGE WHITNEY.  "The Search for the City:  Conservative
     Political Values in Some of the Novels of Evelyn Waugh."  Ph.D.
     dissertation, Boston University, 214 pp.  [DAI 36:1527A.]
        Describes the portraits of politicians, social climbers, and
social reformers in the early novels, together with the discrepancy
between genuine aristocrats and the manipulators of modern society.
Describes the noblesse oblige motif in A Handful of Dust, and the
inadequacy of an idealism based on admiration of the past; the
sardonic view of left-wing causes of the 1930s and fascination with
the "new men" emerging; power without grace in Brideshead and
Helena; and the taking up of the theme of a serving aristocracy in
Sword of Honour, with the conclusion that the most honorable ideals
will collapse in an amoral world.

2   MACHON, DANIEL JAMES.  "The Failure of the Ironic Mask:  Irony
    as Vision and Technique in the Early Novels of Evelyn Waugh."
    Ph.D. dissertation, Temple University, 174 pp.  [DAI 36:3733A.]
        Says that as his career proceeds, Waugh discovers the inade-
quacy of the ironic mask he has assumed.  Yet the ironic vision
remains; even in Brideshead, Providence is enmeshed in the con-
tingencies of the world, so that there are really no absolutes.
Counters the view of Waugh as an absolutist by going to his non-
fictional works to demonstrate his possession of the basic machin-
ery needed by a modern ironist.

3   PHILLIPS, GENE D.  Evelyn Waugh's Officers, Gentlemen and
    Rogues:  The Fact Behind his Fiction.  Chicago:  Nelson-Hall,
    180 pp.
        Discusses Waugh's transformation of his own experiences into
fiction, his evolving personal vision, and the importance of his
Diaries in illuminating his writing.

4   SYKES, CHRISTOPHER.  Evelyn Waugh:  A Biography.  London:
    Collins, 468 pp.  Reprint.  Harmondsworth and New York:  Penguin,
    1977.
        As authorized biographer, Sykes is able to supplement his own
knowledge of Waugh and his circle of friends with a great deal of
documentary material; in spite of complaints about its omissions
and interpretations, the book contains a wealth of essential information about Waugh and his works.  Has a surprisingly detached
view of Waugh's literary position:  "I am as aware of his glaring
literary errors as I am of his shining virtues, and I have sought
to show both while not pretending to a high position in literary
criticism."

5   TOSSER, Y.  "Le sens de l'absurde dans l'oeuvre d'Evelyn Waugh."
    Ph.D. dissertation, University of Rennes, 423 pp.  [DAI 5:70C.]
        Aims to show that Waugh's portrayal of the Absurd cannot be
explained without reference to the traumas and existential crises
which marked his life.  Studies his social, cultural, and family
background.  Also aims to bring to light structures in his imaginary universe which are connected with his quest for meaning.
Says that a Waugh text speaks at once to our hunger for order and
harmony and the reality of our extravagances and follies.  Revised
for publication:  1977.A3.


B.  SHORTER WRITINGS

1   AMIS, KINGSLEY.  "Waugh's Warts."  Observer (London), 28
    September, p. 24.
        Reviews Sykes' Biography (1975.A4), commenting on Waugh's
unfailing outrageousness, Catholic snobbery, and blend of flaws
and attractiveness.

1a     ANON. "Evelyn Waugh." In Obituaries from the Times, 1961-1970,
       compiled by Frank C. Roberts. Reading: Newspaper Archive
       Developments, pp. 823-24.
            Reprint of 1966.B10.

2      BURNS, TOM. "Waugh, Warts and All." Tablet 229 (4 October):
       942-43.
            Notes difficulties of writing Waugh's biography, such as
       Sykes' friendship with his subject, and Waugh's protean personality.
       Praises Sykes' achievement in conveying Waugh's personal complexity
       and literary importance.

3      CLARK, JOHN R. "Symbolic Violence in Vile Bodies." Studies in
       Contemporary Satire 1, no. 2:17-27.
            Defends Vile Bodies against academic neglect. Examines
       Waugh's blend of reserve and an accelerated pace to create violent
       effects, and the symbolic immolation of Agatha Runcible.

4      CLARKE, GERALD. "Waugh Stories." Time 106 (8 December):58-60.
            Review of Sykes' biography (1975.A4), criticizing the biog-
       rapher's dullness and coyness. Summarizes Waugh's life and work,
       noting his taste for anarchy and blended humor and melancholy.

5      DAVIS, ROBERT MURRAY. "Muddling Through: Sykes on Waugh--A
       Review Essay." SHR 9 (Fall):303-8.
            Evaluates Evelyn Waugh: A Biography (1975.A4) as it partial-
       ly presents Waugh's social and private personalities. Criticizes
       Sykes' literary attitudes, his ignorance and oversights, and his
       sloppiness.

6      _____. "Two Suppositious Letters by Evelyn Waugh." EWN 9
       (Spring):3-5.
            Transcribes two anonymous 1945 letters regarding Marshal
       Tito's regime, and explains why they are likely to have been writ-
       ten by Waugh.

7      DRIBERG, TOM. "Pop for Chaps at White's." New Statesman 90
       (3 October):410-11.
            Praises Sykes' biography (1975.A4) for its veracity. Gives
       anecdotes about Waugh, and comments on his snobbery, religiosity,
       reactionary politics and love of fantasy.

8      FARR, D. PAUL. "The Novelist's Coup: Style as Satiric Norm in
       Scoop." Connecticut Review 8 (April):42-54.
            In spite of Waugh's statement that he regards writing as an
       exercise in the use of language, his prose has never been treated
       to systematic analysis. Scoop is most appropriate for detailed
       examination because it concerns itself with the anatomy of style:
       it displays the norm of good style while satirically exposing the
       vulgarity of the journalese which permeates the modern world.
       Analyzes diction, imagery, and rhetorical devices in the novel.

9   FUSSELL, PAUL.  The Great War and Modern Memory.  New York and
    London:  Oxford University Press, pp. 53-55, 107, 109, 176,
    185-86, 220, 318.
        Lists Waugh among those seeing the two world wars as virtual-
    ly a single historical episode; the irony of Gervase Crouchback's
    death in the First World War prepares us for the ironic treatment
    of his brother Guy in the Second.  Also says that Sword of Honour
    does for the Second World War what Robert Graves did for the First;
    to derive Waugh's trilogy, one would superadd the farce in Good-bye
    to All That to the moral predicament of Ford Madox Ford's Tietjens
    in Parade's End.

10  HANTSCH, INGRID.  Semiotik des Erzählens:  Studien zum
    satirischen Roman des 20. Jahrhunderts.  Munich:  Wilhelm Fink
    Verlag, pp. 49-54, 247-67, 277-306.
        Comparing Waugh to Voltaire and Aldous Huxley, discusses the
    narrative pattern of Decline and Fall ("sequence orientation"), use
    of an ingénu hero, and use of an external view.  Discusses the sa-
    tiric reduction of personality, with or without authorial irony.
    By close technical analysis of the dialogue, illustrates that Waugh
    anticipates Harold Pinter and Eugène Ionesco in conveying grotesque
    and absurd behavior in a dramatic mode, through commonplace speech.
    Waugh depicts wasteland characters typical of their times, remind-
    ing us of Eliot's line, "We had the experience but we missed the
    meaning."

11  HEATH, JEFFREY M.  "Brideshead:  The Critics and the Memorandum."
    ES 56 (June):222-30.
        Discusses hostile reactions to Brideshead and Waugh's response.
    Critics dislike Charles Ryder, identifying him with Waugh; Waugh
    meant to treat him ironically, in his usual satiric manner, but
    over-estimated his audience.  Prints the hitherto unpublished
    "memorandum" from Waugh to potential film producers of the novel,
    in which the focus moves from Ryder to the Flytes.

12  _____.  "Evelyn Waugh:  Afraid of the Shadow."  EWN 9 (Winter):
    1-4.
        The epigraph to A Handful of Dust from The Waste Land, with
    its reference to fear and shadows, is more than a source for a
    title.  It is a comment on Waugh's polemical aim and satiric method:
    by making the reader uneasily aware of shadows, Waugh tries to lead
    him towards conversion.  Quotes a passage which appears only in the
    first edition of Brideshead about abstractions and shadows in sup-
    port.  Says the frightening symbiosis of self and shadow which
    Waugh diagnoses makes A Handful of Dust one of the most unnerving
    books of the century.

13  _____.  "The Year's Work in Waugh Studies."  EWN 9 (Spring):1-3.
        Surveying a "slim but interesting year," quotes a striking
    description of Waugh by Leo Rosten, and calls attention to the im-
    portance of the Waugh-Dudley Carew correspondence at the University
    of Texas (see 1974.B5).

14    HECK, FRANCIS S.  "Brideshead, or Proust and Gide Revisited."
      EWN 9 (Autumn):4-7.
          Notes thematic similarities between Brideshead and Proust's
      À la recherche du temps perdu:  childhood innocence, snobbery, in-
      ability to know another person fully, and the importance of memory.
      Also notes an analogy between the conversion theme in Brideshead
      and Andre Gide's La porte étroite.

15    HOLLIS, CHRISTOPHER.  "Saint and Sinner."  Spectator 235 (4
      October):442-43.
          Reviews Sykes' biography (1975.A4), noting Waugh's faults
      and virtues and his religious attitudes.  Indicates some of the
      biographer's errors.

16    JOHNSON, PAUL.  "The Ordeal of Evelyn Waugh."  Daily Telegraph
      (London), 11 October, p. 10.
          Publication of Sykes' biography (1975.A4) has released a tide
      of anecdotes about Waugh's horrid behavior, reinforced by Sykes
      himself.  Waugh's significance resides in the greatness of his
      literary achievement.  Discusses Waugh's character in relation to
      his fiction.

17    KNIGHTLEY, PHILIP.  The First Casualty:  From the Crimea to
      Vietnam:  The War Correspondent as Hero, Propagandist, and Myth
      Maker.  New York and London:  Harcourt, Brace, Jovanovich, pp.
      171-81, 185-86.
          Says that Scoop was hailed as a brilliant parody of the war
      correspondents' experiences at Abyssinia; as only they could know,
      it was actually a piece of straight reportage, thinly disguised as
      a novel.  Describes Waugh's failure as a correspondent; when he
      sent a long cable predicting the Italian invasion, sending it in
      Latin to keep the story from prying eyes, a puzzled subeditor on
      the Daily Mail was trying to work out the cable when the war started
      and the scoop was lost.

18    KUNKEL, FRANCIS L.  Passion and the Passion:  Sex and Religion
      in Modern Literature.  Philadelphia:  Westminster Press, esp.
      pp. 157-68.
          Includes Waugh in a list of writers who in one place or
      another equate religion with sex; does not give specific examples
      from Waugh.  Calls him a life-defeating writer, ranged on the side
      of death.  Says Mauriac and Waugh confuse love with cannibalism.
      Also includes Waugh among those who agree in theory that super-
      natural love is superior to natural love, but who trim God to fit
      man.

19    La FRANCE, MARSTON.  "Sword of Honour:  The Ironist Placatus."
      DR 55 (Spring):23-53.
          Considering three common views of Waugh--as comedian, snob,
      and Tory satirist--says none fits well.  Analyzes Sword of Honour
      as the struggle of an ironist--one who perceives a double realm of

values and thus feels melancholy and nostalgia--to resolve the
contradictions he perceives. Sees the ironic contrasts of the Paul
Pennyfeather and Basil Seal archetypes being successfully resolved
in Guy Crouchback.

20  LANE, CALVIN W. "Evelyn Waugh's Radio and Television Broadcasts,
    1938-1964." EWN 9 (Autumn):1-4.
        Discusses the eight or more B.B.C. interviews and broadcasts
    Waugh was involved in. Describes in detail a "Frankly Speaking"
    interview in 1953 by three insolent interrogators; the famous John
    Freeman "Face to Face" telecast in 1960; and the last interview
    with Elizabeth Jane Howard in 1964.

21  MARCUS, STEVEN. "Evelyn Waugh and the Art of Entertainment."
    In Representative Essays on Literature and Society. New York:
    Random House, pp. 88-101.
        Reprint of 1956.B9.

22  McDONALD, HORACE THELTON. "Africa as a Fictive World. Seven
    Modern Responses from Joseph Conrad to Graham Greene." Ph.D.
    dissertation, Southwestern Louisiana University, 241 pp. [DAI
    36:7440A.]
        Discusses seven novels, including two by Joyce Cary and two
    by Waugh (Black Mischief and Scoop) as well as one by Conrad and
    two by Greene. The objective world reflected in these seven novels
    parallels physical Africa, but the fictive world is alive with dra-
    matic tensions reflecting the distinct psyche of each author. For
    Waugh, Africa is a metaphysical jungle of chaos and confusion
    threatening established values and the individual.

23  QUINTON, ANTHONY. "A Risky Friendship." Listener 94 (9
    October):483-84.
        Praises Sykes (1975.A4) for his balanced portrait of Waugh
    and for his literary criticism.

24  RATCLIFFE, MICHAEL. "Plain Clothes." Times (London), 2 October,
    p. 9.
        Comments on Waugh's mastery of prose and uncompromising self-
    knowledge, in reviewing Sykes' biography (1975.A4), which he criti-
    cizes for sentimentality and verbosity.

25  REES, JOHN O. "'What Price Dotheboys Hall?' Some Dickens
    Echoes in Waugh." KanQ 7 (Fall):14-18.
        Traces correspondences between Waugh and Dickens, and allu-
    sions in Waugh's fiction to Dickens's writings, to argue for the
    kinship of their imaginations.

26  RODWAY, ALLAN. English Comedy: Its Role and Nature from
    Chaucer to the Present Day. Berkeley: University of California
    Press, pp. 217-18, 243-49, 265.
        Crotchety discussion in which Waugh is called cynical and

amoral; a reactionary anarchist; a person who has no consistent
comic vision but only a set of prejudices; a writer whose work is
really hollow-centered, and beneath whose cool surface beats a
heart of stone. Compares The Loved One to Joseph Heller's Catch-22,
finding the latter bigger and greater.

27    SCHEIDEMAN, J.W. "Miss Vavasour Remembered." EWN 9 (Winter):
      4-8.
      Finds an antecedent for Miss Vavasour in Sword of Honour in
the Vavasor sisters in Trollope's Can You Forgive Her? She could
be a representative forgotten (and easily forgettable) genteel
lady, with chivalrous pretensions as inappropriate as Guy
Crouchback's own.

28    SHRAPNEL, NORMAN. "A Needless Excess." Manchester Guardian
      Weekly, 11 October, p. 26.
      Reviews Sykes' biography (1975.A4), commenting on Waugh's
self-punishment and cruelty to others. Sykes reveals Waugh's theatrical impulse and unquenchable romanticism.

29    SPEAIGHT, ROBERT. "Evelyn Waugh, Who 'Could Do Nothing by
      Halves.'" Catholic Herald, 3 October, p. 6.
      Praises Sykes biography (1975.A4) for its veracity, research
and literary criticism. Discusses Waugh's character and Catholicism.

30    STANSKY, PETER. "Evelyn Waugh." New York Times Book Review,
      30 November, pp. 2-3, 58-59.
      Sykes biography (1975.A4) is important, but disappointing
in its reticence and occasional vagueness. Comments on Waugh's
"nasty" personality and his melancholy, and his literary achievement.

31    THIEME, HANS OTTO. "Evelyn Waugh: A Supplementary Checklist
      of Criticism." EWN 9 (Winter):8-9.
      Annual bibliography of items published since 1973, including
those previously omitted.

32    VOORHEES, RICHARD J. Review of Evelyn Waugh: A Biography, by
      Christopher Sykes and Evelyn Waugh's Officers, Gentlemen, and
      Rogues: The Fact Behind His Fiction, by Gene D. Phillips.
      MFS 22 (Winter):664-66.
      Comments on Waugh's contradictory personality, and the re-
lationship between his life and his writings. See 1975.A3-4.

33    WAUGH, AUBERON. "Stillingfleet's Revenge." Books and Bookmen
      21 (October):7-9.
      In reviewing Sykes biography (1975.A4), Waugh's son comments
on the lifelong misinterpretations of his father's personality.
Lists resources used and ignored by Sykes, and blames him for un-
derestimating Waugh's literary talents and overestimating his

faults. Defends Waugh against charges of cruelty, arrogance and aggressiveness, and explains his love of the certainty and permanence of Catholicism.

34   WAUGH, MARGARET. "Life with Father." Observer (London), 28 September, p. 19.
     "At meal times there were terrible rages, chilling depressions, jolly jokes and tipsy revelry." In a memoir of him introduced by Christopher Sykes, Waugh's favorite daughter declares that she would never have chosen a different father. Reprinted as an appendix to Sykes' Evelyn Waugh:  A Biography (1975.A4), pp. 451-55.

35   WICKER, BRIAN. "Waugh and the Narrator as Dandy." In The Story-Shaped World. London: Athlone Press, pp. 151-68.
     In the face of a descent into barbarism, the only sane attitude to adopt is that of the dandy, a man not interested in conveying a message of salvation or hope but in striking an attitude of defiance and finding a personal style. Waugh's contribution to the literature of dandyism was his creation of the dandyish narrator. When he revealed his own inner agony, as in The Ordeal of Gilbert Pinfold, or found a cause, as in Brideshead and Sword of Honour, he lost his sense of poise and comic autonomy.

36   WILSON, ANGUS. "The Evelyn Waugh Play." TLS, 3 October, pp. 1116-17.
     Reviews Sykes' biography (1975.A4), noting Waugh's capacity for transforming experience into his "own special play," for acting out fiction in his life as well as vice versa. The entertainer became the victim-hero of his novels. Sykes fails to come to grips with Waugh's complexity.


                                   1976

1    ANNAN, NOEL. "The Possessed." New York Review of Books, 5 February, pp. 19-22.
     Reviewing Sykes' biography (1975.A4), finds the keys to Waugh's life in his religion and his artistry. Discusses his personality, his "Augustinian" Catholicism, and the hostility of critics to him. Also reviews Gene D. Phillips's Evelyn Waugh's Officers, Gentlemen and Rogues (1975.A3) noting Waugh's consistent moral emphasis.

2    AUSTIN, RICHARD. "Huge Shipwreck of Esteem." Month, n.s. 9 (October):354-55.
     Diaries usually create an imaginary self; so too with Waugh's Diaries, which reveal an unattractive persona devised to protect his vulnerability and say little of his aesthetic and religious beliefs.

3    AUTY, SUSAN GARIS. "Language and Charm in Brideshead Revisited."
     DQR 6 (Winter):291-303.
         Analyzes the imagery and language of Brideshead to demonstrate
     their contribution to the meaning and effect of the novel and an
     understanding of Charles Ryder. The civilization represented by
     the Marchmain estate is both admired and rejected: its charm is
     destructive. Yet it is Ryder's susceptibility to charm which shows
     him capable of religious fulfilment.

4    BELL, PEARL K. "Boys Will Be Boys." New Leader 59 (5 January):
     14-15.
         Criticizes Sykes' biography (1975.A4) for dullness, irrele-
     vancies, reticence, and snobbery. Criticizes Waugh himself for
     snobbery and religiosity, cruelty and immaturity.

5    BLAYAC, ALAIN. "Evelyn Waugh: A Supplementary Bibliography."
     Book Collector 25 (Spring):53-62.
         A bibliography of Waugh's nonfiction (1929-42), aimed at re-
     vealing the underlying seriousness of his social views. Includes
     some fiction, as well as reviews, articles, and radio broadcasts.

6    CARENS, JAMES F. Review of Evelyn Waugh's Officers, Gentlemen,
     and Rogues, by Gene D. Phillips. EWN 10 (Spring):7-9.
         Calls Phillips's book (1975.A3) a sympathetic account of
     Waugh's fiction in terms of Catholic theology and morality, but
     raises questions about the use of biographical material, especially
     the way in which Waugh transmuted his own experiences into fiction.

7    CAREY, JOHN. "How the Style Refines." New Statesman 92
     (3 September):309-10.
         Reviews Waugh's Diaries, noting his evolution as a major
     novelist and the development of his characteristic style to expose
     the absurdity of existence.

8    CHRISTOPHER, MICHAEL. "Up Against the Waugh." U.S. Catholic
     41 (April):48-51.
         Discusses Sykes' biography (1975.A4) and Waugh's literary
     reputation.

9    DAVIS, ROBERT MURRAY. "Evelyn Waugh's Juvenilia." EWN 10
     (Winter):1-7.
         Though Waugh deprecated his juvenile work, a survey of the
     forty-odd pieces in the Waugh collection at the University of Texas
     shows him experimenting with various genres in interesting ways and
     foreshadowing his mature achievement.
10   _____. "'A Flat in London' and 'By Special Request': Some
     Variant Readings." PBSA 69 (Summer):565-68.
         Revisions of "A Flat in London," the final section of the
     Harper's Bazaar version of A Handful of Dust, for the version en-
     titled "By Special Request" in Mr. Loveday's Little Outing and
     Other Sad Stories, indicate that even in relatively minor work

Waugh tried to make the smallest elements of style and detail exactly convey his meaning.

11    DAVIS, R[OBERT] M[URRAY]. Review of Evelyn Waugh's Officers, Gentlemen, and Rogues, by Gene D. Phillips. JML 5 (supp.), pp. 823-24.
       States that Phillips's book is no more than a pleasant survey with plot summaries of Waugh's life and work; it contains some serious errors and some real howlers. See 1975.A3.

12    DONALDSON, FRANCES. "How Beastly to Know Mr. Waugh?" Sunday Telegraph (London), 5 September, p. 11.
       Calls Waugh's Diaries "the angry jottings of an introvert," much unlike his personal presence.

13    DOOLEY, D.J. "The Dandy and the Satirist." EWN 10 (Winter): 7-10.
       Summarizes Brian Wicker's discussion of Waugh in The Story-Shaped World (1975.B35), in which the excellence of the early novels is viewed as the result of a policy of nonintervention: Waugh is a dandy, interested in the achievement of a personal style, rather than a satirist, measuring failings against a standard. Argues that this is precisely where Sykes went wrong in his biography, seeing Waugh as skimming over surfaces, and that Waugh was writing in the satiric tradition of Pope, with a depth of meaning present all the time.

14    DOYLE, PAUL A. "Some Unpublished Waugh Correspondence." EWN 10 (Spring):5.
       Transcribes two Waugh letters from March, 1931 and 9 January, 1954.

15    DRABBLE, MARGARET. "A Tale of Gloom." Listener 96 (2 September):283-84.
       Unlike his exhilarating novels, Waugh's Diaries are depressing in their record of punitive self-indulgence. Compares them to his fiction.

16    EDWARDS, A.S.G. "A Source for A Handful of Dust." MFS 22 (Summer):242-44.
       Points out several parallels between the novel and Peter Fleming's Brazilian Adventure (1933), which contains an account of a search for a lost English explorer. See 1978.B17 (p. 3) for comment on this by Jeffrey Heath.

17    FORBES, ALISTAIR. "All About Evelyn." TLS, 3 September, pp. 1074-75.
       Reviews Waugh's Diaries, commenting on the author's reputation, and relating details of his life to his writings. Says that the Diaries are mainly a writer's notebook and memoranda.

18    FULLER, EDMUND. "Evelyn Waugh and the Sun Children." <u>Wall</u>
      <u>Street Journal</u>, 2 March, p. 22.
           Reviewing Martin Green's <u>Children of the Sun</u> (1976.B21) to-
      gether with Sykes' biography of Waugh (1975.A4) and Phillips's
      <u>Evelyn Waugh: Officers, Gentlemen, and Rogues</u> (1975.A3), calls
      Green's book a substantial contribution to the cultural and social
      history of Britain between the wars, and Sykes' a fine, detailed
      study of his long-time friend. Ends with discussion of Waugh's
      development as a conservative, with a quotation from him about man
      being an exile on earth and the inequalities of wealth and position
      being inevitable.

19    GALBRAITH, JOHN KENNETH. "An American View." <u>Books and Bookmen</u>
      22 (November):8-9.
           Waugh is a serious diarist in only two respects, his travels
      and the war.

20    GINDIN, JAMES. "Anecdotal Biography." <u>MQR</u> 15 (Fall):460-66.
           More social and political than literary or psychological,
      Sykes' biography (1975.A4) fails to illuminate the author or his
      works. He "mediates" between Waugh and the reader, telling anec-
      dotes but offering little insight or explanation.

21    GREEN, MARTIN. <u>Children of the Sun. A Narrative of "Decadence"</u>
      <u>in England after 1918</u>. New York: Basic Books, passim.
           Describes a twentieth-century dialectic in which dandyism was
      the cultural thesis and Orwellism its antithesis. Waugh was the
      man of greatest intelligence involved in the dandy enterprise, and
      its keenest observer--though it finally led him to blindness and
      fatuity. Says <u>Brideshead</u> reveals in mythic form why he failed as
      an artist: just as Charles Ryder rejected the aesthete Anthony
      Blanche for the aristocrat Sebastian Flyte, so Waugh and his gener-
      ation preferred the playfulness of English aristocrats to the ex-
      perimental dandyism of international aestheticism.

22    GREENE, GRAHAM. "Both Dross and Gold." <u>Books and Bookmen</u> 22
      (October):19-21.
           Criticizes Michael Davie (editor of Waugh's <u>Diaries</u>) for
      sloppy indexing and footnoting, and for failing to edit more rigor-
      ously. Tedious passages bury sections of real significance. The
      <u>Diaries</u>, however, do not assist in explaining Waugh's personality.

23    GERSH, GABRIEL. "A Self-Made Aristocrat." <u>Modern Age</u> 20
      (Spring):222-24.
           Reviews Sykes' biography (1975.A4), noting Waugh's outrageous
      persona, his virtues and vices. Largely derived from Anthony
      Burgess's obituary and his review of <u>A Little Learning</u>.

24    HEATH, JEFFREY M. "Concluding <u>Helena</u>." <u>EWN</u> 10, no. 2 (Autumn):
      4-5.
           Waugh first thought of writing <u>Helena</u> in 1935. In the book's

reworked conclusion, we can see how concerned he is to point up
the conflict between fact and delusion with a measure of subtlety.

25 _____. "The Private Language of Evelyn Waugh." ESC 2 (Fall):
327-38.
Neither a thinker nor a propagandist, Waugh is engaged in the
time-honored pursuit of producing effects; he achieves his most
telling ones through cadences and allusions embedded in a deceptive-
ly simple prose. Shows by numerous examples that Waugh's personal
shorthand and mythology convey values and meaning through what appears to be a prose of complete moral neutrality.

26 _____. "Waugh and the Pinfold Manuscript." JML 5 (April):
331-36.
Describing Waugh's major fictional strategy as the "persona's
quest to escape from the condition of a cartoon," traces manuscript
revisions of The Ordeal of Gilbert Pinfold to show how Waugh ac-
centuates the thematic pattern.

27 _____. "The Year's Work in Waugh Studies." EWN 10 (Spring):
1-4.
The most important event in a busy year was the publication
of Sykes' biography of Waugh; finds the anecdotes the best part,
the critical judgments capricious and feeble. Calls Gene D.
Phillips's Evelyn Waugh: Officers, Gentlemen and Rogues (1975.A3)
a very successful introduction to Waugh's fiction. Discusses other
books and articles more briefly.

28 HOLLIS, CHRISTOPHER. Oxford in the Twenties: Recollections of
Five Friends. London: Heinemann, 72-93, et passim.
Intimate revelations of Waugh at Oxford by a very close
friend, who says that it never occurred to his associates at the
time that Waugh would turn out to be the best-known undergraduate
of his generation.

29 HUGHES, CATHARINE. "Reign of the Esthetes." SatR 3 (7 February):
30-31, 34.
Reviews Martin Green's Children of the Sun (1976.21) and
Sykes' Evelyn Waugh (1975.A4). Comments on Waugh's contradictory
personality and the central importance of his conversion.

30 HYNES, SAMUEL. The Auden Generation: Literature and Politics
in England in the 1930s. London: Bodley Head, pp. 20, 25-26,
57-64, 228.
Waugh is the first English novelist of the time to see his
period as one between wars. In Vile Bodies, he undertakes the
task of defining and explaining the younger generation as a princi-
pal subject. The novel is a surreal or expressionist attempt to
record reality at a time when everything seemed unreal. The term
bogus is a generation's judgment on a world emptied of significance.

31    JOOST, NICHOLAS. "A Handful of Dust: Evelyn Waugh and the
      Novel of Manners." PLL 12 (Spring):177-96.
           Argues that Waugh is not only concerned with manners as vio-
      lence, but also with the traditional novel of manners; his work
      poses the question, "Will the world and its values, which manners
      represent and reflect, withstand the attempt to explode its in-
      tegrity?" Says Waugh is as allusive as Henry James, and cites
      references to Eliot, Proust, Dickens and others to show how he
      builds upon the bare bones of his structure.

*32   KOSOK, HEINZ. "Die Darstellung des Zweiten Weltkrieges im
      Romanwerk von Evelyn Waugh." Literatur in Wissenschaft und
      Unterricht 9 (August):85-99.
           Source: EWH 11 (Winter 1977):9; 1977.B46.

33    LINCK, CHARLES E., Jr. Review of Evelyn Waugh: A Biography,
      by Christopher Sykes. EWN 10 (Spring):6-7.
           Puzzled that Sykes ignored factual data available to him--
      which gives him little ground for mocking American scholarship in
      the way he does. Does have some good things, if we could trust
      them. See 1975.A4.

34    _____. Review of Evelyn Waugh: A Biography, by Christopher
      Sykes. JML 5 (supp.):824-26.
           Sykes (1975.A4) fails to satisfy the scholar's desire to know
      the details of Waugh's life, which were absorbed into his writings.
      He sometimes enlightens, but he provides only a partial portrait.

35    LORD, GEORGE. "Heroic Games: Homer to Waugh." College
      Literature 3:180-202.
           Examines the Sports Day at Llanabba School (Decline and Fall)
      to prove it parodies the games proclaimed by Achilles in the Iliad.

36    MacSWEEN, R.J. "Evaluating Evelyn Waugh." Antigonish Review
      25 (Spring):41-50.
           Reviewing Sykes' biography (1975.A4), says it fails in
      sympathy and enthusiasm. Compares Sykes' treatment of Waugh to
      that of other friends, Frances Donaldson and Dudley Carew. Dis-
      cusses Waugh's satiric weapons, "the glare and the dead pan,"
      which antagonized his critics, and evaluates his achievement.

37    MANNING, GERALD F. "The Weight of Singularity: Meaning and
      Structure in Put Out More Flags." ESC 2 (Summer):225-34.
           Waugh's sixth novel is important not only because of its
      transitional place in the author's development and its picture of
      England at the start of the war; it is a novel with great tonal
      subtlety and thematic complexity. Basil Seal and Ambrose Silk,
      though polar opposites, are strikingly linked by their singularity.
      The tone progressively deepens; the novel chronicles a transition
      to a new kind of sobriety and realism--to which Basil can adapt
      himself, but not Ambrose.

38   McCABE, BERNARD. "An Ungentle Gentleman." <u>Commonweal</u> 103
     (16 January):52-54.
        Reviews Sykes' biography (1975.A4), commenting on Waugh's
     rancorous and vindictive personality, which contrasts with the
     youthful image of him as a prancing faun. Discusses his contrast-
     ing Apollonian and Dionysian elements, which carry over into his
     fiction.

39   MEYERS, JEFFREY. Review of <u>Evelyn Waugh:  A Biography</u>, by
     Christopher Sykes. <u>ELN</u> 13 (June):313-17.
        Calls Sykes' work (1975.A4) unsatisfactory because of its
     discursive, anecdotal, reticent form. But Sykes has genuine af-
     fection for his loathsome subject.

40   MITTLEMAN, LESLIE B. Review of <u>Evelyn Waugh:  A Biography</u>, by
     Christopher Sykes. <u>Books Abroad</u> 50 (Summer):664-65.
        Sykes fails to integrate Waugh's various personalities into
     a portrait of the artist, and so his biography is disappointing.
     See 1975.A4.

41   MOORE, HARRY T. Review of <u>Evelyn Waugh:  A Biography</u>, by
     Christopher Sykes. <u>New Republic</u> 174 (17 January):38-40.
        Calls Sykes' biography (1975.A4) clumsy but informative, and
     comments on the upsurge of interest in Waugh.

42   MOULIN, ANDRÉ. Review of <u>Pikareske Thematik im Romanwerk Evelyn
     Waughs</u>, by Kurt O. Wyss. <u>ES</u> 57 (February):87-89.
        Agrees with Wyss that the picaresque tradition, as adapted
     and transformed by Nashe, Defoe, Fielding, and Smollett, does pro-
     vide an explanation for some aspects of Waugh's work. Agrees as
     well that Waugh, unlike Fielding, does not offer wry or ironic
     comments, but contends that he has less obtrusive ways of communi-
     cating attitudes to his readers.

43   MUGGERIDGE, MALCOLM. "Ordeal of Evelyn Waugh." <u>Observer</u>
     (London), 5 September, p. 24.
        Calls Waugh's <u>Diaries</u> strangely uninformative and inaccurate,
     and preoccupied with Waugh's fantasy self. There are no diary
     entries for the crucial times in his life--Oxford, the end of his
     first marriage, and his conversion. But says he was so much a man
     of our times, in his virtues and defects, that the <u>Diaries</u> are
     likely to go on being thumbed for years.

44   NYE, ROBERT. Review of <u>The Diaries of Evelyn Waugh</u>. <u>Scotsman</u>
     (Edinburgh), 4 September, weekend supp., p. 5.
        Says that all through this volume, the gay drunk and desper-
     ate addict does a dance of death with Waugh the immortal soul;
     Waugh emerges as a very torn and tortured human being. The only
     real coherence emerges in the major novels, where he turns his
     divisions into laughter. Those divisions are sufficiently the
     problems of the rest of us to make it likely that his work will
     live.

45   POWELL, ANTHONY. <u>Infants of the Spring</u>. Vol. 1, <u>To Keep the</u>
     <u>Ball Rolling:  The Memoirs of Anthony Powell</u>. London:
     Heinemann, pp. 154-68, et passim.
         Anecdotes of Waugh at Oxford, describing his unpredictable
     moods, his extraordinary powers of improvising antics when not
     suffering from melancholy, and his drawing for the <u>Cherwell</u>.  Says
     that so far as <u>Brideshead</u> presents a naturalistic picture of the
     University, it is closer to the time when Waugh used to return to
     Oxford to see old friends than to his days as a student.

46   PRITCHETT, V.S.  "Books:  Evelyn Waugh."  <u>NY</u> 53 (16 January):
     89-93.
         Reviews Waugh's <u>Diaries</u>, connecting the author's experience
     with the fictional world he created.  Says Waugh's puzzling persona
     is demonstrated but not explained.  His snobbery was romantic in
     origin, though it hardened into reactionary dogma.

47   QUENNELL, PETER.  "The Diary to End All Diaries."  <u>Punch</u> 271
     (15 September):442-43.
         Criticizes the length of Waugh's <u>Diaries</u>, for they are not
     entertaining, introspective, or reflective.  Little is learned of
     Waugh's literary methods and struggles.

48   _____.  <u>The Marble Foot:  An Autobiography, 1905-1938</u>.  London:
     Collins, pp. 97-98, 116-25.
         Reminiscences of Waugh, especially at Oxford.  Describes him
     as a protean character, with a lively wit and a sharp tongue and
     startlingly original opinions, but also with a pensive romanticism.

49   RAPHAEL, FREDERIC.  "Portrait of the Artist as a Bad Man."
     <u>Sunday Times</u> (London), 5 September, p. 27.
         Waugh lacks literary prestige because of his greatest talent:
     humor.  His divided personality becomes apparent in the <u>Diaries</u>.
     His "awfulness" is transformed only by his art.

50   RATCLIFFE, MICHAEL.  "Hoping for Trouble."  <u>Times</u> (London),
     2 September, p. 6.
         Waugh's <u>Diaries</u> reveal his consistent, angry seriousness,
     his blend of pity and disgust.  The life described in them is
     clearly linked to Waugh's imaginative art; this makes them invalu-
     able and entertaining.

51   RICKS, CHRISTOPHER.  Review of <u>Evelyn Waugh:  A Biography</u>, by
     Christopher Sykes.  <u>Critic</u> 34 (Spring):70-72.
         Praises Sykes' biography (1975.A4) for its affectionate dig-
     nity in dealing with Waugh's complex personality.  Complains, how-
     ever, that Sykes does not face the central question of "What was
     wrong with Waugh?"

52   RILEY, JOHN J.  "Gentleman at Arms:  The Generative Process of
     Evelyn Waugh and Anthony Powell before World War II."  <u>MFS</u> 22

(Summer):165-81.
Contends that the generative artistic processes of the two
authors were similar, and that a competitive tension existed between them. Both were influenced by Ronald Firbank, both use telephone dialogue, and the artist manqué in Afternoon Men, Raymond
Pringle, seems to be a disguised literary assault on Waugh and Vile
Bodies.

53   RYAN, JOAN. "New Waugh-Betjeman Correspondence." EWN 10
     (Spring):5.
     Describes the expansion of the Waugh-Betjeman correspondence
at the University of Victoria; seven letters and ten postcards
(1940-1966) have been added.

54   SISSMAN, L.E. "Books: The Oddest of Men." NY 5 (9 February):
     106-8.
     Reviews Sykes' biography (1975.A4), noting Waugh's life-long
arrogance and eccentricity, and observing that his reputation as
ogre was well earned.

55   STANNARD, MARTIN. "No Admittance on Business." Essays in
     Criticism 26 (April):182-88.
     Sykes' biography (1975.A4) deals tactfully with an oblique
and obstructive personality, but suffers from factual error and
reticence. Suggests Waugh was unbalanced all his life in his assumption of public roles. Analyzes his life and his aesthetic and
political views.

56   STINSON, JOHN J. "Waugh and Anthony Burgess: Some Notes Toward
     an Assessment of Influence and Affinities." EWN 10 (Winter):
     11-12.
     Though Burgess is much more interested than Waugh was in ex-
ploring the limits of the novel form, there are essential similarities between the two in attitude and outlook; certain Burgess novels have close affinities to Waugh's; and many parallels of style,
incident, and theme can be found between other Burgess and Waugh
novels.

57   TANNER, RALPH (interviewed by Peter Buckman). "I Was Evelyn
     Waugh's Batman." Punch 271 (November):960-61.
     Denies rumors of Waugh's unpopularity in the army, his
drunkenness, and his rudeness. Says that Guy Crouchback is a
fairly accurate portrait of Waugh during the war.

58   THIEME, HANS OTTO. "Evelyn Waugh: A Supplementary Checklist
     of Criticism." EWN 10 (Winter):12-13.
     A continuation of earlier checklists, including chiefly
items published since 1974.

59   TOMALIN, CLAIRE. "Waugh to the Roots." Evening Standard
     (London), 7 September, p. 17.

Notes that Waugh's Diaries provide a mass of routine details over a forty-year span. Further anecdotes about Waugh by David Malbert appeared 9 September, p. 17.

60   Van ZELLER, DOM HUBERT. "The Agreeable Mr. Waugh." Critic 35
      (Fall):36-41.
         Reminiscences of Waugh, noting his wit, kindness, charm, and sensitivity to reviews of his books; anecdotes revealing his response to contemporary writers. Defends Waugh against charges of drunkenness and irascibility.
         Letters from readers attacking Waugh led to further defense of his religious sincerity and personal integrity in "More Waugh" (Spring 1977), p. 12.

61   VOGEL, JOSEPH F. "Waugh's The Loved One:  The Artist in a
      Phony World." EWN 10, no. 2 (Autumn):1-4.
         The Loved One is often criticized for superficial satire and a weak structure, but the criticism misses the mark.  The book is about attractive illusions masquerading as truth, and Dennis Barlow is an absolute realist:  the artist is confronted by illusions others accept, but must penetrate through them rather than let them cloud his vision of truth.

61a  VOORHEES, RICHARD J.  Review of Evelyn Waugh:  A Biography, by
      Christopher Sykes and Evelyn Waugh's Officers, Gentlemen, and
      Rogues, by Gene D. Phillips. MFS 22 (Winter):64-66.
         Though Waugh was marvellously inventive, palpable fact and direct experience were more often than not the stimuli of his invention.  Therefore a full-length biography and a study of the connections between his life and work ought to be of interest. Sykes' biography (1975.A4) is by no means a monument raised by uncritical piety.  Phillips's book (1975.A3) will not alter anyone's judgment of Waugh as a novelist but clearly demonstrates the inconsistencies in his character.

62   WALKER, KEITH. "Waugh Belittled." New Society 37 (2 September):
      510.
         The editor of Waugh's diaries implicitly belittles him; many names are not explained.  Finds the Lancing diaries the most interesting; otherwise there is little that is unfamiliar.

63   WAUGH, AUBERON. "Entries and Exits." Spectator 237 (4
      September):13-14.
         While criticizing Sykes' biography (1975.A4), reviews Waugh's Diaries, giving information about their editor, Michael Davie, and recounting the history of their publication. Says they obscure Waugh's life as a family man.

64   WHITTINGTON-EGAN, RICHARD. "Evelyn Waugh's Diaries."
      Contemporary Review 229 (December):372-73.
         Says Waugh's position in English letters seems secure, but

questions whether the diaries were worth publishing in extenso.
Their chief interest is in the unvarnished self-portrait of a very
unhappy man, whose judgments of people were often grotesque.

65   WICKLOW, Earl of (WILLIAM CECIL JAMES HOWARD). "A Man Possessed."
        Month, n.s. 9 (February):68-69.
             Praises Sykes' biography (1975.A4) for its realistic and at
        times merciless treatment of Waugh.

66   WIMSATT, MARGARET. Reviews of Evelyn Waugh: A Biography, by
        Christopher Sykes and Evelyn Waugh's Officers, Gentlemen, and
        Rogues, by Gene D. Phillips. America 134 (7 February):101-2.
             Both Sykes and Phillips try to relate Waugh's novels to the
        facts of his life; both emphasize his eccentricity and egocentrici-
        ty. Sykes' book commits many sins of omission and commission. See
        1975.A3-4.

67   WOODRUFF, DOUGLAS. "DW loquitur." Tablet 230 (5 June):552-53.
             Contains an account of Waugh's controversy with the editor
        of the Tablet, Earnest Oldmeadow, over Black Mischief, and of a
        change in the proprietorship and editorship of the paper as a re-
        sult.

68   ____. "A Handful of Dust." Tablet 230 (18 September):905-6.
             Reviews Waugh's Diaries as highly relevant to his fiction.
        Comments on his distress at liturgical change within the Chruch.

69   WYKES, DAVID. Review of Evelyn Waugh: A Biography, by
        Christopher Sykes. DQR 6 (Autumn):334-41.
             Waugh's official biographer had to decide how much silence
        was necessary. Sykes omits crucial periods in Waugh's life, but
        deals well with his political and religious views, and with his
        streak of cruelty. His literary criticism is unhelpful. See
        1975.A4.

1977

A.  BOOKS

1   DARMAN, KATHLEEN EMMET. "Evelyn Waugh: Problems of Dandyism."
        Ph.D. dissertation, Tufts University, 221 pp. [DAI 39:7354A.]
             Considers that Waugh's imaginative strengths and literary
        strategies are misunderstood by those who describe him as a satir-
        ist preoccupied with the wasteland or a novelist concerned with
        religious matters. When too much stress is put on his moral seri-
        ousness, his comic techniques are misrepresented; his fragmentary,
        preposterous plots are read as dark visions; and his deliberately
        flat characters are seen as savage caricatures. Repudiating the
        moral realism of nineteenth-century fiction, he embraced the

dandyism of the 1920s, though moral seriousness kept creeping in. Serious Waugh is never as effective as comic, divided Waugh.

2   LYNCH, RICHARD PAUL.  "Parody as Structure and Motif in the Novels of Evelyn Waugh."  Ph.D. dissertation, Southern Illinois University at Carbondale, 206 pp.  [DAI 38:807-8A.]
     Says the shape of Waugh's novels and the recurring motifs in them were determined largely by parody of the romance form.  Such parody reflected his basic conflict:  romantic nostalgia for Victorian and Edwardian ideals mingled with a postwar rebellion against them.  It also enabled him to reject Victorian conventions of realism without accepting modern alternatives, such as internal monologue.  In the later novels, there is a straightforward presentation of ideas formerly conveyed implicitly through parody--with loss of subtlety and effectiveness.

3   TOSSER, YVON.  Le sens de l'absurde dans l'oeuvre d'Evelyn Waugh.  Lille:  Atelier Université de Lille; Paris:  Champion, 423 pp.
     Revision of 1975.A5.

B.  SHORTER WRITINGS

1   ATKINS, JOHN.  Six Novelists Look at Society:  An Enquiry into the Social Views of Elizabeth Bowen, L.P. Hartley, Rosamond Lehmann, Christopher Isherwood, Nancy Mitford, C.P. Snow.  London:  John Calder, passim.
     Makes frequent references to Waugh, using his standards of craftsmanship and social attitudes as measuring sticks or poles, especially in a chapter on Nancy Mitford and in the chapter "Democracy and Inequality."

2   BARNARD, ROBERT.  Review of Evelyn Waugh:  A Biography, by Christopher Sykes.  ES 58 (April):172-74.
     Reviews Sykes' biography (1975.A4) and evaluates Waugh's literary status.  Says the biography lacks shape and focus, though it contains a wealth of information, anecdote, and character sketches.  Sykes underestimates Waugh's consistent self-dramatization.

3   BARRETTE, CRAIG RICHARD.  "Three Modern Novelists as Biographers:  E.M. Forster, Virginia Woolf, and Evelyn Waugh."  Ph.D. dissertation, Southern Illinois University at Carbondale, 146 pp.
     Says Waugh's lack of interest in depicting the inner man prevented him from using many fictional devices.  Calls Edmund Campion his most successful biography, but has major criticisms of Rossetti and Ronald Knox.  Concludes that all three of these novelists are more cautious in use of fictional techniques in biography than professional biographers are.

4    BELL, ALAN. "A Life Recorded." <u>SR</u> 85 (Spring):xxvi, xxviii,
     xl.
          Reviewing Waugh's <u>Diaries</u>, notes that the <u>Observer</u> had pub-
     lished excerpts in 1973, Sykes had used them for his biography,
     and extracts from the full diaries had appeared in the <u>Sunday Times</u>.
     Little remained to be extracted, except for a richer portrait of
     Waugh.

5    BLAYAC, ALAIN. Review of <u>Le sens de l'absurde dans l'oeuvre</u>
     <u>d'Evelyn Waugh</u>, by Yvon Tosser. <u>EWN</u> 11 (Spring):9-10.
          Reviews a thesis which attempts to find in Waugh's private
     life the sources of the absurd in his fiction, and to uncover the
     structures of his imaginary universe and recapture the personality
     behind them. Questions the focus on the absurd as the central ele-
     ment of Waugh's philosophy, but says this comprehensive study probes
     unexplored areas and contains some distinguished criticism. See
     1977.A3.

6    BURGESS, ANTHONY. "Occasional Waugh." <u>Observer</u> (London), 18
     December, p. 24.
          Reviews <u>A Little Order</u>, noting Waugh's literary and religious
     attitudes, and his confusion of aesthetics with theology. Re-
     printed: 1978.B6.

6a   BURNETT, HUGH. "Face to Face with Waugh." <u>Listener</u> 98
     (11 August):174.
          Recalls John Freeman's interview with Waugh (1960.18), and
     his own association with Waugh. Comments on the omission of Waugh's
     remarks on J.B. Priestley at the end of the interview.

7    CLEMONS, WALTER. "The Misanthrope." <u>Newsweek</u> 90 (31 October):
     102, 105.
          Waugh's <u>Diaries</u> contain long stretches of tedium between the
     interesting parts, but his formation of a chill comic prose can
     clearly be traced.

8    DAVIS, R[OBERT] M[URRAY]. "Muddling Through:  Sykes on Waugh--
     A Review Essay." <u>SHR</u> 11 (Summer):303-8.
          Sykes' biography of Waugh (1975.A4) will not satisfy the
     general reader, the devotee, or the scholar; if Waugh emerges as
     an interesting figure, it is because of his inherent power rather
     than Sykes' art. He fails to give a coherent picture of Waugh as
     man or artist, he is too reticent, and he is incredibly ignorant
     of important evidence, especially American scholarship on Waugh.
     He missed many good things by not visiting the Humanities Center
     at Texas.

9    DAVIS, ROBERT MURRAY. "Shaping a World:  The Textual History
     of <u>Love Among the Ruins</u>." <u>Analytical and Enumerative</u>
     <u>Bibliography</u> 1 (Spring):137-54.
          Traces the stages through which this brief work went before

Waugh was satisfied with it; it took him three years to complete
it. Calls it "not one of Waugh's best," but "one of his most
polished" works.

10      _____. "Title, Theme and Structure in Vile Bodies." SHR 11
        (Winter):21-27.
        Argues that Vile Bodies is more than just a social satire;
Waugh saw the novel's events in a Christian perspective, and the
book is about a world where grace is being ignored or refused.
Suggests the structure can be seen in liturgical terms--pre-Advent,
Advent, and Christmas--and that the action of the novel is a traves-
ty of what ought to occur at those times.

11      _____. "Vile Bodies in Typescript." EWN 11 (Winter):7-8.
        Describes an incomplete manuscript of Vile Bodies at the
University of Texas, and variations between it and the first
edition.

12      DENNIS, NIGEL. "Fabricated Man." New York Review of Books,
        8 December, pp. 3, 4, 6.
        Relates Waugh's Diaries to his fictional creations. What he
chose to suppress does much to explain what he expressed:  a fabricated man, created to protect his vulnerability. Yet the diaries
fall short only of the very greatest, and present a period picture
which no other diaries have yet given us.

13      DOYLE, PAUL A. Review of A Fragment of Friendship, by Dudley
        Carew. EWN 11 (Spring):10.
        Comments that Carew's brief monograph (1974.A1) is written
to correct Waugh's gloomy impressions of his Lancing years, and
also demonstrates that Waugh was much more friendly with Carew than
he later remembered.

14      GALBRAITH, JOHN KENNETH. ". . . and Great Comic Novels."
        Washington Post Book World, 20 November, pp. E1, E6.
        Praises Waugh's honesty and skills as a novelist describing
his compulsion to adopt socially unacceptable attitudes. Waugh
was against everything, and for nothing. Reprinted in Manchester
Guardian Weekly, 4 December, p. 18.

15      GALLAGHER, DONAT. "Chris, A Distant Relative of Bill Sikes?"
        EWN 11 (Autumn):1-4.
        Shorter version of a commentary on Sykes' biography (1975.A4)
that appeared in an Australian journal, Quadrant. Indicates major
reservations about Sykes' aim and scope, method of narration, and
accuracy. Waugh's life offers near-insuperable problems of understanding and exploration, which this biographer certainly could not
handle.

16      _____. "Early Waugh Fare." SoRA 10 (March):92-97.
        Reviewing new editions of Rossetti and Labels, says both

books still make interesting reading and do much to illuminate Waugh's novels, which extreme economy and allusive technique often render less clear than they seem. Describing the composition and publication of Rossetti, calls attention to Waugh's striking ability to translate visual impressions into words. Calls Labels his most successful travel book, precisely because it gives widest scope to his disparate talents.

17   GREEN, MARTIN. "Of Drinks and Drunkenness." SatR 5 (11 December):26.
      Essentially private documents, Waugh's Diaries are at times a writer's notebook, making public his narrowly defined inner self. Most interesting of all is his process of self-stylization.

18   ____. Transatlantic Patterns:  Cultural Comparisons of England with America. New York:  Basic Books, esp. pp. 37-100, 149-63.
      Just as Lawrence led the erotic movement towards naiveté, Waugh superseded Twain and led humor toward sophistication and dandyism. Since the sixties, his style of humor has held sway; yet it is directed against the major faiths of our life. It is ironic, defensive, antimodern, antifuture; it loves the past and the defeated, and it shows life as subordinate to death. Though his humor really develops out of Shaw, Waugh is one of the most brilliant artists of this century in any language. He is a major artist when he delights in the people and events he is presenting --not, therefore, in A Handful of Dust, Brideshead, and the war trilogy, which are dull and obsessive. He delights in satire with no moral touchstone.

19   GREENE, DONALD. "Who was Father Rothschild?" EWN 11 (Autumn): 7-9.
      Questions the flat assertion in EWN 11 (Spring):10 that Father Rothschild was based on Father Martin D'Arcy, and suggests a literary antecedent--Father Holt in Thackeray's Henry Esmond.

20   HEATH, JEFFREY [M.]. "Waugh's Scoop in Manuscript." EWN 11 (Autumn):9-11.
      States that the most significant variation between the manu-script of Scoop and the Chapman and Hall first edition occurs at the end; shows why the changes represent an improvement. Comments on other revisions, and suggests there are similarities between Scoop and A Handful of Dust.

21   HEATH, JEFFREY M. "The Year's Work in Waugh Studies." EWN 11 (Spring):4-8.
      Discussion of the Diaries, which he finds inadequately edited, leads to perceptive questioning of the relation between these ex-traordinary diaries and Waugh himself. Says Martin Green in Children of the Sun (1976.21) misunderstands his subject in a stimulating way. Survey of a number of important articles, includ-ing, surprisingly, the first extended stylistic analysis of a Waugh novel, D. Paul Farr's on Scoop (1975.B8).

22    HEWISON, ROBERT. <u>Under Siege: Literary Life in London 1939–1945</u>. London: Weidenfeld & Nicolson, 217 pp.
         Provides useful social and historical background for this period of Waugh's life and writing. Refers briefly to his war novels.

23    HIGHAM, T.M. "Captain Grimes's Revenge." <u>London Magazine</u> 17 (April–May):65–73.
         Says that the man who served as the model for Grimes in <u>Decline and Fall</u> wrote a detective novel in 1934; argues that both novels are set in the same school and that the later one contains a portrait of Waugh as schoolmaster.

24    HUNTER, JEANNE CLAYTON. "The Character of Language in <u>Decline and Fall</u>." <u>EWN</u> 11 (Spring):8–9.
         Waugh deliberately uses language as a tool of separation in his first novel, and therefore social relations are abortive and verbal intercourse sterile.

25    HUTTON-BROWN, CHARLES. "Sebastian as Saint: The Hagiographical Sources of Sebastian Flyte." <u>EWN</u> 11 (Winter):1–7.
         Notes that each member of the Flyte family is accorded a precise role in <u>Brideshead</u>, in contributing to Waugh's theme of the power of faith. Taking a hint from the name of Sebastian's teddy bear, suggests there are many parallels between the life of Sebastian and that of St. Aloysius of Gonzaga.

26    HYNES, SAMUEL. "Evelyn Waugh's Sad Mean Life . . ." <u>Manchester Guardian Weekly</u>, 4 December, p. 18.
         Neither comic nor witty, Waugh's <u>Diaries</u> provide few clues to his writing; they do reveal why he was not a greater writer. The final impression is one of misery. Reprinted in <u>Washington Post Book World</u>, 20 November 1977, pp. E1, E6.

27    KERMODE, FRANK. "Writer's World." <u>New York Times Book Review</u>, 16 October, pp. 1, 49.
         Waugh's <u>Diaries</u> require more vigorous editing to avoid repetition and tedium. They illustrate the interaction of his peculiar genius with upper-class Bohemia, and provide the blueprints for his self-created fictional world. It now seems obvious that he was one of the three or four best novelists of his generation.

28    LASSETER, VICTOR. "Anglo-American Confidence Men: the Theme of Fraud in <u>The Loved One</u>." <u>Studies in Contemporary Satire</u> 4, no. 2:14–20.
         Discusses Waugh's satire on the fraudulent values of modern culture in this novel, which shows how society prefers varieties of "the con artist" to truth in cultural, religious, and aesthetic matters.

29    LENTFOEHR, SISTER THÉRÈSE. "My Meeting with Evelyn Waugh."

EWN 11 (Spring):1-4.
Describes a meeting with Waugh in Milwaukee in 1949 during which he was surprisingly gracious and amusing. Records remarks about Thomas Merton, Ronald Knox, and Graham Greene, and includes two letters she later received from Waugh.

30   LEVIN, BERNARD. "Gilbert Pinfold sees it through." Sunday Times (London), 18 September, p. 35.
Michael Hordern gives a magnificent performance as the haunted hero of The Ordeal of Gilbert Pinfold; the stage version is strong, spare and lucid.

31   LODGE, DAVID. The Modes of Modern Writing: Metaphor, Metonymy, and the Typology of Modern Literature. London: Edward Arnold, pp. 50, 210-12, 270.
Calls Waugh a conservative anarchist, and so more sympathetic than his left-wing contemporaries to the despair of secular progress underlying much modern writing. But Waugh renounced the modernists' subjectivity--especially the limited point of view and stream-of-consciousness. He renders the collapse of value dramatically through conversational nuances and ironic juxtapositions, but remains objective--morally, emotionally, and stylistically. In the 1930s, when compassion, moral indignation and democratic sentiment were at a premium, he was an isolated figure. Gives a brief survey of his fiction, noting his changes in style and technique: the abandonment of detachment, and eventual return to a modified form of his earlier technique.

32   MacKINNON, A.A. "Evelyn Waugh: Public and Private." QQ 84 (Autumn):476-81.
Reviews both Waugh's Diaries and Sykes' biography (1975.A4), noting the links between the author's life and fiction. These two books support the claim that Waugh was his own best character creation.

33   MALLOWAN, MAX. Mallowan's Memoirs. London: Collins, pp. 19-20.
Brief reference to Waugh by a distinguished archaeologist who was in the same house as Waugh at Lancing. Says Waugh was popular because he was amusing and always ready to lead others into mischief; but he had a way of escaping the consequences himself. He was witty and courageous, but cruel; he cared nothing about humiliating his companions as long as he could expose them to ridicule.

34   MATTHEWS, PETER. "Waugh-fare." America 137 (10 December): 424-25.
Despite his wit and literary talent, Waugh appears in his diaries as a thoroughly disagreeable man.

35   MAYER, DAVID. "The Ordeal of Gilbert Pinfold." Plays and Players 25 (November):25.
In the dramatic version of Waugh's novel, Michael Hordern

gives a lustrous performance which both amuses and terrifies. For
all the virtuosity, however, Pinfold fails as a play:  something
is missing.  Ronald Harwood cannot be blamed for his adaptation;
Waugh himself is the culprit, since the real characters of the
novel are as shadowy as hallucinations.  Pinfold alone holds our
interest, and that in steadily diminishing quantities.

36  MECKIER, JEROME.  "Evelyn Waugh."  ConL 18 (Winter):98-109.
        A cantankerous man and a brilliant writer, Waugh was an un-
usual modernist, a rational and Apollonian man in an increasingly
Dionysian and irrational world.  Sykes' biography (1975.A4) gives
no overview; in fact it misunderstands and misinterprets him.

37  MOSLEY, DIANA.  A Life of Contrasts.  London:  Hamish Hamilton,
        pp. 75-79, 196, 214-15, 226.
        Reminiscences by a friend to whom Waugh dedicated two books.
Says there was no hint of painful depression even after the break-
up of his first marriage; with him it was impossible to be dull for
a moment.

38  MYERS, WILLIAM.  "Potential Recruits:  Evelyn Waugh and the
        Reader of 'Black Mischief.'"  RMS 21 (Special number):40-51.
        Waugh's first two novels disconcert and delight, without pro-
viding real basis for judgment; Black Mischief remains comic, but
gives intimations of a serious concern with issues, especially that
of barbarism versus civilization.  The novel's triumph is that it
refuses to be didactic; Waugh shows himself capable of being in
the midst of flagrant contradictions without reaching inelegantly
toward ways of resolving them.  His art was fueled by contradiction.
What Catholicism gave him was the assurance that such contradictions
were not freakish but built into the order of things.  Revised:
1978.B26.

39  NARDIN, JANE.  "The Myth of Decline in A Handful of Dust."  MQ
        18 (Winter):119-30.
        Argues that the myth of decline as formulated by David Lodge
and others does not explain this novel:  the characters, not the
author, believe that the past was better than the present.  Tony
Last's journey into the past does not suggest decline, but the essential similarity between past and present.  Waugh undermines
Tony's belief that the orderly Victorian Age was a satisfying time
to live.

40  PRINGLE, JOHN DOUGLAS.  "Vile Bodies."  Quadrant 21 (February):
        74-75.
        Waugh's Diaries give little new information about the author;
they do not record crucial events in his life.  Analyzes Waugh's
personality, his boredom and melancholy.

41  PRITCHARD, WILLIAM H.  Seeing Through Everything:  English
        Writers 1918-1940.  New York:  Oxford University Press,
        pp. 178-91.

In a chapter on satire and fiction in the 1930s, compares Waugh to Huxley, Wyndham Lewis, and others. Says his early novels make gestures towards a real world, but humor and fantasy change them into extravagant art; the author's virtuoso performance nearly obliterates their "real world" truth. A Handful of Dust showed him going beyond this, though as in The Waste Land, the novel possesses tensions which are not resolved, and the term satire no longer strictly applies.

42   RABAN, JONATHAN. "Misericords." New Statesman 94 (23 December): 902-4.
       Reviews A Little Order, commenting on Waugh's journalistic skill, and his clarity and certitude even in his novels. Notes the difficulty of interpreting his "outrageous" statements. His comedy fuses knockabout farce with theological ice; Catholicism provided him with a line of cold and sometimes preposterous logic.

43   SAVAGE, D.S. "Death and Evelyn Waugh." Critical Review, no. 19, pp. 88-105.
       The difficulty in coming to critical terms with Waugh's fiction arises from his uncertainty in the realm of feeling: he either writes heartless comedy or allows only negative or sentimental feelings to appear. Bondage to childhood mars his serious fiction; his Catholicism is linked to immaturity and snobbery; his innocence is impervious. Discusses the death-wish theme in him.

44   SHELENY, HARVEY. "Some Aspects of Brideshead Revisited: A Comparison with Henry James' The American." EWN 11 (Autumn): 4-7.
       Finds many parallels between the two novels, especially in the situations of Mme. de Cintré and Julia.

45   SHEPPARD, R.Z. "An Establishment of One." Time 110 (17 October):83-84.
       Distinguishes between Waugh's reputation as man and as artist, commenting that Catholicism provided the framework for his deep pessimism. Reviews the Diaries, as offering a portrait of his unfavorable qualities.

46   THIEME, HANS OTTO. "Evelyn Waugh: A Supplementary Checklist of Criticism." EWN 11 (Winter):8-9.
       Annual checklist of items published since 1975, as well as items previously omitted.

47   THORNBER, ROBIN. "Hordern as Waugh." Manchester Guardian, 2 October, p. 21.
       Says the Royal Exchange Theatre Company in Manchester has created from a slight, dubious exercise in psychological flashing (The Ordeal of Gilbert Pinfold), a fascinating evening's theatre.

48   WARDLE, IRVING. "The Ordeal of Gilbert Pinfold, Royal Exchange,

Manchester." Times (London), 16 September, p. 7.
Despite being a treacherous subject for the adaptor, the
dramatic version of the novel succeeded beyond his hopes.  It came
off best in the encounters between Pinfold and his "ghosts"; Michael
Hordern portrayed a deliciously laughable and easily dislikeable
figure, discovering the courage to face his demons.

49    WATKINS, ALAN.  "Craftsman and Classicist." Spectator 237
      (31 December):15.
      Reviews A Little Order, discussing how Waugh himself provokes
anecdotes about his outrageous behavior.  Comments on his craftsmanship and religious melancholy, observing that his classical
prose conflicts with his taste for the ornate.

50    WATSON, GEORGE.  Politics and Literature in Modern Britain.
      London:  Macmillan, pp. 12-13, 88-89, 90-92.
      Compiles a list of writers to disprove Orwell's statement in
1940 that "There is now no intelligentsia that is not in some sense
'left.'"  Includes Waugh in this list.  Also uses him as an example
of the obtuseness of intellectual conservatism in modern Britain--
as in his praise of Mussolini for conquering Ethiopia and thereby
bringing civilization to a dark continent.

51    WILSON, EDMUND.  Letters on Literature and Politics, 1912-1972.
      Edited by Elena Wilson.  New York:  Farrar, Straus & Giroux,
      pp. 386, 428-29, 496, 682.
      Calls Waugh a very complex person who dramatizes the various
elements in his own nature in a way that makes it difficult to say
that he is in sympathy with one character rather than another.  In
1944, writes that he has never been able to see any Catholic point
of view in Waugh's novels:  "If I had not been told that he was a
Catholic convert, I should certainly never have known it from reading his books."  When Brideshead appears, he calls it extremely
trashy and unintentionally comic.  He has similarly disparaging
remarks about Helena, calling it snobbish.

52    WYKES, DAVID.  "Evelyn Waugh's Sword of Volgograd." DQR 7,
      no. 2:82-99.
      Traces the factual history of the Sword of Stalingrad to
illustrate Waugh's method and intent in Unconditional Surrender.
Connects it with Sir Roger of Waybroke's sword to indicate Guy
Crouchback's disillusionment.


1978


A.  BOOKS

1    KLOEFKORN, JOHNNY LEE.  "The Protagonist as Structural Device
     in Evelyn Waugh's Novels."  Ph.D. dissertation, University of

Denver, 243 pp. [DAI 39:2292A.]
    Examines ten novels to show how they are constructed around
a central character. Also focuses on the way Waugh alters his
protagonists to meet his changing fictional and ethical require-
ments.

2   MIDDENDORF, MARILYN ANN. "The Circular Worlds of Evelyn Waugh:
    Satire Approached Through Structure." Ph.D. dissertation,
    University of Wisconsin, 361 pp. [DAI 40:2665A.]
    Reversing the conventions of traditional satire, modern sa-
tires are often highly structured and devoid of moralizing. Waugh's
major novels all employ a circular plot; by the end almost nothing
has been effected by the frantic actions of the characters. Even
though World War II changes the spirit and manner of Waugh's fiction, the circular structures continue--until Guy Crouchback breaks
out of the futile circle that Waugh imposes on his heroes. The war
forces Waugh to confront the nature of human experience and see
what can be learned from seemingly futile repetitions.

3   SAMUELS, JEFFREY BERNARD. "There Are No Clean Wounds: A
    Literary Biography of Evelyn Waugh in the Pre-War World." Ph.D.
    dissertation, Columbia University, 403 pp. [DAI 40:2669A.]
    Each of Waugh's books was an intensely private creation, a
manifestation of the hidden Waugh. By writing he saved himself,
not from self-revelation, but from self-destruction. Each novel
was a step towards self-understanding.


B.  SHORTER WRITINGS

1   AMIS, KINGSLEY. "Fit to Kill." New Statesman 96 (22 September):
    384.
    Reviews a new issue of Decline and Fall, noting that Waugh
tried to make cruel things funny and thus more tolerable. The
novel is only incidentally satiric; even the satirical attack on
Sir Wilfrid Lucas-Dockery's liberal ideas of prison reform strikes
at the heart of a cruel, arbitrary universe rather than at progressive reformers.

2   ANON. Review of A Little Order. Sunday Times (London), 5
    March, p. 40.
    States Waugh accused himself of "bombast and exaggeration,"
faults to which he remained liable, but at his best he was lucid,
elegant, and individual. His journalistic prose is plain and ser-
viceable; his opinions notoriously are not.

3   BEATON, CECIL. The Parting Years: Diaries 1963-74. London:
    Weidenfield & Nicolson, pp. 37-38, 50.
    "So Evelyn Waugh is in his coffin. Died of snobbery."
    "Now that he is dead, I cannot hate him: cannot really feel
he was wicked, in spite of his cruelty, his bullying, his caddish-
ness."

4    BELL, ALAN. "Reproofs and Virtues." TLS, 3 February, p. 113.
        A Little Order is not a representative selection of Waugh's
journalism, but it aids understanding of his life and works, particularly in his roles of spokesman for youth, craftsman, and dandy.

5    BLAYAC, ALAIN. "'Bella Fleace Gave a Party,' or The Archetypal
        Image of Waugh's Sense of Decay." SSF 15 (Winter):69-73.
        Calls this Waugh story not only an essential link between
Vile Bodies and A Handful of Dust but also an archetypal illustration of Waugh's embittered human and religious stances, of the decline and fall of man in modern times.

6    BURGESS, ANTHONY. Review of A Little Order. Critic 36 (Summer):
        81-83.
        Reprint of 1977.B6.

7    CADOGAN, MARY, and PATRICIA CRAIG. Women and Children First.
        London: Gollancz, pp. 193-94.
        States that Waugh's satiric method in Put Out More Flags is
exactly appropriate to render the experience of anticlimax and
frustrated patriotism. It is a wartime novel, not a war novel.
The most important writers of the 1940s, including Waugh, found
their subject matter in the day-to-day experiences of wartime behavior.

8    CRAFT, ROBERT. "Too Little Waugh." New York Review of Books,
        9 March, pp. 39-40.
        Reviews A Little Order, noting Waugh's elegance and marksman-
ship in journalism, and criticizing the editor's omission of certain articles and his arrangement of those included. Waugh's views
are more widely accepted now than in his own day.

9    DAVIS, ROBERT MURRAY. "'Clarifying and Enriching': Waugh's
        Changing Concept of Anthony Blanche." PBSA 72 (Third Quarter):
        305-20.
        Notes that since there are at least twelve versions of
Brideshead, a study of its textual history would need a full-length
book. Observes that Anthony Blanche is important not just as a
character but as the first and most consistent critic of the Flyte
family. Apparently Waugh came to believe he had made him too appealing; in the 1960 revisions he emphasized his oddness, and
strengthened his portrait as a prophet who could view only the
secular world, not the spiritual, but could still offer an ironic
corrective to other characters.

10   _____. "An Early Portrait of Waugh." EWN 12 (Spring):6-7.
        Notes that in Dudley Carew's "Justly obscure" novel, The
Next Corner (1924), there is a character, named Dick Hirst who
seems modelled on Waugh.

11   _____. Review of The Diaries of Evelyn Waugh. World Literature

Today 52 (Autumn):635-36.
Praises the work of Michael Davie in editing Waugh's Diaries.

12  _____. "Scott-King's Modern Europe: A Textual History." EWN
     12 (Winter):1-3.
     Waugh never regarded this book as more than a jeu d'esprit,
but its complex textual history reveals the process by which he
attained meaning in all his novels. He worked over it carefully;
the ending reveals significant revision, and for the first time
Waugh showed a secular hero not merely retreating from the world
but positively rejecting it.

13  DOYLE, PAUL A. "'The Man Who Liked Dickens' on Television."
     EWN 12 (Autumn):1-3.
     Describes Robert Tallman's successful television version
(October 1953) of this Waugh story, which became substantially
chapter six of A Handful of Dust. Prints a letter from Tallman
describing work on the script and the difficulties which Waugh
raised over the rights in the adaptation.

14  EAGLETON, TERRY. "A Touch of the Pinfolds." Month 239 (March):
     106-7.
     Reviews A Little Order, defining Waugh's paradoxes as art-
fully comic epigrams, combining seriousness with self-mockery.
This quality overrides the predictable banality of his social and
religious attitudes.

15  FRIEDMAN, ALAN WARREN. Multivalence: The Moral Quality of
     Form in the Modern Novel. Baton Rouge: Louisiana State
     University Press, pp. 96, 100-107, 181.
     Takes Sword of Honour as an example of a hybrid form: we
identify outselves with the protagonist, but we also view him in
a detached way from above. Finds many similarities between Waugh's
trilogy and Ford Madox Ford's Parade's End tetralogy: in both
there is a structural antagonism between the protagonist's perspective and that of the world at large; in both there is life-
affirming action at the end; in both form beautifully follows function.

16  HARWOOD, RONALD, and JOHN SELWYN GILBERT. "A Sense of Loss;
     the Ordeal of Evelyn Waugh." Listener 100 (26 October):528-29.
     Regarding three of Waugh's books, asks what happened to the
man, and what the artist made of the experience. The authors
establish through interviews that the school in North Wales where
Waugh taught was not like Llanabba, the infamous Captain Grimes
did not resemble his prototype, and the fountain in Brideshead is
not that at Castle Howard but one in the Piazza Navona in Rome.
They emphasize the sense of self-hatred evident in The Ordeal of
Gilbert Pinfold, and conclude that Waugh possessed a desperate
need to be loved, as though there were an icy void in him.

17    HEATH, JEFFREY M.   "The Year's Work in Waugh Studies."  EWN 12
      (Spring):1-6.
          Gives special attention to Martin Green's Transatlantic
      Patterns, which views Waugh as a part of recent cultural history
      in an interesting but somewhat quirky way.   Calls attention to a
      number of articles on A Handful of Dust, especially Nicholas
      Joost's, which claims that Waugh is as allusive as Henry James.
      Comments on biographical articles by T.M. Higham and Dom Hubert
      van Zeller, and on reactions to Waugh's diaries, especially Frank
      Kermode's statement that Waugh was one of the three or four best
      novelists of his generation and Nigel Dennis's that the diaries
      give us a "fabricated man."

18    HUNTER, JEANNE CLAYTON.   "Uneventful Order:   The End of Decline
      and Fall."  EWN 12 (Autumn):7-8.
          At the end of this novel, a learning process is going on for
      Paul Pennyfeather, however comic; Christian doctrine is being ap-
      plied, however haphazardly.   Paul is wise:   he metaphorically dies
      to absurdity to resurrect to stability.

19    JOHNSON, PAUL.   "Star Waughs."  Punch 274 (11 January):73.
          Reviews A Little Order, which shows Waugh's journeyman prose
      in various styles, and his own literary progress.   Notes contradic-
      tion between his public and private personalities, and his consis-
      tent concern for literary quality and integrity.

20    JONES, D.A.N.   "Humble Waugh."  Listener 99 (9 February):186.
          Reviews A Little Order, comparing Waugh's essays to those
      of Graham Greene, specifically in their attitudes to Ronald Knox.
      Both writers were attracted to the humility of the Roman Catholic
      church in England.   Compares Waugh to Hilaire Belloc and G.K.
      Chesterton.

21    JONES, RICHARD.   "Evelyn Waugh:   A Man at Bay."  VQR 54 (Summer):
      503-17.
          Discusses Waugh's clouded reputation, noting the hostile re-
      action to his Diaries, which reveal the souring of his career and
      the decline of his character.   Comments on his attempt to create
      an aristocratic persona, his vulgar romanticism, and his melan-
      choly; questions whether he was tragic or merely pathetic.   Many
      of the diaries are tedious; the effect is like that of reading the
      time-table for a disused railway.


22    LOVAT, LORD.   March Past:   A Memoir.  London:   Weidenfeld &
      Nicolson, pp. 175, 233-35.

Identifies some of Waugh's characters.  Gives a military appraisal of this misfit personality who made no attempt to train or learn his trade, was cordially disliked by every combatant officer in the brigade, and was the world's biggest snob.

23    MECKIER, JEROME.  "Evelyn Waugh."  ConL 18 (Winter):98-109.
      Calls Sykes biography (1975.A4) frank and interesting but ultimately inadequate; it is bland fare, contains few imaginative insights, and possesses no organizing thesis.  Waugh knew precisely why the world was falling apart:  having lost its religious framework, it had become a perverse secular parody not only of more civilized eras but of the City of God.

24    MOORE, T. STURGE.  "Fifty Years On."  TLS, 12 May, p. 526.
      Reprints part of the anonymous review of Waugh's Rossetti: His Life and Works (1928.11), and identifies the author as T. Sturge Moore.

25    MYERS, WILLIAM.  "Potential Recruits:  Evelyn Waugh and the Reader of Black Mischief."  In The 1930s:  A Challenge to Orthodoxy.  Edited by John Lucas.  Sussex:  Harvester Press; New York:  Barnes & Noble, pp. 103-16.
      Revision of 1977.B38.

26    NOBLE, DONALD.  "Life of a Great Novelist and Great Boor."  SWR 63 (Winter):100-102.
      Adverse review of Sykes' biography of Waugh (1975.A4).  Calls it irritating and amateurish.  Says Waugh's novels are brilliant, but he was bad-tempered, narrow-minded, and snobbish.

27    PHILLIPS, GENE D.  "Big Screen, Little Screen:  Adaptations of Evelyn Waugh's Fiction."  Literature Film Quarterly 7 (Spring): 162-70.
      Notes Waugh's scorn for films based on books, and shows how well Tony Richardson's version of The Loved One justified it.  Considers Sword of Honour on BBC TV the finest adaptation of Waugh's fiction to the screen, big or little.

28    POWELL, ANTHONY.  To Keep the Ball Rolling:  The Memoirs of Anthony Powell.  Vol. 2, Messengers of Day.  London:  Heinemann, pp. 18-24, 62-69, 128-38, et passim.
      Describes Waugh's cheering up London life for him when he was at Duckworth's in 1927.  Says that the high life described in Decline and Fall came from hearsay and gossip columns; Waugh's first-hand experience of this life came later.  Discusses the composition of Rossetti and of Decline and Fall, Waugh's first marriage and its break up, meetings with him during the war and in 1965, when Waugh was physically ill.

29    RILEY, JOHN.  "The Two Waughs at War."  EWN 12 (Autumn):3-7.

("Part I--A Reassessment of Put Out More Flags"); EWN 12
(Winter):3-9 ("Part II--A Reassessment of Brideshead Revisited").
Considers that the major conflict in Put Out More Flags, ex-
ternalized in Ambrose Silk and Basil Seal, is really between two
sides of Waugh, the aesthete and the man of action. Brideshead
does not deal with the man of action but the artist. It is the
artist's self-purgation; he attempts to efface all that has gone
before except one justification for life itself, his conversion.

30    SHORTER, ERIC. "Plays in Performance." Drama, no. 127
      (Winter):67-69.
      Describes Ronald Harwood's adaptation of Waugh's The Ordeal
of Gilbert Pinfold, in which Michael Hordern gave an outstanding
performance. For all its ingenuity in describing a fashionable
author verging on mental breakdown, the episodic treatment of what
was almost a sustained soliloquy lacked theatrical impulse; the
voyage in the play, though not without incident, was merely a pre-
text for Waugh's essentially private meditations and musings.

31    SHRAPNEL, NORMAN. "Cold Waugh." Manchester Guardian Weekly,
      22 January, p. 22.
      Reviews A Little Order, noting the sensationalism of Waugh's
early journalism, and the persistent confusion about his relative
seriousness in public statement.

32    SNIDER, NORMAN. "Evelyn Waugh." Globe and Mail (Toronto),
      23 March, p. 25.
      Reviews A Little Order, noting Waugh's reputation as a bully,
bigot and gourmand, and his role as a "vicious careerist." Discusses his current popularity.

33    STANNARD, MARTIN. "Work Suspended: Waugh's Climacteric."
      Essays in Criticism 28 (October):302-20.
      The revisions to the novel attempt to disguise deep-rooted
aesthetic problems; by 1939, Waugh faced an artistic dilemma which
he did not fully understand, though he glimpsed the necessity of
introducing a positive element into his work. He never completed
the novel because he failed to resolve the problem of rendering
the subjective objectively. In his postwar work, objectivity means
the assumption of a higher reality governing human actions; since
no such dimension had been built into Work Suspended, the external-
ized analysis of behavior became meaningless.

34    STRATFORD, PHILIP. "Evelyn Waugh and 'The Loved One.'"
      Encounter 51 (September):46-51.
      Describes Waugh's 1947 visit to Hollywood, his excitement at
discovering Forest Lawn Memorial Park, and the process of his writing The Loved One. Contrasts the Horizon text with the British
and American editions, which also differ from each other.

35    THIEME, HANS OTTO. "Evelyn Waugh: A Supplementary Checklist

of Criticism." EWN 12 (Autumn):9-10.
Continues earlier bibliographies, dealing with books and
articles published since 1976, and including previously omitted
items.

36  TRILLING, DIANA.  Review of Brideshead Revisited.  In Reviewing
    in the Forties.  New York and London:  Harcourt, Brace
    Jovanovich, pp. 140-43.
        Reprint of 1946.22.

37  VOORHEES, RICHARD J.  "Evelyn Waugh's Travel Books."  DR 58
    (Summer):240-48.
        The travel books are entertaining documents that reveal
    Waugh's principles and convictions and possess significant links
    with his fiction.  His traveler-persona explodes the myth of ro-
    mantic expeditions, and is fascinated with contrasts and bizarre
    experiences.  Civilization is not very different from barbarism.

38  WALKER, RONALD G.  Infernal Paradise:  Mexico and the Modern
    English Novel.  Berkeley:  University of California Press,
    pp. 198-202, et passim.
        Compares Waugh's Robbery under Law with Graham Greene's
    Another Mexico (British title, The Lawless Roads), finding Greene's
    book more balanced.  Says that Waugh's is more tendentious and
    oversimplified, and that evidently Mexico did not engage his
    novelist's imagination.

39  WAUGH, ALEC.  The Best Wine Last:  An Autobiography through the
    years 1932-1969.  London:  W.H. Allen, passim.
        Contains many biographical anecdotes concerning Evelyn.  In
    an appendix prints Evelyn's sketch of him, page seven of the newly
    begun volume of autobiography which was to have been called A
    Little Hope, found on Evelyn's desk at the time of his death;
    finds it very moving.

*40  WELLS, WALTER.  "The Loved One as a Headstone for a Dead
     Civilisation."  Los Angeles Times, 27 August, p. 3.
         Reflections on The Loved One on its thirtieth birthday.  En-
     shrines it in the tradition of the Hollywood novel, and then claims
     that Waugh internationalized the tradition:  Fitzgerald, West, and
     others used Hollywood as a metaphor for the collapse of the American
     dream, but Waugh expanded the metaphor to embrace all western civi-
     lization.  Says that Scott-King's Modern Europe clarifies The Loved
     One:  Hollywood and Neutralia are sister metaphors, opposite sides
     of the same coin.  Source:  EWN 13 (Spring 1979):5.

41  WOLFF, GEOFFREY.  "The White Mischief of Evelyn Waugh."  New
    Times 10 (23 January):58, 63.
        Reviews Waugh's Diaries, stressing his snobbery and racism,
    his early failures and dissipation, but stating that he was a
    writer of extraordinary gifts.  Reviews his early novels, praising
    his courage, generosity, and energy.

42   YOUNG, VERNON. "Declarations of Waugh." HudR 31 (Autumn):
     500-506.
        Reviewing the Diaries, says that all of Waugh is present in
     the first entry: snobbery, cruelty, intolerance, and boredom.
     The diaries fill in the gaps between books; they are pregnant with
     history being made. Discusses Waugh's personality, noting that his
     comedy is born in disdain.

43   ZOGHBY, MARY DOLORES. "Metaphoric Structure in the War Novels
     of Ford Madox Ford and Evelyn Waugh." Ph.D. dissertation,
     Georgia State University, 238 pp. [DAI 39:879A.]
        Concludes that Ford's Parade's End tetralogy has a greater
     impact than Waugh's war trilogy because the metaphoric pattern is
     better integrated. The recurring images in Waugh's novel are not
     always allied closely to the main plot or the development of the
     central character. Ford's Christopher Tietjens is a highly intel-
     ligent and imaginative person; Waugh fails to make his Guy
     Crouchback interesting enough, and digresses into the comic ex-
     ploits of minor characters.


                              1979


A.   BOOKS

1    ADCOCK, JAMES PATRICK. "From Satirist to Seer: The Novels of
     Evelyn Waugh." Ph.D. dissertation, East Texas State University,
     183 pp. [DAI 40:5446A.]
        Identifies the narrative point of view in each of the novels,
     to show the resultant emphasis. Concludes that the early narra-
     tives strike a pose of detached amusement. Eventually Waugh de-
     velops a narrative technique which enables him to blend the farce
     and irony of the early novels with his conservative views, and
     thus becomes an important spokesman for those who question twenti-
     eth-century progress.


2    GARNETT, ROBERT REGINALD. "The Early Life and Writings of
     Evelyn Waugh." Ph.D. dissertation, University of Virginia,
     336 pp. [DAI 40:5064A.]

Concludes that the first five novels represent a complex response to English life between the wars. Waugh takes a strong delight in energy and in the eccentricity of individual characters; he is attracted to the disorderly vitality of human nature. But in each novel an isolated rural setting offers a sanctuary from urban civilization, indicating an impulse of retreat, a wistful desire for pastoral simplicity and harmony on Waugh's part.

3   KUPERSMITH, LEONARD RONALD. "The Uses of Counterfeit in the Novels of Evelyn Waugh." Ph.D. dissertation, Kansas State University, 275 pp. [DAI 40:3317A.]
    Concludes that satire is generated in Waugh's novels through counterfeits--negations or displacements of a standard, by which the surrogate becomes normative. These are of three kinds:  institutional counterfeits (first explored in detail in Decline and Fall); verbal counterfeits, in which the devaluation of language reflects the epistemological and moral disorders of Waugh's society; and counterfeits of the physical world, as man remakes it to suit his own vanity. Sees Sword of Honour as consummating Waugh's career by integrating the three types of counterfeit with a protagonist who matures through his confrontation with them.


B.   SHORTER WRITINGS

1   BARNARD, ROBERT. "What the Whispering Glades Whispered." ES 60 (April):176-82.
    Explains the fascination of Forest Lawn Cemetery for Waugh; like Hollywood, the cemetery deals with illusion and observes reality. Waugh's message is both social and religious in The Loved One. Stresses that Dennis Barlow is an artist gathering his material; by the end of the book, he has made significant discoveries.

2   DAVIS, ROBERT MURRAY. "Evelyn Waugh's Helena and the Problem of Proofs." PBSA 73 (Fourth Quarter):481-83.
    Urges Waugh scholars to watch for proof copies, since they can indicate revisions in texts; he also made corrections in typescripts. Cites examples from the proof copy and first edition of Helena to show revisions.

3   _____. Review of Evelyn Waugh: A Little Order, edited by Donat Gallagher. World Literature Today 53 (Winter):120-21.
    Discusses Waugh's role as man of letters, suggesting articles to be included in a second collection of his journalism.

4   DEEDES, WILLIAM. "The Abyssinian Waugh." Spectator 242 (5 May):32.
    Describes the background of Scoop, arguing for a factual basis for the novel.

5    DOYLE, PAUL A.  "Evelyn Gardner as Journalist."  EWN 13
     (Winter):4-5.
         Brief discussion of an article in the London Evening Standard
     on parents and children written by Waugh's first wife not long
     after she had left him.

6    FINNEY, BRIAN.  Christopher Isherwood:  A Critical Biography.
     New York:  Oxford University Press, passim.
         Contains numerous incidental references to Waugh, and de-
     scribes Isherwood's involvement with the movie script of The Loved
     One.

7    GREEN, CARLANDA.  "The Bohemian Milieu in the Novels of Huxley,
     Waugh, and Lawrence."  Ph.D. dissertation, University of Alabama,
     234 pp.  [DAI 41:260A.]
         Largely in response to the concentrated nihilism they saw in
     the bohemians around them, Lawrence turned to nature, Huxley to
     mysticism, and Waugh to religion.  The early novels of Waugh show
     the ultimate degradation of the bohemians into hedonism and deca-
     dence; the aristocracy offers hope for regeneration, but must re-
     turn to traditional values.  But Waugh never completely turns away
     from his friends.  The Bright Young Satirist has an ambivalent at-
     titude to the Bright Young People.

8    GREENE, DONALD.  "The Great Long Beach Waugh Memorial."  EWN
     13 (Winter):1-4.
         Provides evidence to indicate that the great trans-Atlantic
     liner described in Brideshead is the Queen Mary, now permanently
     fixed to the harbor of Long Beach, California.

9    GREENE, GRAHAM.  "Remembering Evelyn Waugh."  Listener 102
     (11 October):482-83.
         Recalls the shock of Waugh's curious, perhaps macabre, death:
     in the lavatory, on Easter Sunday 1966.  Says Waugh's romanticism
     conflicted with his satire; perhaps it helped to kill him.  He
     expected too much of his friends, his Church, and the army, and
     therefore experienced disillusionment.  The satire began with the
     end of Waugh's first marriage.  Discusses his own changed evalua-
     tion of Brideshead, his favorite Waugh novels, and the curious ab-
     sence of Guy Crouchback in the latter part of Sword of Honour.
     Compares Waugh to Swift.

10   HEATH, JEFFREY.  "The Lush Places."  EWN 13 (Autumn):1-4.
         Boot Magna in Scoop is the quintessential false refuge in
     Waugh's novels, but there are many others--secular refuges which
     turn out to be prisons.  Brideshead House is an elaborate false
     sanctuary, but now imprisonment in the lush secular place is pre-
     sented as a necessary forerunner to discovery of a true refuge in
     the Church.  Though the lush places are spiritual dungeons, Waugh
     could not root their attractiveness out of his heart.

11    ____. "The Year's Work in Waugh Studies." <u>EWN</u> 13 (Spring):
      1-6.
          Calls the year's collection small but distinguished, begin-
      ning with Donat Gallagher's collected journalism in <u>A Little Order</u>.
      Refers to a piece by Susan Auty as the most intelligent essay yet
      written on <u>Brideshead</u>, and points out that in a review of Sykes'
      biography (1975.A4) Jerome Meckier launches into his own most re-
      warding discussion of Waugh.

12    KEMPTON, MURRAY. "Diction of a Just Man." <u>National Review</u> 31
      (30 March):431-32.
          For all his care to distract us with the disguise of his
      spite, Waugh could never quite conceal from us the fact that he
      was a just and loving man. Despite his attempt to estrange us
      through the <u>Diaries</u>, he ends up endearing himself to us.

13    KING, FRANCIS. "Plays of the Books." <u>Sunday Telegraph</u>
      (London), 18 February, p. 14.
          Says that Ronald Harwood's dramatic version of <u>The Ordeal of</u>
      <u>Gilbert Pinfold</u> stands up with impressive solidity; it was an act
      of courage for Waugh, a proud and private man, to reveal the cir-
      cumstances of his breakdown, and Michael Hordern in the leading
      role makes sure that this courage shines out.

14    MECKIER, JEROME. "Cycle, Symbol, and Parody in Evelyn Waugh's
      <u>Decline and Fall</u>." <u>ConL</u> 20 (Winter):51-75.
          Calls the novel a parody of the <u>Bildungsroman</u>; if protagonists
      do not mature, only parodies of coming-of-age are permissible. Ex-
      cept within a religious framework, virtues and temporal values are
      hopelessly profane, in fact liabilities. Grimes is a prisoner of
      life, able to rise again but kept from genuine transcendence;
      Prendergast is a parody of spiritual man, having a fervor without
      faith; Pennyfeather himself acquiesces in life's preference for
      mismatch and incongruity. Dickens's world is also satirized by
      Waugh; Victorian hopes for a semi-Christian, humanistic world are
      as futile as Prendy's empty religion. Symbols are always the key
      to Waugh's art; here he shows that the art forms and apparently
      saner beliefs of an earlier time survive only parodically.

15    MEIXNER, SUSAN TURNQUIST. "Partisan Politics and the Sequence
      Novels of Evelyn Waugh, C.P. Snow, and Anthony Powell." Ph.D.
      dissertation, University of Kansas, 260 pp. [<u>DAI</u> 41:262A.]
          Writing about the same society, all three see its ruling
      class changing and the "New Men" coming up. But their political
      attitudes differ, and so do their conclusions. Waugh's Guy
      Crouchback faces a world abandoning Tory values. A private act
      of charity establishes his connection with his father's faith,
      and his return to the family estate reaffirms his connection with
      England's Tory traditions.

16    MORRISS, MARGARET. "Critical Responses to <u>Labels</u> and <u>Remote</u>

People." <u>EWN</u> 13 (Autumn):1-4.

Reviews of Waugh's first travel books show the development of his reputation. By 1930 he was regarded as a fashionable writer of the Mayfair set. The reviews of <u>Remote People</u> were more serious and critical than those of <u>Labels</u>; he began to be blamed for his opinions while at the same time being praised for his technique and style. So began his life-long ordeal of reviewers commenting more fully on his personality and beliefs than on his literary skill.

17      . "Evelyn Waugh: A Supplementary Bibliography." <u>EWN</u> 13 (Spring):7-9 (pt. 1); <u>EWN</u> 13 (Autumn):9 (pt. 2); <u>EWN</u> 13 (Winter): 7-8 (pt. 3).

Lists primarily review articles of Waugh's books, found in British and American magazines and newspapers.

17a MULRAIN, MARY ANN. "British Novels between the Two World Wars with the City of London as Metaphor." Ph.D. dissertation, Tulsa University, 135 pp. [<u>DAI</u> 40:5860A.]

If James, Conrad, and Greene recorded the insecurity of the poor, Virginia Woolf, Waugh, and Henry Green disclosed the agitation felt by the upper class in the aftermath of the Great War. These people took refuge in parties to assuage their loneliness and loss of a sense of purpose. Sensitive to the unrest and disillusionment of the period, these novelists felt the approaching shadows of crisis or apocalypse. London provided rich material for their art.

18 O'CONNOR, FLANNERY. <u>The Habit of Being</u>. Letters edited and with an introduction by Sally Fitzgerald. New York: Farrar, Straus, Giroux, pp. 33-35, 79, 98, 159-60, 236, 357, 469, 522, 570.

Quotes Waugh's comment on one of her books, "If this is really the unaided work of a young lady, it is a remarkable product." References to him as a leading Catholic writer. Says he has too narrow a definition of a Catholic novel, does not think any of his early writings are in the same class as the war trilogy, and finds him much more readable than Ford Madox Ford.

19 PRITCHARD, WILLIAM H. "Waugh Revisited." <u>New Leader</u> 62 (24 September):18-19.

Describes Waugh's post-<u>Brideshead</u> books as lame in prose style and wit, in contrast to his earlier fiction. Discusses the failure of his hero-victims to come alive, yet admits that Waugh's limitations are inextricable from his virtues.

20 ROBSON, W.W. "No Offense." <u>PR</u> 46 (Spring):138-42.

Largely favorable review of Sykes' biography of Waugh (1975.A4), praising the research and anecdotes but criticizing the literary analysis. Comments on Waugh's personality, arguing that Catholicism was an abiding strength.

21   SCHLUND, MARIANNE. Studien zur "language of love" im modernen englischen Roman. European University Papers, ser. 14, vol. 72. Frankfurt: Peter Lang, pp. 2, 120-35, 232-81 passim, 325-28.
Discusses Vile Bodies as an illustration of one kind of twentieth-century departure from the conventional language of love. The monotones and fashionable jargon of the Bright Young People do not convey emotion but suppress it; they find it embarrassing. Waugh captures the tone of an epoch in which people find it impossible to express their feelings.

22   SHEPPARD, R.Z. "Fifty Years of Total Waugh: The Greatest Comic Genius since Shaw Is Still in Style." Time 113 (12 February):72, 74.
Waugh fortified himself against his time with a moat of disdain, crenelated views, and a keep of private devotions. Little, Brown's re-publication of his dozen best novels provides an opportunity to appreciate how skillfully he balanced between satire and romance. His vitality, matchless craftsmanship, audacious imagination, and perceptions have not dated.

23   WÖLK, GERHARD. "Evelyn Waugh: A Supplementary Checklist of Criticism." EWN 13 (Winter):5-6.
A continuation of earlier checklists; includes mainly books and articles published since 1977.

24   WOOD, MICHAEL. Review of Men at Arms, Officers and Gentlemen, and The End of the Battle. New Republic 180 (12 May):28-31.
War is the apparent subject of the trilogy but Catholicism is the real one: Waugh is more concerned with Guy Crouchback's innocence, and the loss of honor and grace, than with military matters. His parable turns on the distinction between the will to win and the acceptance of sacrifice.

## 1980

A. BOOKS

1   BLAYAC, ALAIN. "Evelyn Waugh, romancier satirique, 1903-1942." Thesis for Doctorat d'État, Université Paul Valéry, Montpellier, 933 pp.
Makes use of Waugh's manscripts, correspondence, and diaries to give a biographical account and an account of Waugh's early career, followed by an extensive discussion of six novels written between 1930 and 1942, which he regards as a homogeneous entity. Also discusses comedy, and modes and methods of the satiric novel. Views Waugh as a Catholic and Tory humanist, "a clown and a thinker," "a satirical novelist and a passionate militant." Sources: see discussion by Yvon Tosser in 1981.B28.

2   JAMKHANDI, SUDHAKER RATNAKAR. "The Rhetoric of War:  An
    Evaluation of Evelyn Waugh's Military Novels." Ph.D. disserta-
    tion, Texas Christian University, 235 pp. [DAI 42:226A.]
        In Waugh's novels, we find the mind of the last romantic who
looked on war with a crusader's zeal, only to find that war cannot
cleanse a civilization of its ills.  Yet Waugh is able to envision
a new and better England through the acceptance of the New Man by
the old Catholic aristocracy.  His fullest realization of the novelist's art occurs when he gives order to one of the most chaotic and
catastrophic moments in man's history.  Through his adherence to
Catholicism, his art gains universality, a vision of a truth.

3   McCARTNEY, GEORGE P. "Confused Roaring:  Evelyn Waugh and the
    Modernist Tradition." Ph.D. dissertation, City University of
    New York, 265 pp. [DAI 41:1613A.]
        States that Waugh does not set out to correct morals and
manners by measuring them against a standard, but really calls into question the epistemological assumptions of modern art:  rela-
tivism, and the supreme importance of releasing the self from social constraint.

4   MORRISS, MARGARET EILEEN. "Prejudice and Partiality:  Evelyn
    Waugh and his Critics (1928-1966)." Ph.D. dissertation,
    University of Toronto, 452 pp. [DAI 42:229A.]
        A study of the development of Waugh's reputation reveals
curious paradoxes.  Critics often misinterpreted his books because
of hostility to his political and religious views.  Considering
his later serious novels marred by pessimism and dogmatism, they
asked him to return to the method of his early comedies.  Thinking
that he had lost ironic detachment once and for all with Brideshead,
they neglected the development of a more humane irony which included
both commitment and compassion.  With few exceptions, they failed
to notice his genuine technical advances.  There was a great disparity, therefore, between his own aims and achievements and critical response to his novels.


B.  SHORTER WRITINGS

1   ANON. "Waugh's Fare, All's Fair." Economist 276 (13 September):
    109.
        Love is not the virtue most frequently associated with Waugh's
name.  But the letters reveal a dutiful son, a devoted husband, a
man fundamentally and surprisingly good.  His best comic creation
was himself; his letters are spiced with self-mockery.

2   BERGONZI, BERNARD. "A Conspicuous Absentee:  The Decline and
    Fall of the Catholic Novel." Encounter 55 (August-September):
    44-56.
        Notes that by the early 1950s reviewers were taking the
"Catholic novel," as written by Waugh, Graham Greene, and François

Mauriac, seriously. But it declined quite rapidly; by 1968, David
Lodge said that it was largely a thing of the past (see 1968.B32).
It apparently represented only a phase for Greene, and Waugh did
not attempt a large-scale Catholic novel after Brideshead.

3   BOSTON, RICHARD. "Waugh in Pieces." Punch (10 September):
    410-11.
        Ironically, Waugh protected his private life ferociously dur-
    ing his lifetime, but it has been pushed into the public domain
    since his death. The avalanche of Waugh material seems to compete
    with the Bloomsbury one; but while even a small dose of Bloomsbury
    brings on deep boredom, Waugh remains consistently fascinating.
    We look for him to drop his guard and reveal his real self. This
    never happens; perhaps his face was identical to his mask. The
    letters are revealing about his method of writing, especially his
    achievement of comic effects through exaggeration. Not a nice man
    perhaps, but a fellow of infinite jest.

4   BRAILOW, DAVID G. "'My Theme is Memory': The Narrative Struc-
    ture of Brideshead Revisited." EWN 14 (Winter):1-4.
        Argues that if we pay heed to the narrator's reminder that
    he is telling the story from the perspective of middle age we will
    see that it is better designed than is often thought. The shape
    and logic of the book are intentionally those of human memory, not
    satiric narrative; they reflect Ryder's deep need for stability
    and permanence.

5   BUCKLEY, WILLIAM. "Notes and Asides." National Review 32
    (14 November):1374, 1376-77.
        Declares that Mark Amory, the editor of Waugh's letters, did
    a curiously selective job of presenting Waugh's letters to him; he
    conveyed the impression that Waugh thought poorly of the National
    Review. Publishes letters included in the collection, together
    with some not included, to illustrate that Waugh's attitude to the
    Review changed and matured.

6   BURGESS, ANTHONY. "A Seldom Civil Waugh." SR 7 (October):
    76-77.
        In a typical Waugh letter there is a stuffy ponderousness
    that mocks itself. Some readers will find the religious rigor and
    snobbery offensive, but these are part of the pose of the insular
    Tory. He was less formidable than he appeared; his wartime letters
    to his wife Laura evince a passionate heart. He was the toughest
    Catholic of his age; his own heart was broken when the Church lit-
    urgy was vulgarized. His real nostalgia was less for a Catholic
    aristocracy than for upper-class mindlessness. People who have
    heard of him as disagreeable will be surprised at how charming
    many of these letters are.

7   CONRAD, PETER. Imagining America. London: Routledge & Kegan
    Paul, pp. 168, 241, 251, 303-7.

Discusses Waugh's picture of Hollywood along with Aldous
Huxley's in Jesting Pilate and After Many a Summer.  Notes that
Huxley's friend Christopher Isherwood despised The Loved One as a
facile criticism of California; he got his revenge on Waugh through
the movie script of The Loved One, which he and Terry Southern wrote
for Tony Richardson, and which effectively sabotaged the novel.

8    DAVIS, ROBERT MURRAY.  "Brideshead Revisited and All the King's
     Men:  Towards a Definition of Forties Sensibility."  EWN 14
     (Autumn):1-4.
        Noting similarities between novels by Waugh and Robert Penn
Warren published at about the same time, suggests that the breach
of normal family ties in both is symptomatic of larger social problems, and that the attempt to recover values reflected in both is
central to postwar fiction and drama.

9    DOYLE, PAUL A.  "Evelyn in Arthur's Diary, I."  EWN 14 (Autumn):
     6-8.
        References to Evelyn in his father's diary are frequent in
the period 1930-36 because he used the family home as a base.
There are more diary entries for 1930 than for any other year; in
this article, prints entries from the beginning of the year until
July 31.

10    _____.  "The Year's Work in Waugh Studies."  EWN 14 (Spring):
     1-4.
        In a survey of fifteen items, calls an article on Decline
and Fall by Jerome Meckier (1979.B14) a sine qua non for Waugh
scholars, and also gives special attention to articles on A Handful
of Dust by R.M. Davis (1976.10) and on Work Suspended by Martin
Stannard (1978.B34).

11    FUSSELL, PAUL.  Abroad:  British Literary Travelling Between
     the Wars.  New York and Oxford:  Oxford University Press, pas-
     sim.
        Surveys Waugh's travel books in a chapter entitled "Evelyn
Waugh's Moral Entertainments" (pp. 171-202), but has many other
references to him as well.  Says that as a devotee of the norm,
Waugh calls attention to the anomalies in his travel books; his
comedy ordinarily arises from such disparities, and travel itself
is an implicit quest for them.  Also observes that travel writing,
which requires organization and narrative, is not very remote from
fiction; Waugh is aware that, to be refracted in language, fact
must be fictionalized.

12    _____.  "A Hero of Verbal Culture."  New York Times Book Review,
     2 November, pp. 3, 36-37.
        Sees Waugh as indispensable today because he was a rarity,
a writer who cared about language; to write well, he thought, was
an author's obligation.  His ethical intensity makes his letters
instructive; he saw everything in moral terms, and his comedy was

possible only because of his restless moral imagination.  The letters bring him alive more than the diaries do.  They show that he
has a lot to teach us about writing and the usefulness of the comic
vision in transforming anger into verbal art.

13    GORRA, MICHAEL.  "Waugh in Transition:  Put Out More Flags."
      EWN 14 (Winter):6-8.
           Suggests that in the comic scenes involving the Connolly
      children we feel sympathy for Basil Seal's victims, and this marks
      a change in Waugh:  his early manner is past and done with.

14    GREENE, GRAHAM.  Ways of Escape.  New York:  Simon & Schuster,
      pp. 118, 262-73, et passim.
           Evaluates Waugh's career; concludes he left us an estate to
      walk through.  Says there was always a conflict in him between the
      satirist and the romantic; discusses his characterization of him-
      self, especially in "that very courageous book, The Ordeal of
      Gilbert Pinfold."  Draws an illuminating contrast between Waugh
      and himself as Catholic writers, indicating that Waugh was far
      more committed than he to the work of conversion.

15    HEPPENSTALL, RAYNER.  "Vile Bodies."  New Statesman 100
      (16 September):17.
           Says that apart from paranoia and snobbery, the worst feature
      of Waugh's letters is the indecency in letters to Dorothy and Mary
      Lygon.  The letters provide a good picture of the work of a hard-
      working, hard-living man; but unfortunately he never discusses his
      work, though he criticizes that of his friends.  The letters are
      less interesting than the diaries, so much of the wit being mirth-
      less.  Waugh clearly never had anything to teach us, except that
      a man may be a fool and yet a master of English prose narrative,
      perhaps the finest in the century.

16    HOWARD, MICHAEL.  "In the Parrot-Cage."  TLS, 17 October, p.
      1164.
           Notes that two-thirds of the letters in Mark Amory's edition
      date from the postwar period, twenty years in which Waugh made no
      new friends but chronicled the disintegration of the Bright Young
      Things, the parrot cage in which he had chosen to pass his life.
      Uprooted from the urban culture he despised but on which he was
      dependent, he found no alternative pleasures in the country, in
      art, or even in books; he rejected the world almost as totally as
      if he had entered a monastery, but without finding any alternative
      discipline or peace--not even any consolation in his religion.  By
      his own standards, he was guilty of two of the deadliest sins:
      accidie and despair.

16a   IGOE, W.J.  "Mr. Waugh in Person."  Month 251 (November):392.
           Calls the volume of letters a vastly entertaining and useful
      book, though it has flaws and puzzling omissions, especially of
      letters to close friends.  But it does give a more truthful

revelation of Waugh's character than most of the books published
since his death. Waugh played the part he contrived for himself
all too well; it masked his virtues. His prose is often an exqui-
site kind of courtesy.

17  JOHNSTONE, RICHARD. "Travelling in the Thirties." London
    Magazine 20 (August/September):90-96.
      Describes Waugh, Greene, and Christopher Isherwood as repre-
sentative explorer-artists of a generation on the move. At the
time travel meant inspiration, escape from a purposeless England,
and observation without involvement. Sophisticated, unsentimental,
ungullible, the traveler mocks and congratulates himself. Yet he
commits himself to his nationality even as he abandons England.

18  LARKIN, PHILIP. "A Chatterbox With No Charity." Guardian,
    14 September, p. 22.
      The degree to which Waugh's letters are readable depends on
how far he can convert gossip into his own kind of black comedy.
His piety, dividing people into "Papists & heathens," did little
for his charity. The world his gossip evokes has none of the appeal of Horace Walpole's; it is curt, cheap, brutal.

19  LEITHAUSER, BRAD. "The Letters of Evelyn Waugh." New Republic
    183 (18 October):37-38.
      Notes that the Waugh who emerges in the letters is far more
humane and interesting than that in the diaries; the wide range of
letters to his wife is especially fascinating. A number of his
books may not weather well because of the narrowness of his sympathies, amounting to provincialism. He surmounted his shortcomings
because of his comic power, especially his genius for inverting
things twice over. His letters show better than his other books
how subtly linked both his strengths and weaknesses as a writer
were to his Catholicism. He became an energetic proselytizer; in
fact it is this evangelism which gives Brideshead, the most un-
fairly denigrated of his books, its submerged power.

20  LINCK, CHARLES E., Jr. Review of The Letters of Evelyn Waugh,
    edited by Mark Amory. EWN 14 (Winter):4-6.
      Expresses some reservations about the selection of Waugh's
letters, gives praise to the editor for the mountains of scholarly
data he has provided but withholds judgment as to their accuracy,
and says that the greatest contribution of this selection is to
point up Waugh's extraordinary versatility.

21  MANLEY, JEFFREY A. "Waugh in the Soviet Union--The War Trilogy."
    EWN 14 (Spring):4-16.
      Notes the surprising popularity of Waugh's war trilogy in
the Soviet Union, though says that Waugh would have been amused
at some of the interpretations of his work by Soviet critics--
references to Waugh shamelessly ridiculing English bourgeois society as an alienated, spiritually empty class; to Guy Crouchback's

welcoming the war as a chance to fight against Fascism, which per-
sonified the worst tendencies of the contemporary epoch; and to
the inversion of the significance Waugh gives to the Sword of
Stalingrad.  Gives examples of bowdlerization in the Russian edition.

22   MECKIER, JEROME.  "Why the Man Who Liked Dickens Reads Dickens
     instead of Conrad:  Waugh's A Handful of Dust."  Novel 13
     (Spring):171-87.
          Draws parallels between Waugh's characters in this novel and
     those of Dickens, but contends that for Waugh, Dickens represents
     the defects of Victorian humanism, which tried to preserve the moral
     order by secularizing Christian values:  literature cannot replace
     religion as the source of moral standards.  Similarly, Waugh finds
     the stoicism of Conrad's Heart of Darkness as sentimental as human-
     ism:  Marlow's discovery of life's perversity ought not to assume
     the status of a final wisdom, and again his experiences result in
     a kind of substitute religion.  As Waugh's paradigm, Tony personi-
     fies the incurable hollowness Conrad sensed in secular man but
     immediately obscured.

23   MORRISON, BLAKE.  The Movement:  English Poetry and Fiction of
     the 1950s.  Oxford:  Oxford University Press, pp. 51, 58, 60,
     242, 279.
          Discusses briefly Waugh's attack on "The Movement" or "the
     Angry Young Men" in Encounter, December 1955, and his controversy
     with John Wain over P.G. Wodehouse in the Spectator early in 1956.

24   MORRISS, MARGARET.  "Evelyn Waugh:  A Supplementary Bibliography,
     Part IV."  EWN 14 (Spring):6-8.
          Continues 1979.B17.

25   NUTTGENS, PATRICK.  "Campaign for Rectorship Revisited."  Times
     Higher Education Supplement (London), 28 March, p. 31.
          Describes a campaign by a group of students at the University
     of Edinburgh to have Waugh elected Rector.  Outside the literary
     group to which Nuttgens belonged, however, few students had read
     Waugh's novels; moreover, Waugh made himself unpopular by emphasiz-
     ing his Catholicism.  Nuttgens was set upon by the supporters of
     a rival candidate while he was distributing Waugh posters at night
     and beaten unconscious with hockey sticks.  When a photograph of
     his battered defender was sent to Waugh, he replied "that he was
     glad to see that we were working hard in his cause."

26   POWELL, ANTHONY.  To Keep the Ball Rolling:  The Memoirs of
     Anthony Powell.  Vol. 3, Faces in My Time.  London:  Heinemann,
     pp. 29, 53, 77, 137, 182, 218.
          Mentions Waugh's reviewing for Night and Day, especially a
     favorable review of David Jones's In Parenthesis, a book which did
     not receive much attention when it first appeared.  Also recounts
     an anecdote concerning Waugh and Cyril Connolly which inspired an
     Osbert Lancaster cartoon.

27    POWELL, ROBERT S.  "Uncritical Perspective:  Belief and Art in
      Brideshead Revisited."  CritQ 22 (Autumn):53-67.
           Recalls the vehemence of the criticism of Brideshead when it
      first appeared, and surveys subsequent discussions.  Surprised to
      find commentators on the novel so concerted in their belief that
      it is a Catholic novel.  Maintains that it is less concerned with
      religion than with an aesthetic reaction to Catholicism.  Admires
      Waugh's artistic ability to explore his own possibly illusory be-
      liefs.

28    PRAWER, S.S.  "The Anglo-American-German version."  TLS,
      21 November, p. 1342.
           Reviewing the paperback edition of Peter Gan's Tod in
      Hollywood, expresses regret that no one has revised this very un-
      satisfactory translation of The Loved One in the thirty years since
      it first appeared, so that German lovers of satire could encounter
      Waugh's novel in a form a little nearer to his intentions.

29    PRESCOTT, MARY ELIZABETH.  "The Disembodied Voice:  Changing
      Characterizations of Antisocial Artist and Artifice in Thackeray,
      Wilde, Huxley, Waugh."  Ph.D. dissertation, Brown University,
      152 pp.  [DAI 41:5111A.]
           Says that the antisocial characters of Vanity Fair, The
      Picture of Dorian Gray, Point Counterpoint, and Vile Bodies are
      revealing sopkesmen for their writers and their times.  The char-
      acters in the last three are schizoid--in R.D. Laing's terms, on-
      tologically insecure and preoccupied with self-preservation.  Waugh
      depicts a nightmare of lack of confidence, with disembodied voices
      dissociated from faith and tradition.  His contempt for his char-
      acters reaches its climax in his account of his own schizophrenic
      episode, The Ordeal of Gilbert Pinfold.  The personality he has
      cultivated in schizoid fashion is a caricature of the values he
      professes to uphold.

30    PRITCHETT, V.S.  "Evelyn Waugh:  Club and Country."  In The
      Tale Bearers:  Literary Essays.  New York:  Random House, pp.
      93-103.
           Comments on Waugh's protean development and his skills as
      an impersonator and a craftsman.  Revision of 1961.22 and 1964.B47.

, 30a   QUENNELL, PETER.  The Wanton Chase.  An Autobiography from 1939.
      London:  Collins, pp. 22, 47, 44-49, 175.
           Gives an account of Waugh and his poses at the Paris embassy
      following the Second World War.  Says that the real face and the
      formidable mask were not easily distinguishable.  Gives anecdotes
      to illustrate Waugh's merciless sense of fun, and notes references
      to himself in Waugh's diaries.

31    QUINTON, ANTHONY.  "'No Filthiness with Women While I Am
      Around . . .'"  Listener 104 (4 September):307-8.
           Describes reviewing Waugh's letters as an exercise in

self-indulgence:  all sorts of luxuries are jumbled together in
festal profusion.  Says the backbone of the collection is the letters to women friends like Nancy Mitford, Diana Cooper, and Mary
Lygon; the relations with men correspondents are uneasy, though
Waugh never fell out with Graham Greene and Anthony Powell and
continued to admire their work.  Says the editing is superb, the
footnotes splendidly copious.

32   RABAN, JONATHAN.  "Evelyn Waugh:  The Novelist in the Gymnasium."
     *Sunday Times* (London), 7 September, p. 42.
          The publication of Waugh's letters will add to his stature
     as one of the stranger English characters of the century.  It is
     becoming harder to read his novels without being reminded of his
     character; they were brilliant distillations of a messy and para-
     doxical life.

33   SNIDER, NORMAN.  "A Nasty Man Joins the Ranks of the Exalted."
     *Globe and Mail* (Toronto), 29 November, "Fanfare," p. 7.
          Puzzled by Waugh's current reputation, says he was not con-
     sidered by academics during his lifetime to be of much account.
     But in the age of Ronald Reagan there is many a conservative in-
     tellectual who looks to Waugh as a role model--partly because of
     his dedication to the norm, his celebration of the traditional.
     Discusses his unsurpassed outrageousness, his accomplishments as
     a social climber, and his unparalleled gluttony, and concludes
     that he would have loathed many of his current admirers--homosexu-
     als, Jews, liberated women, Americans.

34   SYKES, CHRISTOPHER.  "When the Going Was Good."  *Tablet* 234
     (27 September):949.
          Waugh's letters become fascinating when he makes interesting
     friendships; some of the best, usually written to women, are far-
     cical and fantastic.  The letters explain a fact of his life, name-
     ly that he was anxious to convert people, though he never succeeded
     in doing so.  The letters of famous humorists are often disappoint-
     ing; some of these are as funny as anything Waugh ever wrote.  This
     is a triumphant book, better than could have been expected.

35   WHEATCROFT, GEOFFREY.  "No Misgiving."  *Spectator* 245 (11
     October):18-19.
          Fourteen years after his death Waugh retains the power to
     captivate and enrage.  He was more than just the first novelist
     of his age:  he was a larger-than-life personality.  The most im-
     pressive letters are those to other writers; the most remarkable,
     about religion (the key to his character)`; the happiest, those to
     or about his children.  Not everyone will enjoy these letters.
     But those who find no charity have chosen not to look for it.

36   WÖLK, GERHARD.  "Eveyln Waugh:  A Supplementary Checklist of
     Criticism."  *EWN* 14 (Autumn):4-5.
          A continuation of earlier checklists published in *EWN*, in-
     cluding mainly books and articles appearing since 1978.

1981

A.  BOOKS

1   DAVIS, ROBERT MURRAY.  A Catalogue of the Evelyn Waugh Collection
    at the Humanities Research Center, The University of Texas at
    Austin.  Troy, N.Y.:  Whitston, 375 pp.
        After Waugh's death, the Center acquired manuscripts of all
    but two of his novels, of all three biographies and his autobiogra-
    phy, of one travel book, of many shorter works--and also of the
    complete contents of his library.  A large body of other material
    supplements the collection itself.  The catalogue is a guide to
    the contents of the collection, but it also provides summaries or
    descriptions of unpublished material, including the 1,400 letters
    by Waugh.

2   _____.  Evelyn Waugh, Writer.  Norman, Okla.:  Pilgrim Books,
    342 pp.
        Using manuscript material, traces the development of Waugh's
    style throughout the composition of his major novels, paying spe-
    cial attention to their textual history and demonstrating the great
    care Waugh took in the revision of his material.  Also shows the
    relationship between Waugh's fiction and his nonfiction.  Says
    many readers assume that Waugh's books came easily to him, but in
    fact he labored endlessly for artistic wholeness and for the effect
    of effortlessness which often deceives the reader.

3   LANE, CALVIN W.  Evelyn Waugh.  Twayne's English Authors Series.
    Boston:  G.K. Hall, 189 pp.
        Intended for the general reader rather than the specialist,
    this study deals with works of major importance rather than with
    all of Waugh's writings.  Stresses that in a highly varied career
    Waugh remained amazingly consistent in his views of the foibles of
    mankind:  he increasingly implied that he was living in a world
    devoid of common sense.  Contains a chapter summing up Waugh's
    views on the craft of fiction, and another assessing his achieve-
    ment as a satiric novelist.

B.  SHORTER WRITINGS

1   AMIS, KINGSLEY.  "How I Lived in a Very Big House and Found
    God."  TLS, 20 November, p. 1352.
        Calls Waugh a marvelous writer able to write a bad book at
    any given moment; Brideshead, his most enduringly popular novel,
    is clearly his worst.  The chief reason for its success is that
    it is a heavily romantic book about the upper class.  It was as
    if Waugh came to believe that wealth, rank, Catholicism, and beau-
    ty were enough to establish his characters as glamorous and moral-
    ly significant.  The Flyte family are a bunch of bores; the actors

portraying them in the television version are clearly underemployed.
Lingering scenes of eventless sightseeing do not establish dramatic
significance; the vacancy at the center of the novel cannot help
being thrown into prominence by the very process of screening.

2    ANON. "Brideshead Revisited." Vogue (London), 138 (April):
     188-95.
         Account of the Granada television production of Brideshead,
including interviews with Derek Granger, the producer; John
Mortimer, the adaptor; and members of the cast.  Contains background photographs and stills from the television film.  Mortimer,
socialist and non-believer, but still a life-long admirer of Waugh,
describes the process of preparing the script, noting that it presented difficulties because so much of the action in the novel hap-
pens off stage, that the novel cannot be effectively condensed or
compressed, and that he hopes Brideshead will revive the nineteenth-
century tradition of the long story which becomes part of the household.  Derek Granger says that the more they dug into the story,
the more extraordinary it revealed itself to be; it is certainly
not an indulgent, romantic study of high life, and the shock of
the ending comes with extraordinary power.

3    BURGESS, ANTHONY. "'Brideshead Revisited' Revisited." Lamp
     (Winter):14-19.
         Sees the novel as a paean to two traditions implausibly
brought together:  Catholicism and the British aristocracy (Protestant since the Reformation).  In the wish fulfilment of the novel,
an ideal aristocratic family adheres to the old faith, and art ful-
fils what history denies.  Waugh is wrong to seek the best of both
worlds; the novel is nostalgic and romantically indulgent.  Yet it
is also "real"; it is an exact record of a particular social class
at a particular time.  The Granada production is probably the finest fictional television ever made; never before has there been
such uncompromising fidelity to a piece of literature.

4    CATALOGUE NO. 28 OF BELL, BOOK & RADMALL, LTD., p. 33.
         Describes a collection of 111 unpublished letters and post-
cards from Waugh to his bookseller, Handasyde Buchanan of Messrs.
Heywood Hill, written between 1948 and 1964.  Includes shafts of
vintage Waugh, as when he refers to a postal strike--"When the
mutiny of the postmen is broken . . ."--or when he tries to sell
Buchanan a copy of Terry Southern's Candy as suitable for resale
to pornophiles.  Says the letters obliquely reveal his kindness,
for example to Alfred Duggan's widow, and sometimes throw surprising light on his literary preferences.

5    DAVIS, ROBERT MURRAY. "Settling the Estate:  Evelyn Waugh's
     Posthumous and Uncollected Work." PLL 17 (Spring):204-19.
         Notes that since the early 1970s most of the wider public
attention has gone to work that reveals more of Waugh as personality than as writer.  Comments on things yet unpublished--some

diary entries, letters, correspondence with his agent A.D. Peters, projected books and articles, a memorandum on Brideshead written in Hollywood in 1947, and manuscripts of novels. Makes suggestions for what a volume of unpublished material should contain; says that fugitive material can be used to understand the contexts out of which the novels come.

6   DOOLEY, D.J.  "Hardy, Douglas, and Waugh's Ironic Searchlight." EWN 15 (Spring):5-7.
    Contrasts two reviews Waugh wrote in 1930.  Reassessing Hardy's Tess of the D'Urbervilles, he found it long, ponderous, and badly written; the central moral problem was avoided, and the irony was on the level of adolescent pessimism.  He was far more tolerant of Norman Douglas's diatribe How About Europe?  Evidently the lesser writer could teach him more than the greater about a way of looking at the modern world and depicting it in his fiction.

7   DOYLE, P[AUL] A.  Review of A Catalogue of The Evelyn Waugh Collection at the Humanities Research Center, The University of Texas at Austin, edited by Robert Murray Davis.  EWN 15 (Autumn): 5-6.
    States that this volume fulfills an indispensable function; every page reveals Davis's total familiarity with and mastery of the material, and for anyone seriously interested in Waugh the book reads like a novel.

8   ___.  "That Poem in The Loved One."  EWN 15 (Winter):6-7.
    Notes that Donald Greene has identified a poem quoted in chapter 7 of the novel--"God set her brave eyes wide apart."  It is Richard Middleton's "Any Lover, Any Lass," found in Stevenson's Home Book of Verse.

9   ___.  "The Year's Work in Waugh Studies."  EWN 15 (Spring): 1-4.
    Describes the appearance of the Letters as the year's high-light.  Also calls attention to Greene's comparison of Waugh and himself in Ways of Escape; Paul Fussell's chapter ("Waugh's Moral Entertainments") in Abroad; and Jerome Meckier's essay on A Handful of Dust in Novel.  Also discusses a controversy in the Irish Times following an article by John Broderick (21 March) praising Waugh's writing but criticizing his behavior.

10  GLENDINNING, VICTORIA.  Edith Sitwell:  A Unicorn Among Lions. New York:  Knopf, passim.
    Contains numerous references to Waugh, beginning from the time of the first performance of Edith Sitwell's Façade in 1923. Describes Miss Sitwell's reception into the Catholic Church, and Waugh's response.

11  GOLDEN, GLEN THOMAS.  "Two Visions of Modern Man and the

Military: Evelyn Waugh's 'Sword of Honour' and James Gould
Cozzens's 'Guard of Honour.'" Ph.D dissertation, University of
Southern California. [DAI 42:1136A.]
   Waugh uses the military structure primarily as a backdrop
from which to explore the idealistic crusade of his protagonist,
whereas Cozzens believes that the military situation offers a
unique setting by which to define the limits of human endeavor
and achievement. Waugh creates an unusual type of hero in
Crouchback, allowing the novelist to make various statements about
modern man, while Cozzens lets the military system assume its own
significance.

12   GRANGER, DEREK. "The Writing of Brideshead Revisited."
     Listener 106 (8 October):394-96.
        "Of all Waugh's books it is the most constantly read." De-
scribes the circumstances of its composition, when Waugh asked for
three months' unpaid leave from the army in 1944, and began writing
his "Magnum Opus" at the rate of 1,500-2,000 words a day. Also describes his trip to Hollywood for the projected filming of the novel in 1946, and a new proposal in 1950 for Graham Greene to write
the script for a movie version. Refers to Waugh's own assessment
in Life magazine in 1946 that this was his best book, vastly more
ambitious than A Handful of Dust.

13   GRIBBLE, THOMAS A. "The Nature of a Trimmer." EWN 15 (Autumn):
     1-5.
        By reference to Halifax's Character of a Trimmer (1688) and
the words of Hugh Latimer to Bishop Ridley, finds literary ante-
cedents for Trimmer in Sword of Honour and other trimmers depicted
by Waugh. Such characters are insubstantial opportunists, people
who have no knowledge of the supernatural and whose lives are
therefore no more than a series of roles or identities.

14   KAPLAN, STANLEY R. "Circularity and Futility in Black Mischief."
     EWN 15 (Winter):1-4.
        The Western ideas with which Seth hopes to bring about his
brave new world violate tradition; they are at a remove from the
core of Judeo-Christian values which sustained the West for centuries, and also from the African society which is struggling out
of barbarism. Seth's downward spiral can be traced through a number of ironic leitmotivs, such as cannibalism and the wrecked motor
car. In fact, since the novel offers no firm base for judgement,
it is not satire but irony—cosmic irony or black comedy.

15   KERNAN, ALVIN. "Well Well Never Again." YR (Spring):416-21.
        Reviewing Waugh's letters, says that late in the century it
seems as if he is going to be seen as the great satirist writing
in English in the modern times. The twentieth century has been
generous in providing material for satire, but the gods have not
been as kind to our satirists. Only Waugh, as the letters make
clear, seems to be perfectly ruthless and realistic in word and

action.  The matter-of-factness of his description of something
outrageous is the true Waugh tone, the basis of his satiric style.
He was blessed with a moment when human triviality mattered, when
great things were breaking up--the period from 1919 to 1945 when
English power came to an end and aristocratic culture gave way to
"the century of the common man."  The readers who conclude that
he was a reactionary snob will not be wrong, but it would be wrong
not to see that unattractive social traits, combined with the right
moment and the right style, can make for great satire.

16    LANE, GEORGE.  "Cynic and Moralist."  Commentary 71 (March):
      72-74.
            The usual view of Waugh as a thundering snob dominated criti-
      cism of the diaries when they appeared; this selection of letters,
      however, has been hailed with nostalgic affection, though it is
      usually the manner which is praised and the ideas overlooked.  The
      comic hyperbole of the letters shows that he was a first-rate en-
      tertainer in private as well as public.  He is a classic English
      eccentric and a master of prose style whose works deserve recon-
      sideration as we continue to slide down the tube.

17    LEWIS, PETER.  George Orwell:  The Road to 1984.  London:
      Heinemann, pp. 13, 77, 111.
            Orwell was suspicious of intellectuals, and had no interest
      in philosophy and little in religion.  Though Waugh, who visited
      him not long before his death, said that he was "very near to
      God," this may have been more Waugh's vision than Orwell's.
      Orwell's view of Waugh was that he was as good a novelist as it
      was possible to be "while holding untenable opinions."

18    LODGE, DAVID.  "Evelyn Waugh:  Habits of a Lifetime" and "The
      Fugitive Art of Letters."  In Working with Structuralism:
      Essays and Reviews on Nineteenth- and Twentieth-Century
      Literature.  Boston and London:  Routledge & Kegan Paul, pp.
      117-27, 128-39.
            Describes first essay as originally published in the New
      Review, and now incorporating part of an earlier essay, "The
      Arrogance of Evelyn Waugh" (1972.B18).  The second essay is a re-
      print of one included in 1973.A2.

19    LUKACS, JOHN.  "Waugh Recrudescens."  National Review 33 (23
      January):41-44.
            Waugh's reputation continues to grow; the consistency of his
      vision shines through the contradictions of his personality.  His
      reactionary stance was apolitical; his views are more palatable
      now than in his own times.  The letters possess an equilibrium he
      failed to find within himself.

20    LYNCH, TIBBIE E.  Review of Evelyn Waugh, by Calvin W. Lane.
      EWN 15 (Winter):6.
            Says the book should intrigue readers new to Waugh and

provide a readable overview for those familiar with his work, even
though it is somewhat limited in scope. Lane gives fullest attention to the fiction, emphasizing the comically incongruous and
tellingly ironic. Commends the assertion that whatever glaring
façade Waugh presented to the world, he never fooled himself; says
the book provides groundwork for a reassessment of Waugh because
of the implied condemnation of the "protestant ethos," which under-
lies the early novels. See 1981.A3.

21    MacSWEEN, R.J. "Evelyn Waugh's Ladies." Antigonish Review 12
      (Winter):43-50.
           Refers to the detachment in Waugh's letters; all has been
      captured, toned, and harnessed by a master of the unobtrusive.
      Notes that most of his correspondents were beautiful and clever
      women, including Diana Cooper, Daphne Fielding, Daphne Acton,
      Clarissa Churchill, Diana Mitford, and his own daughter Margaret.
      He evidently needed "objects of love" as no other man has ever
      needed them.

22    MUGGERIDGE, MALCOLM. "Evelyn Waugh." Muggeridge Ancient and
      Modern. Edited by Christopher Ralling and Jane Bywater.
      London:  British Broadcasting Corporation, pp. 242-44.
           In a radio program broadcast 24 September 1980, Robert
      Robinson asked Muggeridge and Peter Quennell why Waugh took offense
      at them, and they gave replies. Muggeridge gives an account of
      Waugh's putting down his ear trumpet when Muggeridge got up to
      speak at a Foyle's literary luncheon. Says Waugh had a strong
      death wish, because he was leading a fantasy life.

23    _____. Like it Was:  The Diaries of Malcolm Muggeridge. Edited
      by John Bright-Holmes. London:  Collins, pp. 218, 273, 290,
      330, 354-55, 374, 404-5, 435.
           Largely deals with Waugh's snobbishness; calls a novel he is
      reading in 1946 "very vulgar and second-rate"; says later that
      Waugh is a prisoner of his own fantasy and may end in madness.

24    PRITCHARD, WILLIAM H. "Impossible." American Scholar 50
      (Summer):425-29.
           Notes that among notable modern English letter writers,
      Waugh's only rival as an impossible person is Wyndham Lewis; it
      was a role which came naturally to him, one which he worked hard
      to perfect over the years. Like Lewis, however, he manifested a
      wild sense of humor in his letters; the comic energy of their cre-
      ative fantasies outshines their depravity.

25    RABAN, JONATHAN. Review of The Letters of Evelyn Waugh.
      Critic 39 (January I and II):6-7.
           Waugh's art is a fantastic refinement of his life, but his
      troublesome personality interferes with his fiction. The letters
      constitute his experiments with fantasy based on reality. Compares
      Waugh to Swift in the use of self-destructive irony and decline
      into melancholy.

26   ROSS, MITCHELL. "Evelyn Waugh Dusted off for the Ages." <u>Critic</u>
     39 (January I and II):4-6.
         Comments on the resurgence of interest in Waugh. Incapable
     of dullness, Waugh vacillated between satiric and romantic tenden-
     cies, moving from irresponsible hilarity to straight autobiography
     as his career progressed. Hemingway and P.G. Wodehouse were im-
     portant influences on his writing; the pre-<u>Brideshead</u> novels repre-
     sent his highest achievement.

27   SCHIEDER, RUPERT. "The Letters of Evelyn Waugh." <u>Globe and</u>
     <u>Mail</u> (Toronto), 14 February, p. E15.
         The letters are bound to appeal to a wide audience: Waugh's
     novels, his publicized rudeness, and his blatant prejudices have
     kept his name before both those who read the learned journals and
     those who read nothing more than television guides. The selection
     gives a balanced view, including the thoughtful and considerate
     along with the cruel and vitriolic. Fortunately, he lived before
     the long-distance telephone habit reduced letter-writing to a mini-
     mal art.

28   TOSSER, YVON. Review of "Evelyn Waugh, romancier satirique,
     1903-42," by Alain Blayac. <u>EWN</u> 15 (Autumn):6-7.
         Calls this 801-page thesis (plus notes, etc.) (1980.A1) an
     exciting and provocative contribution to Waugh criticism. Its
     first section, dealing with Waugh's early life and apprenticeship,
     makes good use of letters and diaries; the second section analyzes
     six novels in detail, with special attention to the search for
     norms and the creation of modern myths; the third discusses the
     modes and methods of the modern satiric novel. Finds that the
     third section adds comparatively little to previous discussions,
     criticizes the restriction of the central investigation to six
     novels, and says Blayac is sometimes too hard on Waugh. Neverthe-
     less calls the book a source of genuine critical delight.

29   WISE, BRIAN. "Paperback Editions of Waugh Published in the
     U.K. as of December 1980." <u>EWN</u> 15 (Autumn):5.
         Lists and describes paperback editions, most of them pub-
     lished by Penguin.

30   WÖLK, GERHARD. "Evelyn Waugh: A Supplementary Checklist of
     Criticism." <u>EWN</u> 15 (Winter):4-6.
         Includes chiefly books and articles published since 1979.

31   WOOD, CHRISTOPHER. "Evelyn Waugh: A Pioneer Collector."
     <u>Connoisseur</u> 208 (September):30-34.
         Notes that Waugh and his close friend John Betjeman were
     among the first to encourage serious study of Victorian art. His
     own collection was not large, but it included an important group
     of narrative paintings, especially by George Elgar Hicks, George
     Smith, and Rebecca Solomon. Describes some of these in detail,
     and reproduces photographs of them. Waugh liked to give the

impression that his collecting was a light-hearted affair, but he took it seriously.

32   WOODRUFF, DOUGLAS. "Evelyn Waugh." In The Dictionary of National Biography 1961-70. Edited by E.T. Williams and C.S. Nicholls. London: Oxford, pp. 1058-62.
       The amount of space accorded Waugh in this volume (seven columns) is a measure of the importance attached to him. Explains Waugh's rudeness on the basis of his exceptional intelligence: he behaved unpredictably and very rudely in an attempt to make every-day life more interesting and amusing. He looked with horror on Dylan Thomas: "He's exactly what I would have been if I had not become a Catholic."

33   ZIEGLER, PHILIP. "A Bear Hug from Bevin." Sunday Telegraph (London), 27 September, pp. 10-11. Extract from his Diana Cooper (London: Hamish Hamilton, 1981; and New York: Knopf, 1982).
       Describes Waugh as a mischief-maker when visiting the Coopers at the British embassy in Paris. He set himself to bait the other guests, treating Julian Huxley as a crypto-Communist zoo-keeper with no interest in life beyond the diet of his panda. Diana said, "Poor Wu--he does everything he can to alienate himself from the affection he is yearning for." In an added note, "Why Death Has No Fear," Lady Diana says she prays every night, following a frame-work of prayers taught her by Waugh.


                              1982


A.  BOOKS

1   HEATH, JEFFREY. The Picturesque Prison:  Evelyn Waugh and His Writing. Kingston and Montreal:  McGill-Queen's University Press, 374 pp.
       Using both published and unpublished material, examines the entire body of Waugh's work, with special attention to his themes and techniques. Maintains that he was a far more committed and profoundly satirical writer than has been commonly thought, and that even though his aesthetic, historical, and religious views developed, they remained basically consistent. Traces his retreat from a world he came to view as a spiritual dungeon, but contends that the refuge he sought proved also to be a prison.

2   LYNCH, TIBBIE ELIZABETH. "Forms and Functions of Black Humor in the Fiction of Evelyn Waugh." Ph.D. dissertation, Texas A. and M. University, 146 pp. [DAI 43:1968A.]
       Evelyn Waugh not only anticipated the comic apocalyptic manner of Joseph Heller, John Barth, and others, but was the first contemporary writer to produce a sustained black comic novel.

Examination of patterns of dialogue, narrative structure, and parody
in his first six novels shows him to be a forerunner of this sub-
genre.  Though his Catholicism may seem to contradict a black comic
view, it really helped him to use black humor as an escape from the
vision of the gap between human striving and perfection.

## B.  SHORTER WRITINGS

1   AMORY, MARK.  "Never the Twain."  London Review of Books 4
     (4-17 March):17.
          Shows how thriving the Waugh industry is, but observes that
     though its English and American branches are superficially polite
     to each other, contempt lurks beneath the surface:  "We produce
     works that they think insubstantial and sloppy; they describe
     minutely and accumulate so many tiny shrubs that the outline of
     the forest is lost."  Says that Robert Murray Davis's Evelyn Waugh,
     Writer (1981.A2) is firmly in the American school.  Though the book
     is full of information which is valuable or at least incidentally
     interesting, the author rarely strays from his close examination
     of the texts, and he leaves an English reader wishing that he had
     written a different kind of book.

2   ANON.  "In Search of God."  Economist 283 (26 June):101-2.
          Sixteen years after his death, Waugh's reputation as a seri-
     ous novelist remains uncertain.  Can a plausible case be made for
     him as a writer possessed by a deeply religious vision which domi-
     nates and unifies his work?  Jeffrey Heath's presentation of this
     thesis (1982.A1) is attractive and persuasive.  His analysis of
     individual novels is less than convincing:  he makes mountains of
     symbols from handfuls of dust.

3   BELL, ALAN.  "Waugh out West."  TLS, 21 August, p. 967.
          Criticizes R.M. Davis's catalogue of the Waugh collection at
     the University of Texas (1981.A1) for omitting any account of
     Waugh's own library and furnishings, for omitting archival informa-
     tion about the provenance of the documents catalogued, and for er-
     rors and misprints in dates and publication data.

4   BELL, QUENTIN.  "Visionary Vanity."  TLS, 12 November, p. 1253.
          The thirty pages of Waugh in his PRB:  An Essay on the Pre-
     Raphaelite Brotherhood, 1847-54 are not so much slim as anorexic;
     a pair of Christophers (Sykes and Wood) have to be brought in to
     bear the juvenile Waugh on their devoted shoulders.  One looks for
     some amusing treatment of the brethren, but the author is too seri-
     ously concerned with doing justice to his kinsman Holman Hunt to
     be funny--though his depiction of Rossetti walking with a sailor's
     roll is a touch of Wavian fantasy.

5   BILLINGTON, RACHEL.  "Waugh's Way."  Financial Times (London),
     26 June, p. 10.

Critics say one thing, an author another; Waugh is probably
the worst kind of author for a serious critic because the ghost
of his own irreverence mocks the academic scholar. Yet The
Picturesque Prison (1982.A1) is a sensible book in which the intellectual gears do not grind too often. Caught by the demon of unhappiness, Waugh at a very early age was ready for the way to
Christian salvation, death.

6   BOLD, ALAN. "Studying Waugh in Pieces." Scotsman (Edinburgh),
    12 June, p. 5.
        Jeffrey Heath (1982.A1) invites us to think of Waugh as a
profoundly religious writer whose sense of moral outrage results
in satire. Interpreting his work in terms of a see-saw contest
between art and action, he brings out the manic depressive element
in Waugh's artistic approach. His stimulating book brings out the
contrast between Waugh's sense of failure as a man and his triumph
as an artist: what grace the man had went into his writing, and
it is his art that survives.

7   BRODERICK, JOHN. "Masked Man." Irish Times (Dublin), 26 June,
    p. 4.
        The most dedicated wearer of masks among recent literary men
was Evelyn Waugh. It is a pity that this greatly gifted man had
to suffer so much for his art and for the persona he so painfully
constructed. The later novels from Brideshead on are all informed
by a sense of worldly failure. It is interesting to see that academic critics like Jeffrey Heath are now prepared to accept Waugh's
"warning" that in Brideshead he is attempting to trace the divine
workings in a pagan world--a perfectly legitimate theme for a serious writer, but one that the reviewers of 1945 could not stomach.
The Picturesque Prison (1982.A1) is an excellent introduction to
Waugh and his work, especially for the more scholarly reader.

8   BROPHY, BRIGID. "The Riskiest Way of Writing Novels." Times
    (London), 18 August, p. 7.
        Investigates Waugh's approaches to war in Put Out More Flags.
He uses Firbankian techniques of excising connective passages, jux-
taposing stark images and laconic narrative. These strategies are
risky, like a commando raid. But Put Out More Flags is more effective than Brideshead.

9   BROYARD, ANATOLE. "Books of the Times." New York Times, 22
    November, p. 16.
        Reviewing Charles Ryder's Schooldays and Other Stories, finds
the stories predictable and trivial; they show one of the century's
best writers writing badly.

10  BURGESS, ANTHONY. "On the Waugh-path." Observer (London),
    20 June.
        Waugh, being dead and probably great, has to submit to the
kind of close critical analysis which is rendering Joyce's centenary

so gloomy. Heath's analysis of his symbolism is both sensible and
useful, but we have cause to fear for the future. But since Waugh
subscribed to the Thomistic view of art as not an end in itself
but a way to God, the later books will never make complete sense
unless we relate them to a rigorous Catholicism which was an onto-
logical reality rather than an authorial pose. In his book The
Will to Believe, Richard Johnstone calls faith "a safety net against
despair"--a gross understatement of a positive radiance that only
made Waugh despair of the world that would not accept it.

11    CARENS, JAMES F. Review of Evelyn Waugh, Writer, by Robert
      Murray Davis. EWN 16 (Spring):5-7.
            Notes that Davis's study (1981.A2) is not theoretical, but
      concentrates on precise aspects of composition, excision, and amp-
      lification. Says Davis sees Black Mischief as a pivotal novel; in
      it Waugh began to adopt a method more substantial and particularized
      in its rendering of social content than he had used before. Davis's
      chapters on the intense labors Waugh expended on the composition
      of his works recreate the conditions under which each book was
      crafted: even quite popular writers, Davis reminds us, take great
      trouble sometimes in this matter.

12    CHAMPLIN, CHARLES. "A Novel Narrator Years before 'Brideshead.'"
      Los Angeles Times Book Review, 3 October, p. 3.
            Referring to "Charles Ryder's Schooldays," says that the de-
      scription of a regimen supposed to build character seems to demon-
      strate that it achieved the opposite effect, burning off spontaneity
      and individuality to achieve a sheen of mannered snobbery.

13    CLARKE, GERALD. "Memories of a Golden Past." Time 119 (18
      January):58-59.
            Calls Brideshead an odd book by one of the century's oddest
      writers, but says that the lavish and beautiful television series
      reveals why a book so often derided is often loved. Finds that
      the story's focal point and vitality depart when Sebastian leaves:
      Charles Ryder, the narrator, is only a reactor, who responds to
      people more interesting than himself.

14    CLEAVE, MAUREEN. "Acton in Aspic." Observer (London), 21
      February, p. 25.
            In an interview, Harold Acton gives reminiscences of Waugh--
      "Not a very interesting life; a charming witty original person, a
      good writer, one of our best writers, but not a fascinating life."
      Remembers reciting poems and delivering a lecture on charm, as
      Anthony Blanche did in Brideshead. Calls Waugh susceptible but
      disciplined: "Religion saved him from every point of view."

15    COWARD, NOEL. The Noel Coward Diaries. Edited by Graham Payne
      and Sheridan Morley. Boston: Little, Brown, pp. 122, 200,
      279, 490, 581, 596.
            Recalls that in his earlier books Waugh had zest and brevity

and was irresistibly comic. Finds <u>Unconditional Surrender</u> sadly
disappointing. There are gleams of the old magic, but tracts of
well-written boredom; the novel is shadowed by a dark cloud of
Catholicism which suffocates humor and interferes with the story.

16   DONALDSON, FRANCES. "Old Young Waugh." <u>New York Times Book
     Review</u>, 14 November, p. 25.
          States that Waugh has passed the tests that ensure a place
     in posterity. Commends <u>Charles Ryder's Schooldays</u> for its reprint-
     ing of eleven stories not easily available and for the title story
     alone, even though it offers little more than a glimpse of life in
     an English public school.

17   DOYLE, PAUL A. "The Year's Work in Waugh Studies." <u>EWN</u> 16
     (Spring):1-4.
          Comments on a number of articles growing out of the televi-
     sion production of <u>Brideshead</u>. Describes Robert Murray Davis's
     <u>Evelyn Waugh, Writer</u> (1981.A2) as a landmark in research, and such
     a brilliant and intriguing essay that anyone interested in Waugh
     will find it hard to put down. Also mentions Davis's catalogue
     of the Waugh materials at Texas (1981.A1) and his article in
     <u>Papers on Language and Literature</u> (1981.B5) on Waugh's uncollected
     work. Describes Calvin Lane's book on Waugh (1981.A3) as a very
     successful introduction to Waugh's literary career. Also discusses
     the controversy surrounding Richard Huggett's impersonation of
     Waugh on the London stage.

18   ELMEN, PAUL. "'Brideshead Revisited': A Twitch upon the
     Thread." <u>Christian Century</u> 99 (26 May):630-31.
          Commenting on the American success of the televised <u>Brideshead</u>,
     says that Waugh, a "spoiled priest," created a camouflaged sermon
     in it, culminating in Lord Marchmain's deathbed. Discusses the
     history and theology of deathbed repentance.

19   FEATHERSTONE-WITTY, MARK. "Names to Set the Blood Racing."
     <u>Times Educational Supplement</u> (London), 10 September, p. 32.
          Waugh's letters are tedious and disappointing because he
     says nothing about writing.

20   FULLER, EDMUND. "The Man behind 'Rumpole': Evelyn Waugh
     Revisited." <u>Wall Street Journal</u>, 11 October, p. 20.
          <u>Charles Ryder's Schooldays</u> is a literary scrap, published
     opportunistically, for the fans and students of Waugh, not begin-
     ners.

21   GALLAGHER, DONAT. "Black Majesty and Press Mischief." <u>London
     Magazine</u> 22 (October):25-38.
          Claims that accounts of Waugh's coverage of Haile Selassie's
     coronation, such as one by William Deedes in the introduction to
     the 1981 Folio Society edition of <u>Black Mischief</u>, are not accurate;
     neither is Waugh's own account of his Abyssinian experiences in

Remote Places and When the Going was Good.  The true story has not
yet been told; Waugh's own stories about his naiveté as a reporter
are not to be trusted.

22   GREENE, DONALD.  "Evelyn Waugh's Hollywood."  EWN 16 (Winter):
     1-4.
        Traces the Los Angeles locations of the settings in The Loved
One.

23   HART, JEFFREY.  "Brideshead Indeed Revisited."  National Review
     34 (14 May):540-42.
        Contrasts the two images of early and late Waugh, and says
his evolving fiction is the only clue to his emotional and spiritual development.  Brideshead is his transitional novel, and
Marchmain's deathbed is crucial to understanding the shape and
meaning of Waugh's entire oeuvre.  Both Edmund Wilson and Conor
Cruise O'Brien misread this scene.

24   HILL, SUSAN.  "Evelyn Waugh Revisited."  Daily Telegraph
     (London), 29 July.
        Jeffrey Heath gives a succinct and not unsympathetic, though
by no means uncritical, portrait of Waugh from childhood to death,
and treats each of the major novels to a detailed analysis.  The
reader who is approaching Waugh for the first time will find The
Picturesque Prison (1982.A1) a sound introduction, though he might
feel like skipping the more elaborate and far-fetched passages of
critical speculation.  Perhaps Heath does not convey clearly what
a tremendously enjoyable novelist Waugh is, though he does present
him as a great stylist and comic satirist with a serious moral purpose.

25   HURST, MARY JANE, and DANIEL HURST, M.D.  "Bromide Poisoning in
     The Ordeal of Gilbert Pinfold."  EWN 16 (Autumn):1-4.
        Interpretations of the novel to date have not noted the sig-
nificance of bromide poisoning in the life of Waugh and in the creation of Gilbert Pinfold.  The Ordeal, a chronicle of bromide poisoning, is a landmark in the literature of the arts and in the
literature of psychiatry.  Bromide poisoning has a lengthy list of
symptoms, and readers of Waugh will recognize all of them as problems of Mr. Pinfold.  Four bromide psychoses, or stages of mental
disorder, have been recognized, and three of these appear in
Pinfold.  The fact of bromide poisoning does not lessen Waugh's
achievement, but does change the focus for critical response to
the novel.

26   INVERARITY, GEOFFREY.  "Evelyn Waugh Revisited."  Kingston
     Whig-Standard Magazine, 5 June, p. 18.
        Jeffrey Heath's The Picturesque Prison (1982.A1) is a much-
needed guide to Waugh for the general reader, and a valuable study
for the literary specialist.  Rejecting the criticism that Waugh's
satire, especially in the early novels, lacks a stable set of

values and therefore is irresponsible and cruel, Heath shows that
the assertion of order and discipline in Brideshead is implied in
the early works.  But he does perceive an ambivalence in Waugh's
attitudes to his own life and writings which has disconcerted many
readers.

27    JOHNSTONE, RICHARD.  The Will to Believe:  Novelists of the
      Nineteen-Thirties.  Oxford:  Oxford University Press, pp. 79-97,
      et passim.
          Contends that religious belief--Waugh and Greene's Catholi-
      cism, Christopher Isherwood's Vedanta--survived the thirties better
      than political commitment because religious belief more easily al-
      lowed scepticism and faith to coexist.  Once adopted, the religious
      belief could be left out of sight, a safety net against despair.

28    JONES, LEWIS.  "The Iron Mask."  New Statesman 104 (6 August):
      21-22.
          In The Picturesque Prison (1982.A1), Jeffrey Heath argues
      that in the novels up to Work Suspended Waugh was attacking the
      legacy of his father's generation.  The detachment of the early
      novels, he contends, was implicit in their style--which embodied
      propriety and restraint.  His description of the later novels as
      "affirmative parodies" of the earlier ones is odd.  His bio-critical
      portrait is a convincing one, up to a point--the point where man
      and books meet.  Having based his view of the man on the novels, he
      constructs for Waugh's last years a fiction of lurid and dubious
      character.

29    KENNEDY, PACIFICUS, O.F.M.  "Romance and Redemption in Brideshead
      Revisited."  America 146 (1 May):334-36.
          Quotes excerpts from a memorandum Waugh wrote for MGM Studios
      when he went to Hollywood to discuss the possibility of filming
      Brideshead.  Hollywood wanted to produce a love story, but Waugh
      explained that the theme of the novel was the operation of divine
      grace on a group of diverse but closely connected characters.  The
      television version preserves the original theme, showing that
      there is no stereotyped religious habit of life but that in diverse
      ways God calls souls to Himself.  Suggests that Anthony Blanche is
      demonic and foments perversion in the novel.

30    LEITHAUSER, BRAD.  "Brideshead Revisited."  New Republic 186
      (27 January):27-30.
          Reviews past efforts to film Brideshead, mentioning that
      problems arose in the 1940s and 50s because the viewing public was
      opposed to multiple adulteries and homosexuality and because of
      the Catholicism.  Says that to understand Brideshead we must under-
      stand how Waugh links religion and sex.  Since it shows holy people
      as pious fools, Catholics are uncomfortable with the book--as are
      atheists.  Mentions the rich theme of wasted male beauty, and the
      prevailing idea that love of individuals must yield to love of the
      divine.

31    LYNCH, TIBBIE E.   Review of <u>The Picturesque Prison</u>, by Jeffrey
      Heath.   <u>EWN</u> 16 (Autumn):6-7.
         Heath's emphasis on the connection between biography and
      aesthetic criticism, and on the organic consistency of Waugh's
      work are not new, but he formulates an original and compelling
      thesis concerning Waugh's search for a refuge from contemporary
      life.   A great strength of the book is its effective blending of
      biography and criticism to provide evidence of saving values in
      the early satires.   Heath's periodic confusion of terminology ren-
      ders his thesis less convincing than it ought to be, and some of
      the diffuseness in the analyses of individual works might have
      been eliminated, but the book is a major contribution to Waugh
      studies.   See 1982.A1.

32    McCARTNEY, GEORGE P.   "At Waugh with Himself."   <u>National Review</u>
      34 (29 October):1356-58.
         Though Waugh thought that art that did not fulfill its theo-
      logical responsibilities was not true art at all, he was thoroughly
      a man of the world, who took delight in portraying the roguish and
      flamboyant figures of fashionable society.   One Waugh was a
      Dionysian reveler, the other the prophet of a new dark age, and
      the special energy of his fiction came from the clash of the two,
      as Jeffrey Heath shows.   Tact and insight also enable him to show
      that Waugh, despite his poses, was always a deliberate artist whose
      fiction deserves close attention.

33    MITCHENER, CHARLES.   "Charles before Brideshead."   <u>Newsweek</u> 99
      (22 March):76.
         The televised <u>Brideshead</u> makes explicit much that was im-
      plicit in the novel.   Ryder's enigmatic personality is also clari-
      fied by reference to "Charles Ryder's Schooldays," a novel fragment
      begun and abandoned by Waugh in 1945; he appears as a romantic
      aesthete who is cold at the core.

34    MONTGOMERY, ROBERT L.   "In Course of Composition."   <u>TLS</u>, 9
      July, p. 746.
         In his <u>Evelyn Waugh, Writer</u> (1981.A2), Robert Murray Davis
      ties the finished novels to an account of the deliberate, system-
      atic processes of thought he observes in the act of composition:
      Waugh was primarily a craftsman.   Comments especially on the dis-
      cussion of <u>Brideshead</u>, which Waugh evidently saw as a turning point
      in his writing and whose text he could not let alone.   Complains
      about some of the summary critical judgments in the book, and its
      lack of a bibliography and index; also says that sometimes the
      mass of data makes for confusion.   Refers to Waugh's "negative
      vision" of the world.

35    MORTIMER, JOHN.   "Adapting Waugh's <u>Brideshead</u>--Nostalgia Re-
      visited."   <u>New York Times</u>, 17 January, pp. 27, 30.
         States the dramatization is the book and the book is Waugh's:
      he had to let Waugh have his say.   Hopes the television viewer will

have the feeling that he is living through the book and experienc-
ing it in the way the author intended. Also says that though
Waugh's Catholicism is less humane than Graham Greene's, it gives
Brideshead its great dramatic power and fascination, particularly
in the closing scenes.

36   OWEN, I.M. "Leaven of Malice." Books in Canada 11 (June–July):
     22–23.
          For all the shining clarity of his prose, Waugh takes a lot
     of explaining. Heath's The Picturesque Prison (1982.A1) provides
     a coherent explanation of him--in spots too coherent for so wild
     a comic genius. The main theme is Waugh finding his vocation as
     a writer, his attempt to escape from it into a life of action dur-
     ing the war, and his return to it with books for the first time
     explicitly Christian. Occasionally Heath suffers from the academic
     critic's urge to read significance into everything, and he has
     trouble with the vocabulary of religious discussion. But on the
     whole this is an admirable and thorough piece of work.

37   PEARCE, EDWARD. "Brideshead Revisited: Chronicles of a Social
     Alpinist." Encounter 58 (March):48–50.
          Believes that the American debut of the televised Brideshead
     satisfies only snobbish and nostalgic yearnings. It is a desolat-
     ing experience, for aristocracy is the only virtue. Even if the
     soap is from St. James's, Brideshead is a soap opera.

38   REYNOLDS, C.P. "Revisiting Brideshead." Gourmet 42 (February):
     30, 32, 48, 50.
          Describes in some detail the house and grounds of Castle
     Howard, the perfect setting for a vision (in Waugh's words) of
     "very rich, beautiful, high born people who live in palaces and
     have no trouble except what they make for themselves." Shows how
     the house was used for the television version of Brideshead; in-
     cludes photographs.

39   REYNOLDS, STANLEY. "Phoney Waugh." Punch 282 (16 June):994.
          Jeffrey Heath's The Picturesque Prison (1982.A1) challenges
     the critical cliché that there were two Waughs, the one who wrote
     the early comic novels and the Catholic who wrote Brideshead,
     Helena, and the war trilogy. There is much in the book to set
     the English reader's teeth on edge, but it is a work of real schol-
     arship and love. It is clear that Waugh embarked on some sort of
     pilgrim's progress in his novels, and like a Hollywood trial law-
     yer Heath can trace it all step by step.

40   RILEY, ANTHONY W. "Waugh on Germany: An Unpublished Postcard."
     EWN 16 (Winter):4–7.
          Prints a 1959 postcard from Waugh, responding to an enquiry
     about German influences on his writing. Waugh denied any German
     influences on English literature after 1914, and associated Berlin
     of the 1920s with "certain socialist homosexuals." Cites other

evidence from the letters and diaries to modify this response. Also describes Waugh's visit to Munich in 1958, when he gave a disastrous public reading.

41    RODDICK, NICK. "Brideshead Revisited." Sight and Sound 51 (Winter):58-60.

Brideshead is a visual and dramatic masterpiece of awesome proportions. Its stylistic seamlessness consecrates a long-standing tradition of representation: after an early period of experiment with drama, television has settled down to a mode of filmed representation as perfectly sutured as anything Hollywood ever achieved. Its tacit assumption that the ruling classes are more interesting than others tends, paradoxically, to deny the existence of social class as a central part of British experience: these people, like the heroes of classical tragedy, stand for us all.

42    ROUSSEAU, G.S. "Wild Austerities: The Letters of Evelyn Waugh." SAQ 81 (Summer):338-44.

The outrageous writer of these letters complains that he can abide the world only by offending it. This is the ancient stance of the satirist; Waugh belongs to the lineage of great satirists who could reap adoration while they hurled abuse. But the letters show that the outrage stems from an egomaniacal personality incapable of harnessing its own narcissism; unresolved sexual conflict lies at the base of the "offense" after all. Waugh is the twentieth century's most virulent epistolary satirist. Only when the Church is in question does the language of abuse subside.

43    SHERRIN, ROBERT. "The Prison Lurks Behind Brideshead." Calgary Herald, 31 December, p. D9.

In his Picturesque Prison (1982.A1), Jeffrey Heath has performed a great service for those who have always sensed the layers of subtext in Waugh's work but have not been able to mine the strata.

44    SISSONS, MICHAEL. Introduction to "Charles Ryder's Schooldays." TLS, 5 March, p. 255.

Discusses the finding of the manuscript, and raises questions about why Waugh did not proceed with the novel and whether the existing fragment of it was ever submitted to a magazine.

45    SLATER, ANN PASTERNAK. "Waugh's A Handful of Dust: Right Things in Wrong Places." Essays in Criticism 32 (January): 48-68.

Displacement is the recurring motif which unifies the phantasmagoric episodes of A Handful of Dust. The right things--Tony's love for Brenda, his Dream of the City, Hetton Abbey--appear in the wrong contexts. His theme is replayed with inventive precision throughout the novel and illuminates its structure. Waugh has extended and perfected Firbank's method of relating apparently unconnected details; parallel characters and situations and recurring animal motifs complete the thematic structure.

46   SYKES, CHRISTOPHER.  Preface to <u>PRB:  An Essay on the Pre-Raphaelite Brotherhood 1847-54</u>.  Westerham, Kent:  Dalrymple Press, pp. 5-9.

   Disparages Waugh's early writing and yet concludes that he was "probably far and away the best novelist that Britain has produced this century."

47   VOORHEES, RICHARD.  Review of <u>Evelyn Waugh, Writer</u>, by Robert Murray Davis.  <u>MFS</u> 28 (Summer):285-86.

   This is not so much an anatomy of fiction as an embryology. But any specialist in fiction may follow with profit Davis's chart through Waugh's novels and short stories.  No Waugh scholar or critic may ignore his book.  See 1981.A2.

48   WOLCOTT, JAMES.  "Snob Appeal:  Mischief and Malice."  <u>Vogue</u> (New York) 172 (October):126.

   Comments on Waugh's "Years of Practice" in developing his malicious, inconsiderate, snobbish behavior.  Artifice renders Waugh's snobbery inoffensive.  His greatest embarrassment was not social, but literary--the aristocratic excesses of <u>Brideshead Revisited</u>.

49   WÖLK, GERHARD.  "Evelyn Waugh:  A Supplementary Checklist of Criticism."  <u>EWN</u> 15 (Winter):7-9.

   Continues earlier checklists, including items published since 1980, as well as some omitted from previous listings.

50   WOOD, CHRISTOPHER.  Postscript to <u>PRB:  An Essay on the Pre-Raphaelite Brotherhood 1847-54</u>.  Westerham, Kent:  Dalrymple Press, pp. 41-44.

   Praises Waugh for writing about the Pre-Raphaelites when they were in disrepute; he was not merely a pioneer, but a lone voice crying in the modernist wilderness.  Though the essay is rather superficial in the light of modern knowledge, it is a fascinating period piece.

51   YAKIR, DAN.  "Waugh Revisited."  <u>Horizon</u> 25 (January-February): 58-59.

   Commenting on the televised <u>Brideshead</u>, says the novel needs thirteen hours and a huge budget to do it justice.  Waugh's dialogue is used almost verbatim.  The Charles-Sebastian relationship provides the dominant interest.

<u>1983</u>

A.   BOOKS

1   LITTLEWOOD, IAN.  <u>The Writings of Evelyn Waugh</u>.  Oxford:  Basil Blackwell, 249 pp.

Explores related patterns in Waugh's work by linking biographical events to literary practice. Argues that his style of
dealing with experience is defensive; his novels deal with ways of
avoiding reality and surviving despair, through the use of various
narrative strategies. Discusses his nostalgia based on an idealized version of the past, his callous humor, and the tension between the humorist and the devout Roman Catholic. Experience
freed from the constraints of reality leads to comic or romantic
fantasy—not to moral philosophy but to a contrivance which may
involve a distortion of the truth.


B.  SHORTER WRITINGS

1   BANN, STEPHEN. "Mythic elements." London Review of Books 4
    (30 December 1982-19 January 1983):11.
        You have only to glance through Work Suspended and Other
    Stories to sense the very specific formal constraints which a nov-
    elist thinks appropriate to the short story. Waugh's novels usual-
    ly have the crisp, clear, economical structure reminiscent of de
    Maupassant; if they lack it, it is because they have an unresolved,
    problematical relation to a novel, written or about to be written.
    "Work Suspended" and "Charles Ryder's Schooldays" both have this
    rather uneasy status.

2   BUCKLEY, WILLIAM F., Jr. "A Journal." NY 58 (31 January):
    84, 86.
        Discussing his introduction to the episodes of Brideshead on
    WNET television, stresses his desire to counter a possible anti-
    Catholic impact, and quotes acerbic comments on the series from a
    San Francisco columnist, Herb Caen, who called Brideshead Waugh
    at his worship-the-rich-worst.

3   CEVASCO, G.A. "Huysmans and Waugh." EWN 17 (Spring):5-6.
        Makes conjectures about the influence of Huysmans' "black
    romanticism" on Waugh, and shows that the tortoise episode in
    chapter 6 of Brideshead is taken directly from Huysmans' A Rebours.

4   DAVIS, ROBERT MURRAY. "Waugh Memorabilia in Austin." EWN 17
    (Spring):3-5.
        Lists 33 items not included in his Catalogue (1981.A1) to
    indicate the nature of further material in the Waugh Collection
    at Austin.

5   DOYLE, PAUL A. "The Year's Work in Waugh Studies." EWN 17
    (Spring):1-3.
        Gives special emphasis to Jeffrey Heath's The Picturesque
    Prison (1982.A1). Calls Donat Gallagher's "Black Majesty and
    Press Mischief" (1982.B21) a splendid investigative study pointing
    out errors in discussion of Waugh's work as a newspaper correspond-
    ent.

6   FITZHERBERT, MARGARET.  "Waugh Juvenilia."  Spectator 250
    (5 February):24-25.
        In PRB:  An Essay on the Pre-Raphaelite Brotherhood 1847-54,
    Christopher Sykes kills off Waugh's pretensions and Christopher
    Wood kills off the art-historical venture.  The essay has some
    good barbs, but little form or direction; "The Curse of the Horse
    Race," which Waugh wrote at the age of seven, is altogether super-
    ior.

7   JAMES, CLIVE.  From the Land of Shadows.  Picador Edition.
    London:  Pan Books, pp. 34, 95-96, 117-24.
        Rejects a comparison of Waugh to Brian Howard as twin ex-
    emplars of a decayed ruling class, saying that in the long run
    Waugh's social context will not matter:  the context will be gone
    and the work will remain.  In comparing Waugh's Catholicism to
    Graham Greene's, however, suggests that the former compromised his
    religious views by romanticizing the vanishing social order, where-
    as Greene did not.  Calls Waugh's Letters a wonderfully entertain-
    ing volume; even the shortest note is vibrant with his irascible
    temperament and penetrating stare.  There is now no argument about
    his stature; he helped make tolerable the modern age he so abomin-
    ated.  (His review of the Letters originally appeared in the New
    York Review of Books in 1980.)

8   LEVI, PETER.  "Hooperisms."  Spectator 250 (22 January):23.
        Waugh's prose is lucid, biting, modern, and inimitable.  It
    took ambitious study and hard work.  His faults arise from honesty,
    not artifice.  His writing has the style of a joke among intimate
    friends.  The critics always get him wrong, because they are duller
    and more awkward than he.  Ian Littlewood, trying to put an aca-
    demic gown on him, concentrates on the insufferably obvious and
    probes into Waugh's life to no purpose.  Waugh would have seen him
    as a booby.

9   MAGALANER, MARVIN.  Review of The Picturesque Prison, by Jeffrey
    Heath.  MFS 28 (Winter):649-50.
        States that Heath achieves what Jeffrey Meyers does not quite
    attain in his biography of Wyndham Lewis--a representation of the
    essential man.  Each of the major books is discussed methodically,
    intelligently, and with attention to the relation between the life
    of the writer and the literature he was producing.  This study
    should prove influential in destroying the image of the mad satir-
    ist and putting Waugh studies back on track.  See 1982.Al.

10  MANHEIM, LEONARD H.  Review of dramatic performance of A Handful
    of Dust at the Lyric Theatre, Hammersmith, London, November 1982.
    EWN 117 (Spring):7-8.
        Describes an interesting but not entirely successful stage
    rendition of the novel; finds a sameness to the characters and a
    lack of bite to the satire.

11    MARTIN, SANDRA.  Review of <u>Work Suspended and Other Stories</u>.
      <u>Globe and Mail</u> (Toronto), 5 February, p. E12.
          Describes the chapters of "Charles Ryder's Schooldays" as
      not among the best examples of Waugh's work.  Calls "Work Suspended"
      itself far more interesting--crawling with hideous and fascinating
      Waugh creations, and richly embroidered with his commentaries on
      the social customs and snobberies of his day.

12    PORTER, HENRY.  "<u>Work Suspended and Other Stories</u>."  <u>Books and</u>
      <u>Bookmen</u> (January):35.
          Calls "Charles Ryder's Schooldays" a brilliant evocation of
      the unremitting awfulness of schoolboy society; it shows Waugh at
      the height of his powers.

13    RABAN, JONATHAN.  "A la recherche de steak and kidney."  <u>Sunday</u>
      <u>Times</u> (London), 12 June, p. 44.
          Reviewing Anthony Powell's <u>O How the Wheel Becomes It!</u> con-
      cludes that Powell is not, as Waugh was, a great comic stylist and
      inventor.  Finds a strong resemblance between this novel and Waugh's
      <u>Ordeal of Gilbert Pinfold</u>.  Powell's Shadbold and Waugh's Pinfold
      have both fallen out of touch with their own past and survived into
      a rum new world; but Shadbold's ordeal ends with his death offstage,
      whereas Pinfold finds that his ordeal was an unlooked-for gift to
      him as a writer.

14    ROSENTHAL, MICHAEL.  "A Man for No Seasons."  <u>Partisan Review</u>
      50, no. 2:297-300.
          The letters of Joyce, Lawrence, and others considerably en-
      hance our understanding of their art and the minds that produced
      it.  This cannot be said of Waugh's letters.  He does not deal
      with his own work or anyone else's.  We are left in Amory's edition
      with a random sampling of Waugh being his trivial, gossiping,
      wicked, and cutting self.  The astringent ironies he lavishes on
      the flawed humanity around him do not extend however to his pas-
      sionately held Catholicism.  This volume does nothing for his
      reputation.

15    SMITH, ANNE.  "Working on a Dummy."  <u>New Statesman</u> 105 (11
      February):26.
          By academic standards, Ian Littlewood's <u>The Writings of</u>
      <u>Evelyn Waugh</u> (1983.A1) is admirable, but his premise that Waugh's
      books are all strategies of escape is unrealistic and patronizing.
      He fails to grasp Waugh's achievement, especially the satirical
      accuracy of his art.

# Index

1951.14; 1957.10
Mauriac, François, 1945.13;
   1951.13; 1953.B16-17;
   1969.B3; 1975.B18; 1980.B2
Maxwell, William, 1932.12
May, Derwent, 1968.B2
Mayberry, George, 1946.13
Mayer, David, 1977.B35
McAleer, Edward C., 1973.B18
McCabe, Bernard, 1976.38
McCartney, George P., 1980.A3;
   1982.B32
McCay, Robert Dale, 1953.A1
McCormick, John, 1957.20
McDonald, Horace Thelton,
   1975.B22
McDonnell, Thomas P., 1962.B26
McEwan, R.L., 1957.21
McInnes, R.J., 1938.7
McShane, Frank, 1961.20
McWhinnie, Donald, 1970.B25
Meaning of Treason, The, 1956.B8
Meckier, Jerome, 1973.B19;
   1974.B20; 1977.B36; 1978.B23;
   1979.B11, B14; 1980.B10, B22;
   1981.B9
Mehoke, James S., 1965.23
Meixner, Susan Turnquist,
   1979.B15
Menen, Aubrey, 1951.10
Meredith, George, 1972.B15
Merton, Thomas, 1969.B30;
   1973.B10; 1977.B29
Metzger, Joseph, 1937.2
Meyer, Heinrich, 1966.B34
Meyers, Jeffrey, 1976.39
Michener, Charles, 1982.B33
Middendorf, Marilyn Ann, 1978.A2
Middle Age of Mrs. Eliot, The,
   1970.B27
Middleton, Richard, 1981.B9
Mikes, George, 1954.B10; 1973.B20
Millar, Ruby, 1955.B27
Michener, Charles, 1982.B22
Mitford, Diana, 1981.B21
Mitford, Jessica, 1964.B40
Mitford, Nancy, 1967.B23;
   1973.B29; 1977.B1; 1980.B31
Mittleman, Leslie B., 1976.40
Modest Proposal, A, 1948.12
Monod, Sylvère, 1968.B9, B35

Montgomery, Robert L., 1982.B34
Mooney, Harry J., 1968.B24
Moore, Brian, 1964.B41
Moore, Geoffrey, 1955.B28
Moore, Harry T., 1976.41
Moore, T. Sturge, 1928.11;
   1973.B15; 1978.B24
Morley, Christopher, 1945.10
Morley, Sheridan, 1982.B11
Morris, Alice S., 1948.20; 1952.26
Morrison, Blake, 1980.B23
Morriss, Margaret E., 1979.B16-17;
   1980.A4, B24
Mortimer, John, 1981.B2; 1982.B35
Mortimer, Raymond, 1950.14;
   1964.B42; 1967.B31; 1982.B35
Morton, Frederick, 1952.27
Mosley, Diana, 1977.B37
Mosley, Nicholas, 1953.B15
Moulin, André, 1976.42
Muggeridge, Malcolm, 1966.B35-38;
   1973.B21-22; 1976.43;
   1981.B22-23
Muir, Edwin, 1934.14; 1945.11;
   1952.28
Munro, H.H. [pseud. Saki], 1942.7;
   1959.B7; 1968.B18
Murphy, John P., 1960.25
Murray, James G., 1964.B43
Mussolini, Benito, 1977.B50
Myers, William, 1977.B38; 1978.B25
My Grandmother and I, 1969.B18

Nabokov, Vladimir, 1963.B14
Nardin, Jane, 1977.B39
Nashe, Thomas, 1976.43
Neame, A.J., 1953.B15-16
Neill, D.G., 1949.4
Nemerov, Howard, 1957.22
Nemoianu, Virgil, 1968.B36
Nettall, Stephanie, 1964.B51
Nettesheim, Josefine, 1951.11
New, Melvin, 1970.B22
Newby, Eric, 1974.B21
Newby, P.H., 1951.12
Newnham, Anthony, 1970.B23
Next Corner, The, 1978.B10
Nicholls, C.S., 1981.B32
Nichols, Beverly, 1931.5; 1969.B26;
   1973.B23
Nichols, James W., 1962.B27;